"The best"

"A delightful and scientific i   hing,
'Let juice be your medicine   ans
juice of the plants. Juice and   ies,
tonics, and rebuilders, and   ....
It is the best book I hav   ...ine subject in our
current medical literature."

Gabriel Cousens, MD

Director of the Tree of Life Rejuvenation Center

"Important"

"Juice Alive is quite an important book that Dr. Steven Bailey
has compiled with much amazing information. I thoroughly
enjoyed reviewing it. Juice cleansing is a viable and valuable
traditional healing tool for modern medicine. I am excited to
recommend this book to interested readers."

Elson M. Haas, MD, The Detox Doc™

*Author of Staying Healthy with Nutrition
and The New Detox Diet*

"A much-needed book"

"Dr. Bailey's *Juice Alive* book is based on many years
of clinical application to sick bodies with maximal
health restoration from his expertise. Dr. Bailey
knows that these vitally fresh juices are to the
vegetable, fruit and plant worlds, in its life processes,
as the blood and lymph are to the human body in
restoring and maintaining health. You are what you think,
digest, absorb and eliminate. Vital food juices treat
the whole body, not the disease.

May I compliment Dr. Bailey for a much-needed book
that everyone should read to restore and
maintain optimal health."

Ralph Weiss, ND, DC

Physician to Edgar Cayce, "The Sleeping Prophet"

"The Holy Book of Juicing"

"After experiencing *Juice Alive*, I must write that this is 'The Holy Book of Juicing'.... It has been written with love, devotion, patience, knowledge and experience. I can feel Dr. Steven Bailey's holistic brush go through the palette of fruits . . . a real technicolor Dream Coat."

Vaidya Priyanka
Ayurvedic Practitioner, Aum Ayurveda

"Full of insight"

"With his wonderful new book *Juice Alive*, Steven Bailey had written a readable and detailed analysis of the often surprising powers in one of Nature's greatest healing agents. Full of insight and practical information, *Juice Alive* should be on the bookshelf of all nutritionally oriented physicians and consumers. I thoroughly enjoyed it."

Peter J. D'Adamo, ND
Author of Eat Right for Your Type

"A highly recommended book"

"In *Juice Alive,* authors Steven Bailey, ND, and Larry Trivieri provide all the guidance you need to learn how to make a wealth of nutritious and delicious juices, as well as many healthy smoothies. . . . *Juice Alive* is a highly recommended book that all health conscious individuals should have as part of their library. Read it today and learn how to literally drink your way to vibrant health."

Natural Cures Newsletter

Juice Alive

THE ULTIMATE GUIDE TO JUICING REMEDIES

SECOND EDITION

Steven Bailey, ND
Larry Trivieri, Jr.

SQUAREONE
PUBLISHERS

The information and advice contained in this book are based upon the research and the personal and professional experiences of the authors. They are not intended as a substitute for consulting with a health care professional. The publisher and authors are not responsible for any adverse effects or consequences resulting from the use of any of the suggestions, preparations, or procedures discussed in this book. All matters pertaining to your physical health should be supervised by a health care professional. It is a sign of wisdom, not cowardice, to seek a second or third opinion.

Cover Designer: Jeannie Tudor
Steven Bailey Photo Credit: Gila Lane (www.gilalane.com)
Editor: Elaine Weiser
Typesetter: Gary A. Rosenberg

Square One Publishers
115 Herricks Road
Garden City Park, NY 11040
(516) 535-2010 • (877) 900-BOOK
www.squareonepublishers.com

Library of Congress Cataloging-in-Publication Data

Bailey, Steven.
    Juice alive : the ultimate guide to juicing remedies / Steven Bailey and Larry Trivieri, Jr.
        p. cm.
    Includes bibliographical references and index.
    ISBN-13: 978-0-7570-0266-3 (pbk.)
    ISBN-10: 0-7570-0266-8 (pbk.)
    1. Fruit juices—Therapeutic use. 2. Vegetable juices—Therapeutic use.
I. Trivieri, Larry. II. Title.

RA784.B243   2007
641.6'4—dc22

                                                            2006035554

Copyright © 2010 by Steven Bailey and Larry Trivieri, Jr.

All rights reserved. No part of this publication may be reproduced, stored in a retrieval system, or transmitted, in any form or by any means, electronic, mechanical, photocopying, recording, or otherwise, without the prior written permission of the copyright owner.

Printed in Canada

10   9   8   7   6   5   4   3   2

Contents

For my wife, Susan, my daughter, Shayla,
and my greatest teacher, Dr. Ralph Weiss,
my primary inspirations,
each of whom helps me maintain my passions.

—S.B.

For Richard Stark,
a wonderful friend and inspiration,
in appreciation of all that I derive from our friendship.

—L.T.

Acknowledgments

I wish to express my sincere appreciation for my wife, Susan, and daughter, Shayla, for their support, inspiration, and sacrifice in helping the creation of *Juice Alive*.

I also wish to thank my greatest teacher, Dr. Ralph Weiss, for his insight, knowledge, and friendship over the years.

And finally I wish to thank Larry Trivieri, co-writer, and Rudy Shur, publisher, for their excellent work, support, and creativity in bringing *Juice Alive* to fruition.

—S.B.

My thanks to Dr. Steven Bailey, who became my friend during the writing of *Juice Alive*, and without whom this book would not have been possible. And to Rudy Shur, for first suggesting the project to me, as well as his excellent editorial team, who once again have gone beyond the call of duty.

I also want to acknowledge my girlfriend, Marilu, along with my family and many friends, all of whom have supported me throughout all of my creative endeavors. In particular, this time around, I want to thank Steve and Sue Lazarek, great friends and great company.

—L.T.

Together, we also want to thank our editor, Elaine Weiser, for the wise and expert care and attention she brought to our manuscript, ensuring that it reads as well as possible.

Introduction

t's no secret that fresh fruits and vegetables are essential foods for achieving and maintaining good health. So much so, in fact, that today even the American Cancer Society and the National Cancer Institute recommend at least five servings of fruits and vegetables each day as a means of preventing cancer. This is noteworthy because both of these organizations for many years of their existence ignored the importance of a healthy diet in relationship to good health.

What is not as well known, however, is how potent the fresh-squeezed juice of fruits and vegetables can be as a valuable aid for improving and maintaining your health. Yet, fruit and vegetable juices have been used for centuries by healers because of their healing and medicinal properties. In fact, even the word *chemical* is related to juicing. It is derived from the Greek word *chemia*, which means "the juice of a plant."

Preparing your own fresh fruit and vegetable juices is one of the easiest and most convenient methods you can use to take care of your health and the health of your loved ones. By making juicing a part of your daily health practice, you will be obtaining a rich source of vitamins, minerals, enzymes, and other vital nutrients that your body can quickly put to good use without the need for the energy expenditures necessary to digest food. You will also be helping your body to better cleanse and rejuvenate itself, while boosting your immunity and increasing your resistance to harmful microorganisms and environmental toxins.

Regularly drinking fresh fruit and vegetable juices can also increase your stamina and vitality, since such juices are concentrated sources of energy that contain an abundance of life-giving nutrients. The energy benefits that juicing can provide are particularly helpful during times of fatigue, stress, and illness, since fresh juices, unlike foods, do not have to first be digested by the body before the nutrients they contain can be used. The process of digestion requires time and energy. Since fresh juices are virtually self-digesting, the energy that is normally used for digestion is freed up so that your body can use it to repair and maintain itself.

In addition, juicing makes it easier to obtain far greater concentrations of nutrients than fruits and vegetables contain in their solid state. This is because, during the juicing process, the juices that fruits and vegetables contain are separated from fruit and vegetable pulp. This leaves most of the nutrients in the juice, without the bulk and weight of the pulp. For example, it requires approximately 5 pounds of carrots in order to make 1 quart of fresh-squeezed carrot juice. Eating 5 pounds of carrots every day is hardly a realistic option for most people, whereas drinking a quart of carrot juice is realistic.

In this book, you will discover how and why incorporating fresh-squeezed juices into your daily lifestyle can enhance your overall health goals. The information we will share with you is based on over 25 years of clinical experience on the part of Dr. Steven Bailey, a leading naturopathic physician and an internationally recognized authority on therapeutic juicing and fasting. Dr. Bailey incorporates juicing as an integral part of his overall recommendations for nearly all of the patients he sees at his clinic in Portland, Oregon, and is himself an avid juicer with 40 years of personal experience.

In the chapters that follow, we will share with you the "fruits" of Dr. Bailey's clinical and personal experience. In Part One, *The Art of Juicing,* you will discover:

■ Why juicing is so important to good health

■ A history of juicing

■ How to juice

■ How to select the healthiest fruits and vegetables for juicing

■ How to select a juicer that provides the best results and is compatible to what you can afford to purchase

■ How to properly conduct a juice fast and why juice fasting can be so beneficial to your health

■ Delicious and nutritious smoothies and tonics, including "the healthiest smoothie in the world"

■ How juicing can enhance your appearance

■ Healthy eating guidelines that can further improve your health

In Part Two, *Juice Recipes for Health Disorders,* you will learn the specific juice combinations that you can use to help resolve over 120 of the most common health disorders. You'll find an alphabetical listing of conditions and afflictions, and the best juicing recipes to help prevent and/or heal those problems.

As you start to make use of the information we will be sharing with you, you will soon discover that juicing is not only easy to do, but it is also fun. And the results can be delicious! So, if you are ready to literally drink your way to improved health, turn the page and read on.

PART ONE

The Art of Juicing

1

Why Juice?

Anyone unfamiliar with the many health benefits that can be derived from fresh fruit and vegetable juices might wonder why one would go to the trouble of preparing them. It is our hope that after you read this chapter you will have a clear answer to that question. We will begin to answer it by asking you another question: Why experience the precious vitality of true health?

Obviously, all of us want to be healthy, and to enjoy lives that fulfill our potential. To be able to do so, however, requires energy, something that is severely lacking in many—perhaps most—Americans today. So much so, in fact, that lack of energy consistently ranks at the top of the lists of patients' complaints to their doctors. Chronic feelings of fatigue and exhaustion are now so commonplace in our society that they are actually accepted as normal. This goes hand in hand with the fact that most people in our society also equate health with the mere absence of serious disease. Nothing could be further from the truth.

The hallmarks of health are not only a lack of disease symptoms, but also flexibility, mental alertness, emotional balance, and an unlimited flow of life-force energy throughout the body that makes achieving one's goals and dreams easier and far more pleasurable. Does this description match your own experience of health? If your answer is no, you are far from being alone. True health is something that few people know these days, due to the many pressures of modern life, coupled with diets that, even when they are considered healthy, fail to provide all of the vitality that your body needs to optimally function. These reasons alone are enough for us to recommend that you make juicing a daily health habit. As you read on, you will discover many other reasons why you should do so, as well.

In ancient times, the juice of certain fruits was sometimes referred to as "the nectar of the gods." Today, one of the definitions for the word *juice* found in Webster's dictionary is the "current of electricity or charge of batteries." This is an apt metaphor for the easily released energy contained within the juice of fruits and vegetables.

WHY JUICING IS SO IMPORTANT IN TODAY'S TOXIC WORLD

In 1988, C. Everett Koop, then Surgeon General of the United States, issued the *Surgeon General's Report on Nutrition and Health.* In that report, Dr. Koop stated that "more than two-thirds of all deaths in the United States" are directly related to the standard American diet. This figure may actually be a conservative estimate, given how lacking such a diet is in vitamins, minerals, and other vital nutrients that are essential for our bodies' good health. Never before in humanity's history have people consumed the amount of unhealthy and devitalized foods as they do today.

There are many reasons for this sad fact, not the least of which is our tendency to opt for convenient "fast foods," even if they are not healthy, due to our society's increasingly accelerating pace. It's a well-known fact that convenience foods are lacking in vital nutrients. Certainly, they are far more deficient in vitamins and minerals than fresh, whole foods. In addition, many commercial carbohydrate-rich food products are manufactured using refined white flour, which loses as much as 90 percent of its vitamin and mineral content during the refinement process. Overcooking, storage, and shipping procedures further reduce the nutritional value of such foods.

But even when we commit ourselves to eating healthy, doing so is no longer an easy proposition, due to a variety of factors. Chief among them is the fact that the commercial farming industry, which is responsible for the vast majority of food groups raised in the U.S. and around the world, grows its plants in toxic soils that are laced with petroleum and many other unhealthy chemicals that are contained in commercial crop fertilizers. Such farming methods, which first came into vogue in the early 1900s, have been commonplace since the mid-twentieth century. Though commercial farming methods have resulted in an increase in the yield of crops grown each year, they have all but destroyed the biological balance in crop soil, contributing to a depletion of mineral content. The end result is fruits and vegetables that are severely lacking in nutrients.

The late Dr. Linus Pauling, winner of two Nobel Prizes, was keenly aware of the importance of minerals to health. He said, "You can trace every sickness, every disease, and every ailment to a mineral deficiency." Unfortunately, the adoption of commercial farming methods has resulted in a steady erosion of minerals in our nation's farmlands.

In fact, this trend was recognized as early as 1936, at which time loss of farmland mineral content was already so significant that the United States

Senate issued a warning entitled U.S. Senate Document No. 264 to alert the American public. In it, the Senate stated, "The alarming fact is that foods (fruits, vegetables, and grains) now being raised on millions of acres of land that no longer contains enough of certain minerals are starving us—no matter how much we eat." Since that time, the situation has only grown worse.

This fact was confirmed in 2004 by a study published in the *Journal of the American College of Nutrition* that was conducted by biochemist Dr. Donald Davis and his colleagues at the University of Texas at Austin. In the study, Davis and his research team analyzed the nutrient density of 43 fruits and vegetables grown in 1999 compared to the same crops grown in 1950, based on nutritional data for each type of crop in both years. Among their findings was that levels of protein, vitamin C, riboflavin, and the minerals calcium, phosphorus, and iron were significantly lower in the crops grown in 1999 compared to those grown in 1950. Additional research has shown that overall levels of American farmland's mineral content is one-sixth of what it was in 1950 as a direct result of commercial farming methods. As a result, today's commercially grown food crops are deficient in many essential minerals, including chromium, which is necessary to balance insulin levels and to protect against Type II diabetes; zinc, which is required for proper immune function as well as overall neurological function and healthy digestion; and calcium and magnesium, both of which are essential for the health of the body's musculo-skeletal system.

Other Factors That Contribute to Poor Nutrition

Here are some of the other common factors that contribute to the declining nutritional values in our nation's food supply:

■ Commercial meats and poultry are derived from animals raised in unnaturally tight quarters where they live in unsanitary conditions. To protect the animals against infectious agents and illnesses that thrive within such an environment, the animals receive regular antibiotic shots, the residues of which remain in the meats and poultry after the animals are slaughtered. In order to increase animal weight, and therefore greater yields of meats and poultry, the animals are also given harmful steroids. Steroid residues are also common in commercially harvested meats and poultry. Further compounding this problem is the fact that the animals are fed pesticide-rich, nutrient-poor foods.

■ Our seafood supply has also become increasingly contaminated in the last few decades. Today, many types of fish are riddled with heavy metals, such as mercury, due to environmental poisons that have entered our planet's oceans. As a result, many health experts warn against eating popular seafood such as tuna, swordfish, shrimp, and scallops. Farm-raised seafood is also problematic because it contains high amounts of unhealthy and unnatural substances. Farm-raised salmon, for example, is laced with antibiotics and unhealthy food dyes.

Freshwater fish, found in our nation's lakes, rivers, and streams, are also becoming increasingly unfit for human consumption due to the high levels of environmental toxins they contain, including mercury and PCBs, due to environmental pollution and acid rain.

■ Over the last 60 years, there has also been a significant reduction in the broadness and variety of foods that are being grown. This, too, is in large part due to commercial agriculture, which over the years has emphasized the production of only a handful of crops, such as corn, peanuts, potatoes, rice, and tomatoes, as well as select fruits such as apples, bananas, oranges, and a few other citrus fruits. Such foods, along with dairy products and feedlot meats and poultry, comprise the bulk of the standard American diet. This is in sharp contrast to historical traditional diets, which consisted of literally hundreds of different types of foods, all grown and harvested locally and eaten seasonally. Today, the typical Western diet is nearly entirely (90 percent, on average) comprised of fewer than twenty types of food. By limiting our food intake to the same select foods over and over again, we are further depriving ourselves of the wide array of nutrients a more diverse diet provides. In addition, we are also increasing our risk for food allergies and sensitivities, both of which have been shown to be caused, in part, by repetitious eating patterns.

■ Modern food processing, packaging, and shipping methods further reduce the nutrient content of foods. When fresh, natural whole foods are harvested and processed, the nutrients they contained are impaired, and even destroyed, only to be replaced with an array of chemical preservatives, additives, food dyes, and sugars before they are packaged in boxes, cans, and plastics and, in many cases, shipped thousands of miles from where they were grown.

■ In recent years, an additional health threat has arisen in the form of hybrid crops and genetically modified foods. Although the manufacturers of such foods insist they are safe—as does the United States government— many health experts are wary of such safety claims. One reason for their skepticism is the fact that there are no long-term studies to determine the consequences of eating genetically modified foods on a regular basis over time. For this reason, many nations are refusing to allow the introduction of genetically modified foods into their populations, making the United States the uncontested world leader in this dubious endeavor. Adding to the concerns about GMO (genetically modified organism) food crops is a recent study conducted by the Union of Concerned Scientists that found that more than two-thirds of conventional food crops in the U.S. have been polluted with GMO materials due to the drift of engineered genes into adjoining, non-GMO crops.

These and other factors help to explain why a recent analysis of the nutritional status of U.S. citizens, as well as citizens of other affluent Western nations, conducted by the National Institutes of Health (NIH) found that the majority of people in all of these nations are receiving less than 75 percent of the recommended dietary allowances (RDAs) of many essential nutrients.

In light of such facts, it is incumbent upon all of us who desire good health to do all that we can to ensure that we are not part of the nutritionally deficient majority. Drinking fresh fruit and vegetable juices on a daily basis is one of the easiest and most powerful ways that we can do so. The rest of this chapter is devoted to explaining why.

HEALTH BENEFITS OF JUICED FRUITS AND VEGETABLES

There are many reasons why freshly juiced fruits and vegetables can make profound improvements in your health. As delicious supplements to a healthy diet, they have no equal among the many health products on the market. This is because the complete nutritional spectrum of essential nutrients that fresh-squeezed juices contain cannot be condensed into a vitamin pill. In addition, no other health product—or even healthy foods, for that matter—can match how quickly and easily fresh fruit and vegetable juices are digested and absorbed by the body. Here are some of the other major reasons why juices are so nutritious and why they naturally belong in a healthy diet.

Wholesome Nutrition

One of the great advantages of juicing whole vegetables or fruits is that you don't have to "read the label." Organic produce does not contain any hidden or unhealthy ingredients. As long as the produce is fresh, it is rich in vitamins, minerals, enzymes, and other important nutrients. In addition, unlike most forms of cooking, the process of juicing does not significantly destroy any of these nutrients.

During the juicing process, the fiber that fruits and vegetables contain is separated out, leaving a rich array of nutrients in the juice that is produced. The end result is that you have a tasty beverage loaded with nutrients that your body can put to use immediately because fresh-squeezed juice is almost completely self-digesting. In addition, by juicing, you will be able to easily and conveniently consume a much greater volume of fruits and vegetables than you could ever comfortably do by eating them in a raw or slightly cooked form. One quart of vegetable juice, which can easily be consumed by one person in a single day, supplies the nutrition equivalent to approximately five pounds of solid produce.

Concentrated Nutrition

Nearly all of the nutrients essential for good health can be found in the fruit and vegetable kingdoms. Juicing makes these nutrients available in abundant fashion. Juices made from produce grown organically provide a plentiful supply of vitamins, including antioxidants, which are known to reduce the incidence of cancer, heart disease, and a wide range of infectious diseases, as well as to help prevent premature aging. Organic fruit and vegetable juices also provide a wide array of minerals, which, as we've already mentioned, are absent in non-organic and processed foods.

Juicing also makes it very easy to achieve what is sometimes referred to as "rainbow nutrition," a term that reflects the importance of consuming fruits and vegetables of many colors, so as to ensure that you are obtaining the widest possible array of nutrients each day. The many bold colors of fruits and vegetables are generally due to the wide variety of chlorophylls, carotenes, flavonoids, and proanthocyanidines they contain. All of these types of nutrients play important roles in aiding the body to maintain good health. These include acting as antioxidants, anticarcinogens (anticancer agents), detoxifying agents, digestive aids, natural blood purifiers and blood thinners, immune stimulants, and many other functions, as well. Juicing makes it a simple and convenient process to combine many different colored fruits and vegetables to create delicious and nutritious tonic beverages.

Equally important, juicing makes it easy to obtain the minimum of five daily servings of fruits and vegetables that health authorities now advise is an important preventive health measure. Many people in our society fail to live up to even this moderate suggestion. By converting five pounds of fruit and vegetable produce into a quart of fresh juice, it is easy to exceed this recommendation in a single meal, providing added insurance against the early development of the many chronic diseases that are characteristic of Western society.

Nutritional Synergy

The age-old adage "the whole is greater than the sum of its parts" is especially true when it comes to nutrition. Many nutrients depend on other nutrients in order to function optimally in the body. For example, vitamin E works cooperatively with vitamin C and the mineral selenium, while beta-carotene enhances the benefits of zinc and various other nutrients. Similarly, many other nutrients work best in conjunction with each other to support the body's numerous functions.

This synergistic effect of nutrients is a hallmark of nature's many fruits, vegetables, and herbs, all of which contain various nutrients that work together and catalyze each other to efficiently perform their various functions. For tens of thousands of years, the human body has depended on this "whole-food" balance of nutrients in plant foods and herbs to properly function and maintain itself. (See the inset on page 16 for a discussion of the concept of life energy and fresh-squeezed juice.) Yet modern science is still in the very early stages of discovering and fully understanding the vast number of nutritional interrelationships that exist within nature. As a result, both modern medicine and the nutritional supplement industry focus by and large on the "active ingredients" that they derive or synthesize based on their study of fruits, vegetables, and herbs, failing to recognize that each active ingredient depends on myriad other nutrients to do its job. While nutritional supplements certainly can play an important role in helping to achieve good health, they are not a substitute for the naturally occurring nutritional energy that is available from a healthy, organic-based diet.

The synergistic combinations of nutrients that occur in nature is further disrupted and interfered with when foods are processed. To counteract against this, food manufacturers have for years "enriched" such foods with a limited number of vitamins and minerals at a later stage of the manufacturing process. By doing so, however, they are only providing an inferior balance of the nutrients that cannot compete with the whole-food nutrition provided by nature. This is a fact that was proven by the late Dr. Roger J. Williams, a Nobel Prize winner, whose studies led him to refer to "enriched flour" products as "deficient flour." In a series of controlled animal studies, Dr. Williams revealed how enriched flour actually led to an increase in disease and premature death when compared to natural, whole grains. Subsequent experiments by researchers have confirmed these findings.

Juicing is the best way we know of ensuring that you obtain the synergistic nutritional benefits that fruits and vegetables provide. Not only does juicing make it easier for you to obtain nutrients from a wide variety of fruits and vegetables, it also makes those nutrients readily available. For increased benefit, you can even add various nutritionally potent herbs to your juice combinations, such as burdock, cayenne, and ginger.

Increased Bioavailability

Bioavailability is a term used to describe the degree to, or rate at, which nutrients and other substances are digested, absorbed, and become available to the body. Among all foods, fruits and vegetables have the highest rate of bioavailability, requiring as little as 45 minutes to two hours before the body can make use of the nutrients they contain. By comparison, other types of foods take a much longer time before the body can make use of the nutrients they contain, in some cases, as much as eight or more hours. The longer that it takes for your body to digest the foods you eat, the more energy your body has to use in order to do so. By routinely eating foods that require a lot of time to be digested, you are using up a good deal of your body's energy supply. Conversely, by eating foods that require little digestion time, you allow that energy to remain available for other uses.

Further complicating the question of how quickly foods become bioavailable is the fact that digestive problems are extremely common in the twenty-first century. This is due to such factors as over-reliance on antibiotics, which impair the ability of supportive flora in the intestines to aid in the digestion process; the negative health effects that food additives and preservatives have on gastrointestinal function; chronic stress; and diminished enzyme supply caused by overcooking and processed foods. People who suffer from poor digestion are unable to fully make use of the nutrients contained in the foods they eat. Since fresh vegetable and fruit juices are self-digesting, they offer a solution to this problem, providing a rich supply of nutrients that the body can use almost immediately. Moreover, over time, regularly drinking fresh-squeezed juices also helps to reverse sluggish digestion, especially when accompanied by a shift towards eating healthier foods.

Enzyme Support

Fresh juices contain an abundant supply of enzymes. Enzymes are a class of chemicals in fruits and vegetables that act as catalysts for biochemical reactions. Enzymes are also produced by the body and are necessary for every single function that the body performs. Digestive enzymes, produced by the body and found in fruits and vegetables, are necessary to properly digest carbohydrates, fats, fibers, and proteins. Enzymes enable us to convert large food chemicals into much smaller, absorbable nutrients that can then be used by the body for a wide variety of functions.

The actions of digestive enzymes can be compared to oxygen acting on fire. When oxygen is supplied by wind or a bellows, a fire will burn more intensely, with fire burning more rapidly the drier and smaller the wood becomes. Enzyme-rich fruits and vegetables are digested in a similar fashion. Processed, preserved, and packaged foods can be compared to a wet or moldy log, which, when it is set afire, is slow burning, smoldering, and heavy with dense residue. Such foods lack enzymes and are digested by the body in a similar manner. Carrying this analogy further, when food is properly chewed, it is broken down into ever smaller pieces which, like small pieces of kindling, is more easily burned or digested.

Continuing our analogy, wood can act as fuel for fire, and the foods we eat serve as the fuel our bodies need to produce physical energy and heat and maintain its many functions (including mental and cognitive function). In order for wood to burn most efficiently, it is necessary that the fire be stoked at times. Similarly, foods are most efficiently digested and best made use of when there is an adequate "burn factor," which can only occur when a sufficient supply of enzymes is present. This enables large food chemicals to be fully digested so that the nutrients they contain can fully pass through the intestines to go to work throughout the body. Basically, when adequate enzymes are present, the process of digestion moves fast and efficiently.

But when enzymes are lacking, digestion slows, becoming so compromised that an increasing amount of undigested food particles build up inside the gastrointestinal tract and eventually pass into the bloodstream where they do not belong. When foods aren't fully digested, the availability of the supply of nutrients they contain is diminished. These undigested foods will often feed microbial overgrowth, and will also be a source of absorbed (xenobiotic) toxins. In addition, undigested food particles can act to worsen health by triggering chronic low-grade inflammation, food allergies, and other problems.

Based on this, you can see why enzymes are so important to good health.

Enzymes also play another important role in the body, by providing internal support for the prevention of many types of disease. This fact was extensively illustrated by the late Dr. William Pottinger, one of the twentieth century's foremost nutritional experts and researchers. In dietary experiments involving literally thousands of animals, Pottinger observed that when the animals were fed a standard animal diet that included all of their known nutritional needs, they eventually developed cancer, heart disease, and many other common, contemporary degenerative diseases. By adding chopped vegetable greens to the feed of these animals, he was able to eradicate most of these disease conditions from his laboratory environment. Pot-

tinger and other health researchers theorized that much of the health benefits the added food greens provided were due to the enzymes they contained, acting both within and outside of the digestive process. Since
Pottinger's time, we now know much more about the many actions
enzymes perform, including the fact that they do act preventively to protect against many types of disease.

Because of the importance of enzymes to good digestion and overall
health, many holistically oriented health practitioners recommend diges-

Juice and Vital Energy

One of the most interesting and immeasurable qualities of live, raw foods, including fresh-squeezed juice, is the esoteric concept of "vital" or "life energy." This concept can be found in many of our spiritual traditions, and is known by many names.
In traditional Chinese medicine, it is known as *qi,* while in Japan it is called *ki.* In
Ayurveda, the traditional system of medicine in India, which includes yoga, vital
energy is referred to as *prana.* In Hebrew, it is known as *chai,* and the ancient
Greeks called it *pneuma.* All of these terms can be equated with the animating spirit that makes life possible.

We can measure the energetic, vibrational qualities of enzymes and nutrients
that quickly expire with oxidation, but we are no more able to measure the spirit or
vital energy of plants than we are of humans. Yet, simply because our modern science is unable to measure or quantify this energy doesn't mean that it doesn't exist.
In fact, today a growing number of mainstream scientists agree that such a life force
exists even though, overall, it is usually ignored during scientific experimentation.

Vital life energy is also a central element in a variety of non-conventional healing methods, including acupuncture, reflexology, certain types of bodywork, naturopathic medicine, and the emerging field of "energy medicine." Homeopathy also
recognizes the existence of vital energy, both in humans and in primarily plant-
derived homeopathic remedies. Experiments with diagnostic tools such as Kirlian
photography provide a strong indication of life-force energy surrounding all living
beings. Kirlian photographs also reveal that this life force continues to surround
parts of plants even after they are removed.

Throughout history, many pioneering figures in medicine also taught and wrote
of the existence of vital energy. Among them were Hippocrates, the father of Western medicine; Paracelsus, a sixteenth-century Swiss physician and mystic;
Nicholas Culpeper, a renowned English physician, herbalist, and astrologer of the
seventeenth century; and the German physician and chemist Samuel Hahnemann,

tive enzyme supplements for their patients. While such supplements certainly can be useful, they are usually not necessary once people begin to add fresh juice to their diet on a daily basis. Like the other nutrients that fresh-squeezed organic juice contains, the enzymes go to work quickly because juice is self-digesting and immediately absorbed.

CONCLUSION

In this chapter, we addressed some of the main benefits that juicing can pro-

who invented homeopathic medicine at the end of the eighteenth century. In the twentieth century, the famed botanist Luther Burbank also believed in the existence of a vital life-force energy that guided his groundbreaking botanical discoveries.

Paracelsus referred to the vital life force within all living things, including plants, as the *archaeus*. He believed the life force could be conveyed in an ethereal vehicle that he called the *mumia*. According to Paracelsus, archaeus of plants and herbs, via their mumia, could be transferred to humans in the form of extracts, tinctures, and other preparations. The human system could then absorb and divert this energy into healing or restoring their archaeus, promoting physical and spiritual health and balance. Paracelsus also believed in a "doctrine of signatures" that held that plants inform us of their use in medicine through their appearance and energy. Similarly, Culpeper believed in an astrological basis for plant energy and chose his plant and herbal remedies according to the astrological "sympathies" of both plants and each patient's disease.

References to the transfer and blending of plant energies in the medicinal treatment of humans is scattered throughout the written histories of both Western and Eastern healing traditions. Moreover, the juices of certain plants were sometimes referred to as the "elixir of life." While such writings are of a truly esoteric nature, we cannot ignore the fact that so many esteemed scholars and teachers throughout history have taught that this vital life-force energy exists. From their writings, we can also determine that many of them had direct experience of this energy in their own lives.

Whether or not we, too, have such direct experiences, it is clear that freshly juiced vegetables and fruits contain some of the most nutritious and biologically active and bioavailable nutrients of any food source. Based on this fact, it is logical to assume that fresh-squeezed juices also contain some of the most potent life-force energy to be found anywhere. This explains why many systems of healing teach that this vital energy combines with our own life force to promote the best healing and health imaginable.

vide. Based on the various factors that interfere with your health that we also discussed above, it is our hope that you now recognize how powerfully and conveniently a daily regimen of juicing can be for your overall health. In Chapter 3, we will examine even more of the benefits that you can obtain from juicing. First, though, let's examine the history of juicing throughout the ages. You can find that information in the next chapter.

2

A History of Juicing Through the Ages

The word *juice* is derived from the Latin word *jus,* and is primarily defined as "the liquid part of a fruit or vegetable." Other definitions of juice include both "a liquid in or from animal tissue; as gastric juice, meat juice," and "the essence of anything." All of these definitions help to explain why, in ancient Greece, a common medical tenet was "let juice be your medicine." The use of juices as medicine predates written history and was known to ancient cultures throughout the world. In this chapter, we will share with you a brief overview of the history of juices as a primary form of medicine, dating back to biblical times and beyond.

JUICING IN ANCIENT TIMES

The first written records of the medicinal use of juice date back thousands of years, while fruits and vegetables eaten raw clearly predates the discovery of fire. Succulent and easily extracted fruits, such as lemons, oranges, and pomegranates, have been made into beverages by many cultures around the world since the dawn of recorded history. Island cultures, such as those in Polynesia, have also long prepared nourishing beverages from tropical, indigenous fruits, such as noni and xango, the juices of which are recognized today to contain an abundance of vital, health-promoting nutrients. And in Peru, passion fruit has long been mashed and combined with water to make a refreshing, nutritious drink. The use of fruits like these to make juices and other beverages is a natural outgrowth of their ease of extraction, combined with the recognition of native peoples of their delicious taste and health-restorative properties.

Juicing In Biblical Times

In our Western culture, one of the first records of the use of fruits and vegetables for healing can be found in the Bible, specifically in Genesis 1:29 of the Old Testament, wherein it is written, "And God said, 'Behold, I have given you every herb-bearing seed which is upon the face of all the earth, and every tree in thee which is the fruit of a tree yielding seed; to you it shall be for meat." This can be considered the first law given to mankind that can be found in the Bible. (See "Returning to a Natural Diet," below.)

We can also find written passages recommending juices for healing in the collection of writings known as the Dead Sea Scrolls. So named because they were discovered in the mid-twentieth century buried in caves near the Dead Sea, the Dead Sea Scrolls date from 100 BC to approximately 70 AD. Collectively, they comprise a body of religious writings from both the Jewish and Essene traditions. The Essenes were a desert-based community in ancient Israel who are known to have followed a vegetarian diet. Among the health recommendations that can be found in the Dead Sea Scrolls is to make "a pounded mash of pomegranate and fig" in order to achieve "profound strength and subtle form."

Around the same time that the Dead Sea Scrolls began to be discovered (the 1940s), two brothers, Muhammad and Khalifah Ali, came upon a sealed jar at the base of a boulder that had fallen from some ancient caves located above. This jar was another treasure trove of ancient spiritual writings found in the Naj Hammadi region of upper Egypt. Known as the Nag Hammadi Library, these writings contained twelve volumes of scriptural teachings, with part of a thirteenth tucked into the pages of volume six, that date back to the time of early Christianity. Sometimes also referred to as the Gnostic Gospels because of the emphasis they give to *gnosis*, or "direct

Returning to a Natural Diet

Commenting on the Genesis passage in his book *Return to Nature*, Adolf Just, a noted German naturopathic healer of the late nineteenth and early twentieth centuries, remarked that fruits, vegetables, and nuts are the natural foods for all humans. He added that only these foods, which taste good in their natural, raw form, promote health. In Just's view, such foods constitute our "natural diet." In observing that our senses lead us to a healthy and natural diet, he humorously pointed out that none of us have our appetite stimulated by standing near a live cow, while most of us do when we smell the fragrance of ripe fruit. By adopting the "natural diet" that he recommended, Just was able to heal himself of long-standing health problems, and eventually founded the Jungborn Clinic in Germany, where hundreds of patients gained relief from their health complaints following the same diet.

knowledge of spiritual things," the volumes of the Nag Hammadi Library were successfully translated in the 1970s.

Among the volumes the Library contains is the Gospel of Thomas, said to be written by St. Thomas, one of the original twelve apostles of Jesus. In the Gospel of Thomas is the following passage: "For there are five trees for you in Paradise which remain undisturbed summer and winter and whose leaves do not fall. Whosoever becomes acquainted with them will not experience death." The five trees referred to are indigenous to the Middle East and bear fruit continuously without their leaves falling. All five of these fruits can easily be made into juice, or be prepared as delicious, nourishing smoothies. We will discuss them in more detail in Chapter 6.

JUICING IN ANCIENT INDIA

Some of the earliest recorded writings recommending juices for medicinal purposes occur in the healing traditions of Ayurvedic medicine, or Ayurveda, which originated in ancient India. The term *Ayurveda* comes from the Sanskrit language and means "science of life." Along with traditional Chinese medicine, Ayurveda is one of the oldest complete systems of medicine in the world, having been practiced in India for over 5,000 years. Its origins lie in the Vedas, which are considered by historians to be the world's oldest surviving body of literature, and primarily related to spirituality, healing, and man's threefold nature of "body, mind, and spirit."

The earliest Ayurvedic texts were written by the physician sages Charaka and Sushruta, and are known respectively as the *Charaka Samhita* and the *Sushruta Samhita*. Charaka taught approximately 3,000 years ago, and is credited with the discovery that all substances, both organic and inorganic, have definite potential or kinetic attributes. Based on careful observation, Charaka categorized twenty basic attributes into ten opposite pairs that function together, such as hot and cold, wet and dry, slow and fast, and so forth. In the *Charaka Samhita*, he catalogued the medicinal attributes of over 700 plants, and indicated their use both as food and, in many cases, prepared as juices, teas, and other beverages. Sushruta, who was born nearly one-thousand years after Charaka, was very much influenced by him, and added to his compiled knowledge, as well as pioneering many methods of surgery. The writings of both men continue to be used today by students and practitioners of Ayurveda throughout India, and are included in the curriculum of Ayurvedic medical schools.

In the West, meditation and yoga are two of the most popular aspects of Ayurvedic medicine, and in recent decades, a greater understanding of Ayurvedic healing methods have entered into Western cultures, thanks to the writings and teachings of its proponents, such as Deepak Chopra, Dr. Vasant Lad, Dr. Hari Sharma, and Dr. David Frawley. Today, Ayurvedic medicine is recognized by the World Health Organization (WHO), which has recommended that it be included as part of a comprehensive modern medical approach to health.

It is interesting to note that in Ayurveda one of the Sanskrit terms for bodily tissue is *ras,* which means both "life" and "juice." According to Ayurvedic theory, a person's life energy, known as *prana,* and his or her bodily tissues should both be full of juice, flowing properly and abundantly in order to have sound health. Ayurvedic practitioners teach that when a person's life energy is flowing freely, health, happiness, and relaxation result. Similarly, when a person's *ras,* or body tissues, are healthy and free of constriction, he or she will have more energy and is likely to live a long and healthy life.

The pressed juices of fruits, vegetables, and herbs have been used by Ayurvedic physicians for thousands of years. Known as *svarash,* these healing juices were often also extracted using heat, and were sometimes mixed with raw milk (containing over twenty different enzymes) or cultured milk, known as lassi, and honey to make their taste more palatable, especially when administered to children. Among the plants used for this purpose were aloe vera and black nightshade. Because of the potency of such plants, their juices were typically given in small doses. Other Ayurvedic juice remedies include drinking fresh orange or lime juice with a pinch of rock salt to promote recovery from fatigue, and the use of juices that restore the health of the blood, such as pomegranate, grape, or beet juice, in order to treat anemia. Mango juice mixed with warm milk and spices such as cardamom or nutmeg was also used to promote greater energy. For parasitic worms, pumpkin juice was advised, taken on an empty stomach.

Onion is another vegetable that was prized by both Charaka and Sushruta for its many health-promoting attributes. In addition to their recommendation that onion be included in meals to enhance vitality, they also wrote that onion juice mixed with honey could be used for the same purpose. They also recommended onion juice as a topical treatment for head lice, and as a tonic for children suffering from worms in the stomach.

Radish is another vegetable both Charaka and Sushruta wrote about. Among the uses they cited were its effectiveness as a juice for treating stomachache associated with flatulence, and as an aid for kidney and gallstones. Additional juices and their uses mentioned by Charaka and Sushruta include tomato, to treat disease conditions related to excess bile, as a heart tonic, and to treat vomiting and stomach conditions; lemon, to increase energy, relieve inflammation, and to treat malaria; pear, to treat diarrhea and to increase sexual desire; and *amla* (a traditional Indian fruit), to strengthen the heart and to help maintain the health of the female sex organs.

JUICING IN THE TIME OF HIPPOCRATES AND ANCIENT GREECE

The foundations of modern medicine were first laid down in ancient Greece and are based on the Hippocratic writings, named after the Greek healer Hippocrates, who is often referred to as the father of Western medicine. Hippocrates, who lived from 470 to 377 BC, formulated many of the medical teachings that are still taught in today's medical schools. In addition to his famous adage, "Let food be thy medicine, and thy medicine your food," he also counseled his students to, "First, do no harm," advising them to always seek out the most appropriate healing methods most conducive to each patient's specific individual needs and least likely to cause adverse side effects.

The major existing work of Hippocrates is known as the *Hippocratic Corpus*, which historians believe is primarily a compilation of writings by Hippocrates's students, as well as other physicians who practiced medicine according to his teachings. Hippocrates himself wrote little, preferring to pass along his knowledge orally, and only to those students whom he deemed worthy of receiving it, and who could be trusted to keep it secret from those who would misuse it. (This veiled method of teaching was true of Egyptian and Persian physicians as well.) Among Hippocrates's many contributions to medicine was the comprehensive system he developed cataloguing disease conditions and their symptoms. The first such system ever to be developed in the Western world, it provided physicians with a more complete understanding of the nature of their patients' illnesses, enabling them to not only understand the course of a given disease, but also its current symptoms, as well as the symptoms and conditions from the patient's past that had led up to it. This made for a much more accurate prognosis, and therefore a more effective course of treatment.

Hippocrates was a proponent of the use of juices and other beverages for treating diseases, as well as for maintaining heath. This is hardly surprising, given the high esteem that the ancient Greeks gave to juices, wines, and meads, some of which were referred to as the "nectar of the gods." Interestingly, the word *nectar*, which is derived from both Greek and Latin, literally means "overcoming death," and refers to drinks that were considered capable of conferring immortality.

The importance Hippocrates gave to such nectars, or juices, had a twofold basis. Not only did he recognize the restorative healing properties of juices, but he also believed that human life was due to the presence and intermingling of four fluid essences or "juices." The juices were blood, phlegm, and yellow and black bile, which were also known as *humors.* Changes in these humors were considered responsible for the creation of disease. Sick patients were categorized according to the qualities, or flavors, of their humors, such as bitter, sweet, wet, dry, hot, cold, acidic, astringent, and so forth.

Based in large part upon such categorizations, an appropriate course of treatment was planned that would produce an opposite effect. For example, a patient who exhibited fluid retention (superfluous nature) might be prescribed a natural diuretic, or undergo a specific course of bloodletting. (At the time of Hippocrates, the practice of bloodletting was a specific type of surgery with precise indications, something that was far different from the eventual practice of generalized bloodletting, or leeching.) As another example, patients who were determined to be ill due to bitter humors were often given sweet wine or honey-based meads, whereas the "sweet" patient would be prescribed bitter wines or vinegar products.

In his writings, Hippocrates mentioned the use of "drinks made from barley, herbs, raisins, or from the second pressing of grapes, from wheat, thistle or myrtle, pomegranates and the rest." He was also a proponent of the use of juice pressed from the roots or the stalk of the herb silphium, which today is better known as asafetida. Added to the herb purple spurge, Hippocrates recommended this silphium juice as a laxative. He also recommended the juices of various other plants and herbs, as well as strained grains such as barley for a variety of other medical uses, including enemas and to help assist the process of fever. In keeping with his teaching to "above all, do no harm," Hippocrates considered juices and other liquids to be some of the safest medical treatments available in his day. Among his aphorisms, he taught that "Fluid diets are beneficial to all who suffer from fevers," and that, "It is better to be full of drink than full of food."

The use of juices and other beverages for healing continued to be a part of the ancient Greek healing tradition after Hippocrates died. One proponent was Dioscorides, who was born in southeastern Asia Minor in 40 AD. During his lifetime, Dioscorides traveled extensively seeking medicinal substances from all over the Roman and Greek world, and he also served as a physician and botanist for the armies of the infamous Roman emperor Nero. Whereas Hippocrates utilized juices and other beverages based on the function they would provide in the body when consumed—for example, as

Allopathic Medicine

It is interesting to note that from Hippocrates's theory of opposites came the contemporary term *allopath,* a term used to denote the opposite of *pathos,* or disease symptoms. Today, conventional physicians are also known as allopathic physicians. However, the modern practice of allopathic medicine does not seek the original "bringing to a balance" and unfortunately too often ignores another essential element of Hippocrates's approach to healing—the principle of *prognosis.* Today, a patient's prognosis usually means little more than a prediction relating to the likely outcome of his or her disease. To Hippocrates, however, an effective prognosis took into consideration not only a projected outcome, but also a more comprehensive diagnosis of the patient's illness, and an awareness of the factors that caused it to originate.

Allopathic physicians today also often fail to recognize the importance that symptoms of inflammation and fever have in relation to healing. Hippocrates regarded the nature and quality of such symptoms as integral aspects of the healing process and prognosis, and therefore recommended that they be encouraged so that illnesses could more quickly run their course. Today, however, such symptoms are commonly suppressed by doctors, causing them, in many cases, to inadvertently prolong or worsen their patients' conditions.

expectorants or laxatives—rather than as remedies for diseases, Dioscorides and other Greek physicians born after Hippocrates's time began to catalogue particular juice and herbal remedies for specific disease conditions.

Between 50 and 70 AD, Dioscorides developed and wrote a five-volume reference text devoted to cataloguing the preparation, properties, and testing of the medicinal remedies he used, including juices. His work became known, in Latin, as the *De materia medica,* and was used throughout much of Europe and the Middle East for the next 1,600 years as a primary medical reference. Among recommended juice remedies contained in the *De materia medica* are pomegranate juice for gastric ulcers and ulcers of the mouth, cherry juice mixed with wine for kidney stones, and extract of juniper berry mixed with honey for use as a diuretic.

JUICING IN ANCIENT ROME

Physicians in ancient Rome were greatly influenced by Greek healers such as Hippocrates and Dioscorides. Among the most notable of them was Galen of Pergamum, so named as he was born in 131 AD in Pergamum, a part of the Roman Empire that is now known as Bergama, Turkey. Although chiefly known as a physician and biologist, Galen was also a philosopher and a literary scholar, and was deeply influenced by Hippocrates and the *Hippocratic Corpus*. Like Hippocrates, he regarded much of the practice of medicine in his day to be based on superstition, ignorance, and greedy practitioners.

Galen began his medical career as a physician and surgeon tending Roman gladiators in his homeland, during which time he learned much about human anatomy. Four years later, he emigrated to Rome, where he quickly gained a reputation as a brilliant physician. As a result, he counted the Roman emperors Marcus Aurelius, Lucius Verus, Commodus, and Septimius Severus among his many patients.

As he continued his medical research, Galen employed scribes to record his findings and medical opinions. He also wrote commentaries on nineteen Hippocratic texts, elaborating on their meaning. Among these commentaries, he quoted Hippocrates as treating a woman who suffered from heartburn and vomiting with "fine barley meal with pomegranate juice and making one meal of it a day," noting that she warded off the heartburn and that her vomiting ceased. In addition to his many other accomplishments, Galen is credited with discovering that minerals such as calcium, sodium, and sulphur are components of the body's tissues.

While the Roman Empire flourished, its physicians continued to emphasize diet, herbal medicine, exercise, and hydrotherapy as essential elements of their overall approach to healing, largely due to Galen's influence during this period. A variety of juice remedies were also employed by Roman physicians due to Galen's teachings and writings. For example, in his book on foodstuffs, he cites many juices that could be used both for their nutritional values and for their medicinal qualities. These included easily extracted juice obtained from apples, raw grapes, green grapes, pears, and citron, a type of citrus fruit closely related to lemons and limes. Galen also recommended a variety of vegetable juices, including cabbage, celery, and beet juice and stated that it should be used as a medicine and not a food, also noting that, "nothing boiled can preserve the specific juice completely." In this observation, he perceived that overcooking destroys the nutritional value of fruits and vegetables, something that modern science would not know until the discovery of vitamins and enzymes many centuries later.

Galen's influence over medicine lasted for nearly 1,500 years, both in Europe and in Israel, and throughout much of the Arab world. Unfortunately, over time, especially after the fall of the Roman Empire and the dawn of the Dark Ages, much of what Galen taught was overshadowed by superstitions and ignorance. Eventually, the worth of Galen's teachings was all but supplanted with unfounded beliefs and ill-advised medical practices, resulting in a system of medicine that caused harm to a great many people. Even so, the importance of Galen's contributions to medicine cannot be overstated.

JUICING THROUGHOUT THE CENTURIES

Throughout much of the Middle Ages, the medical advances of pioneering physicians such as Hippocrates and Galen were lost or misrepresented as the medical practices in Europe became increasingly steeped in superstition and procedures that often did far more harm than good. Although Galen was still considered the preeminent medical authority nearly 1,500 years after his birth, by the early sixteenth century, the system of medicine that he taught had been obscured by the ignorance that caused so many scientific advancements to fade from memory. Ironically, despite the fact that much of Galen's teachings were ignored, physicians throughout this period regarded any alteration of what they believed to be the Galenic system of medicine to be heretical.

Paracelsus

Such a sad state of affairs might have continued for an even longer period but for the research and advances brought to medicine by Auroleus Phillipus Theostratus Bombastus von Hohenheim, better known today by the name he gave himself—Paracelsus. Born in Switzerland in 1493, Paracelsus was the son of a physician who grew up to become one of the most highly regarded, if controversial, alchemists, surgeons, and physicians of the Renaissance period. A gifted child with a prodigious intellect and curiosity, Paracelsus began his formal medical education at the age of 16, when he entered the University of Basel. While there, he sought to cure illnesses using medicines superior to anything practiced at that time. Among his many achievements, Paracelsus is credited with introducing the use of various chemicals and minerals for use as medicines, including opium, mercury, and zinc (which he named, calling it "zink" because of the sharp pointed appearance of its crystals after smelting, and the fact that "zinke" was the German word for "pointed"). He also exhibited an advanced understanding of the scientific principles of magnetism as they related to health and healing. So impressive were his overall achievements that historian Manly P. Hall described him as "the precursor of chemical pharmacology and therapeutics and the most original medical thinker of the sixteenth century."

Because of his disregard for the accepted medical tenets of his time, Paracelsus ran afoul of the authorities, and, as a result, in 1516 he was forced to flee Switzerland. For the next ten years, he lived a nomadic existence, traveling through Europe, the Middle East, and Asia. In 1526, he settled in Germany, where he took a professorship of physics, medicine, and surgery. Soon thereafter, he publicly denounced the accepted medical practices of his time, going so far as to burn the works of Galen and other medical authorities and infuriating many of his medical peers in the process. It is interesting to note that his high-handed actions led to such behavior being described as "bombastic," a word derived from part of his name (Bombastus). Adding to the envy and ridicule he received from many in the medical field, he gave himself the name Paracelsus, which literally means "superior to Celsus," Celsus being a highly regarded physician during the time of the Roman Empire.

Due to his confrontational nature, Paracelsus did not retain his professorship for long, even though his medical approaches continued to garner him acclaim because of their successful outcomes, especially with European royalty. Soon after his return to Germany, he was once again on the move, spending the next ten years as a traveling healer who continued to be attacked by medical authorities. Yet such attacks did not diminish Paracelsus's reputation as a healer. During this period, he regularly achieved cures that were considered amazing for his time, including a number of severe cases of elephantiasis.

Because of his great skill, as well as his reputation as an alchemist, eventually Paracelsus was invited to settle in Salzburg, Austria by Prince Palatine, Duke of Bavaria, who was also interested in alchemy. Paracelsus died in 1541 after a short illness, and some claim that he was actually poisoned by assassins hired by his jealous medical rivals, although there is no proof that this was so. Although his medical theories and written works were unpopular during his lifetime, after his death his therapies became more widely known and used, leading to a school of medicine known as Paracelsianism.

Like Hippocrates, Paracelsus considered the vital essences of plants and fluids critical to the medicines he prepared. His methods for compounding the extracts of plants were succinct and meticulous and intended to capture the vital life-force energy the plants contained so that they could be put to use as healing aids, often in the form of juices. In considering what constituted human life, Paracelsus used the metaphor of sulphur, mercury, and salt, which was very similar to the ancient Greek concept that "being" was a trilogy of substance, form (or intention), and spirit/soul.

In Paracelsus's view, sulphur was akin to spirit, salt was substance, and fluid mercury served to illustrate the necessary unification of the spirit within and the physical substances of life that made human existence possible. He also taught that both health and sickness in the body were directly related to the harmony or disharmony between man (as microcosm) and Nature (macrocosm), a guiding principle of medicine that can also be found in Ayurvedic and traditional Chinese medicine. Accordingly, he recognized that, for health to be present, his patients required a balance of minerals and other chemicals in their bodies, some of which could be supplied through the plant extracts he prepared.

Although his fame as an alchemist led many to mistakenly assume he was concerned with creating wealth from base metals (and used elemental mercury as a medicine), Paracelsus stated, "Many have said of Alchemy, that it is for the making of gold and silver. For me such is not the aim, but to consider only what virtue and power may lie in medicines."

John Hall

Another famous proponent of juice therapy was the English physician and herbalist John Hall, who was born in 1575. Hall began his medical career at the turn of the seventeenth century, when he was 25. Seven years later, he became William Shakespeare's son-in-law when he married the famous playwright's oldest daughter. Only eleven years younger than Shakespeare, Hall developed a close friendship with him and it is perhaps because of their relationship that Shakespeare's plays contain many positive portrayals of doctors, as well as favorable allusions to herbs.

Medical practice in England during Hall's lifetime was riddled with the same superstitions and unfounded treatments as those Paracelsus encountered in Europe a century earlier. Like Paracelsus, Hall was an exception to this norm, and gained a reputation as a skilled physician and herbalist who exhibited a high degree of compassion and sensitivity to both his patients' physical and psychological needs. In addition to employing over one hundred herbal remedies in his practice, Hall also advised patients about their diet and made use of juice extracts from a variety of plants.

One of the areas in which Hall excelled was in the treatment of scurvy, which was quite common in the England of his day, due to a diet that consisted primarily of salted meat and fish, with few vegetables or fruits. Hall recorded that patients with scurvy suffered from a "general lassitude, filthy yellow jaundice, pains in the loins, weakness of the legs, frequent changes of urine, tumors of the gums, swelling of the fingers, sweating, and wandering pains." He successfully reversed these conditions by preparing a mixture of vegetable juices made from watercress, and the herbs brooklime and scurvy grass, all of which are rich in vitamin C. At times, he also brewed the above plants into a beer flavored with sugar and cinnamon or juniper berries. Hall's treatment of scurvy predated the use of lime juice for scurvy that was popularized by another famous England physician, James Lind, one hundred years later.

The Natural Hygiene Movement and Naturopathy

The medicinal use of juices resurfaced in the nineteenth century with the advent of two related systems of health care—the Natural Hygiene, or Hygienist, movement, and naturopathy—both of which focused on the direct relationship between diet and wellness. The Natural Hygiene movement arose in the United States in the early part of the nineteenth century. Among its earliest proponents was Reverend Sylvester Graham, a Presbyterian minister who invented the Graham cracker.

Central tenets of Natural Hygiene teachings are that the human body possesses the power to heal itself, and that stress and internal toxicity (toxemia) caused by overeating and the eating of unhealthy foods, not germs, are the primary causes of disease. To correct toxemia, Hygienist practitioners often had their patients undergo curative water fasts. However, often patients were unable to undertake water fasts initially because of their overconsumption of processed and denatured foods. Such people were at risk for a toxic healing crisis. As a result, Hygienists typically advised a diet of fresh, whole foods, along with various soups and fruit and vegetable juices.

Arnold Ehret, who was born in Germany in 1866, became a well-known advocate of what was essentially a Natural Hygienist philosophy after he followed such principles to cure himself of a long-standing heart condition. Arriving in the United States at the turn of the twentieth century, Ehret embarked on a nationwide lecture tour teaching others about his healing methods. In his book, *Rational Fasting,* he wrote that many people were too congested with mucus to effectively eliminate toxins through water fasts. For such people, he recommended daily drinks or a total diet of lemon juice (unsugared or with honey) to loosen, thin, and eliminate mucus from their system prior to undergoing a water fast. Other Hygienist practitioners before and after Ehret also promoted the use of fresh juices as a means to greater health.

Naturopathy originated in Austria around the same time that the Natural Hygiene movement was taking shape in America. An early proponent of naturopathy was Father Sebastian Kneipp, an Austrian who, after using hydrotherapy to cure himself of tuberculosis, went on to use naturopathy to minister to the health needs of his sick parishioners. One of his students and former patients, Benjamin Lust, whom Kneipp cured of tuberculosis, introduced his mentor's teachings in the United States and is considered the modern founder of naturopathy. Once in the U.S., Lust expanded the scope of naturopathy far beyond hydrotherapy, adding diet and nutrition, herbology, homeopathy, spinal manipulation, and stress reduction techniques to create a complete system of natural medicine. Also included in Lust's healing regimen was the use of various fruit and vegetables juices for treating a wide variety of health conditions. It is largely through the contributions of natural healers such as Ehret and Lust that the medicinal value of raw juices entered, and remained known at, the dawn of the twentieth century. But it would take the work of another physician, Dr. Norman W. Walker, to bring juicing to the forefront of natural therapy.

JUICING IN MODERN TIMES

Without question, the primary advocate of the health benefits of fresh fruit and vegetable juices throughout the twentieth century was Dr. Norman W. Walker. Born in England on January 28, 1867, Walker lived for 118 years, dying peacefully in his sleep on June 6, 1985 during an afternoon nap, with no indication of illness. His interest in juicing occurred before the dawn of the twentieth century, after he became seriously ill due to overwork and stress. While convalescing in the French countryside, he noticed the moistness under the skin of carrots as they were peeled by a kitchen worker. Curious, he decided to grind them up, creating his first cup of carrot juice.

In his book, *Raw Vegetable Juices,* which he published in 1936, Walker wrote, "My first experiments were made by grating carrots on anything that would reduce them to a pulp, then squeezing the pulp in a cloth, to get the juice. After discovering the miracle of using the juice so simply made, I tried making the carrots into other means until I could make a larger amount of juice for myself in less time and with less effort. I soon discovered that these juices fermented and spoiled unless used immediately, the time element being the factor."

As a result of daily drinking fresh-squeezed carrot juice, as well as adopting a primarily fresh, raw food diet, Walker soon restored himself to health. Convinced of the health-giving properties of fresh juices, Walker termed them "Living Food," and spent the rest of his long life researching, writing, and lecturing to others about the numerous health benefits. He began this career in 1910, after moving to Long Beach, California. With the help of a medical doctor, he opened what was perhaps the first juice bar, offering home delivery to his customers. For the next twenty years, he developed dozens of fresh juice remedies for a variety of health conditions. Always seeking to improve on his methods for preparing fresh juice, in the 1930s, he designed and developed the first modern juicer, known as the Norwalk, a term he created using the first syllable of his first and last names.

Recounting the Norwalk's development, Walker wrote, "Eventually, I discovered a means to triturate [grind] the vegetables almost instantly into a pulp nearly as fine as apple butter, thereby splitting open the interstices of the cells of the fibers, liberating the atoms and molecules. Then, by squeezing the pulp in a hydraulic press, I obtained a virtually complete extraction of the juice and its quality was unsurpassed." The Norwalk is still sold today.

Throughout his lifetime, thousands of people credited Walker's live vegetable juice therapy with helping them recover from serious, and often chronic, health conditions. One of these was Jay Kordich, formerly known as the "Juice Man." In the 1940s, Kordich was diagnosed with cancer. After meeting with Walker, he was inspired to experiment with juice therapy and a raw food diet. The result was that Kordich cured himself. After that, he continued to work with Walker for the rest of Walker's life, and since that time has continued to tout the benefits of juicing.

Today, largely because of Walker's pioneering efforts, juice therapy is used by many practitioners of natural health approaches, and juice bars can be found throughout the United States and abroad. Following the advent of the Norwalk juicer, a number of other juicers have been developed, making it increasingly easy and affordable for anyone to prepare their own fresh juices on a daily basis. (For more information about the types of juicers currently available, see Chapter 4.)

CONCLUSION

As this chapter reveals, the use of fresh juice to maintain health and help treat disease is hardly a new fad. Rather, juices and their health-giving benefits have been recognized by innovative healers for literally thousands of years. Today, the benefits of fresh juice are more important than ever due to a variety of factors. Chief among them is the fact that we have strayed so drastically from the natural, traditional diets of our ancestors. Our modern diets are increasingly comprised of chemically contaminated and genetically altered foods, grown and harvested in unnatural environments, leading to a host of nutritional imbalances and contributing to nearly all disease conditions, including life-threatening illnesses such as heart disease and cancer.

Fortunately, in recent decades, the need for a return to healthier, more natural food production has increasingly been recognized and implemented, so that today it is fairly easy to obtain organically raised food. By preparing fresh juice from organic fruits and vegetables, you can create a bridge back to a state of vibrant health. And upon this bridge, you can regain the benefits of a truly healthy diet so that your food can truly be your medicine, as Hippocrates advised.

3

Powerful Nutrition

N ow that you have a better understanding of how raw fruit and vegetable juices were used for healing by various health traditions throughout the ages, let's return to our discussion of how and why juicing can be so effective as an aid for improving and maintaining health. As we mentioned in Chapter 1, freshly squeezed raw fruit and vegetable juices, once they are consumed, quickly go to work in your body to provide a wide range of health benefits. In this chapter, we will discuss those benefits in more detail.

LIQUID ENERGY

During the juicing process, the cell wall of fruits and vegetables is cut open, releasing an abundance of nutrients, such as amino acids, vitamins, minerals, enzymes, and chlorophyll, all of which are quickly absorbed by the body once the resultant fresh juice is consumed. It is precisely because fresh juices contain such an abundance of nutrients that juicing can create such an energizing effect in the body. To fully understand how this is possible, let's briefly explore the functions of each class of nutrients.

Amino Acids

Amino acids are the building blocks of proteins, which make up over half of your body's dry (non-water) weight. Without an adequate supply of amino acids, many functions in your body cannot be performed or occur at sub-optimal levels. When your body's supply of amino acids is deficient, a host of health problems can result.

Certain amino acids can only be supplied to the body from the foods you eat. For this reason, these eight amino acids are known as *essential amino acids*, and must be obtained in sufficient quantities from your diet to ensure good health. More than a dozen other amino acids are also important for your overall health, but they can be manufactured by your body on its own. The eight essential amino acids are isoleucine, leucine, lysine, methionine, phenylalanine, threonine, tryptophan, and valine.

Amino acids play essential roles in literally thousands of functions that are carried out by your body each and every day, including cellular regeneration and the manufacture of new cells. Amino acids are also needed for the proper buildup and repair of your body's muscles, blood, and organs, as well as for the manufacture of hormones. They are required for healthy digestion, proper immune function, healthy mental function (including memory and mental alertness), proper liver function, proper circulation, restful sleep, and abundant physical and mental energy. Deficiencies in just one amino acid, if left unchecked, can result in a wide range of health problems, ranging from accelerated aging, allergies, and gastrointestinal disorders to sleep disorders, hormonal imbalances, impaired brain function, and an impaired ability of your body to repair and regenerate itself.

By drinking fresh-squeezed juices on a daily basis, you can provide your body with the amino acids it requires in forms that are easily digested and assimilated. The amino acid content found in fresh juices varies, however. For the most plentiful supply, use juices made from dark, leafy green vegetables and sprouts.

Vitamins

As a class, vitamins are perhaps the nutrients most people are familiar with. Vitamins play many vital roles in your body. Like minerals and the essential amino acids, many vitamins cannot be manufactured by the body and therefore must be supplied via the foods we eat.

Vitamins are especially important for the proper performance and regulation of your body's numerous biochemical and metabolic processes and reactions. When vitamins in the body become deficient—a very common condition among people who eat the standard American diet—all of these various biological functions can be impaired. The end result is poor health and, often, the onset of a variety of disease conditions that are specifically related to vitamin deficiencies.

There are two classes of vitamins: fat-soluble and water-soluble. Fat-soluble vitamins get their name because they are capable of being stored in body tissues, where they can be drawn upon when they are not being obtained through diet. The fat-soluble vitamins are vitamins A, D, E, and K. Carrots are an excellent source of vitamin A, as are yellow and dark, leafy green vegetables. Dark, leafy green vegetables are also excellent sources of vitamins E and K. When juiced, these vegetables quickly provide your body with a rich supply of these vitamins.

Another subclass of fat-soluble vitamins is known as *carotenoids*. There are over 500 natural substances that are included in this category, all of which naturally occur in fruits and vegetables. More than fifty carotenoids act as precursors for vitamin A. This means that when such carotenoids, which include beta-carotene, are consumed, they provide the body with the raw materials it needs to convert them into vitamin A. Among the best food sources of carotenoids are yellow and dark green vegetables, orange fruits from the citrus family, cherries, and watermelons. Juicing these fruits and vegetables provides an abundant source of easily assimilated carotenoids, as well as many other vitamins and vital nutrients.

Water-soluble vitamins cannot be stored by the body and so must be obtained on a daily basis from the foods you eat. Water-soluble vitamins include all B vitamins and vitamin C. Vitamin B_1 (thiamine) is contained in all plant foods, and is particularly concentrated in seaweed. Green leafy vegetables are a good source of vitamins B_2 (riboflavin) and B_9 (folic acid or folate), while vitamin B_6 (pyridoxine) is found in bananas, cabbage, and cauliflower. Vitamin C is found in a wide range of fruits and vegetables, including all citrus fruits, cantaloupe, cherries, papaya, strawberries, red and green peppers, parsley, and dark, leafy green vegetables.

Another subclass of water-soluble vitamins is known as *bioflavonoids*. Collectively, bioflavonoids are sometimes referred to as vitamin P because of their ability to increase permeability of the capillary walls, making it easier for other nutrients, as well as oxygen and carbon dioxide, to pass in and out of the capillaries. Bioflavonoids also increase your body's ability to absorb and make use of vitamin C. The best plant food sources of bioflavonoids are the same foods listed above that are rich in vitamin C. As with fat-soluble vitamins, juicing is an excellent way to ensure that your body obtains a rich supply of most water-soluble vitamins.

Minerals

Minerals are another class of nutrients that is essential for good health. Mineral stores in your body's tissues and fluids comprise nearly five percent of your body's total weight. Acting in concert with vitamins, enzymes, and various other substances in your body, including hormones, minerals play an integral role in the literally thousands of functions and processes that occur within your body each day. These include blood formation, energy production, enzyme function, proper metabolism, proper muscle function, nerve transmission, the proper growth and maintenance of your bones and teeth, regulation of body fluids, and the maintenance of acid-alkaline balance. Moreover, without an adequate supply of minerals, vitamins and other nutrients are unable to properly perform their own functions in the body.

In addition, minerals are important for proper cell function, and are required for healthy cellular regeneration as old cells die out and are replaced by new cells, a process that occurs in your body every day. Without an adequate supply of minerals, both existing cells and the cells that replace them can become unhealthy and lose their ability to carry out the many tasks for which nature designed them. When this happens, the stage is set for the onset of chronic and degenerative diseases to take hold within your body.

There are two classes of minerals: *macrominerals* and *trace minerals.* Each class is determined by how much of the total percentage of body weight they comprise. Macrominerals comprise 0.01 or more of total body weight, while trace minerals make up less than that amount. The macrominerals most important for good health are calcium, chloride, magnesium, phosphorous, potassium, silicon, sodium, and sulfur. Ten trace minerals are considered to be essential for health. They are chromium, cobalt, copper, iodine, iron, manganese, molybdenum, selenium, vanadium, and zinc. Other trace minerals, while not considered to be essential, have still been shown to contribute to overall health. They include boron, lithium, nickel, and strontium.

Because minerals are inorganic, they cannot be produced or synthesized by your body. Therefore, it is vitally important that you receive an adequate supply of minerals each day from the foods you consume. Unfortunately, research shows that the vast majority of the population in the United States suffers from some level of mineral deficiencies. In fact, this phenomenon is not new, and was even highlighted by the United States Senate in 1936 when it issued U.S. Senate Document No. 264, which we mentioned in Chapter 1. In addition to warning that, "No man of today can eat enough fruits and vegetables to supply his system with the minerals he requires for perfect health because his stomach isn't big enough to hold them," the document also added, "Our physical well-being is more directly dependent upon the minerals we take into our system than upon calories or vitamins or upon the precise proportions of starch, protein, or carbohydrates we consume." As we also mentioned in Chapter 1, since the Senate issued their warning, the situation has become even worse. As a result, research conducted by the National Institutes of Health (NIH) indicates that, today, the majority of people in both the United States and other Western nations do not even meet 75 percent of the recommended daily allowances (RDAs) for many essential minerals.

In light of the problems of mineral deficiencies faced by so many people, the daily consumption of fresh-squeezed organic fruit and vegetable juices is all the more important. Trying to eat enough fruits and vegetables each day in order to provide your body with an adequate mineral supply is no longer feasible for most people, due to the diminished mineral content in plant foods. This is so even for fruits and vegetables grown organically (although organic fruits and vegetables by and large have significantly higher amounts of minerals and other nutrients than non-organic fruits and vegetables). Juicing provides a solution to this challenge because, by juicing, you can easily and conveniently consume a much greater volume of fruits and vegetables than you can by eating them in solid form. As we stated in Chapter 1, a single quart of vegetable juice, which can easily be consumed by one person in a single day, supplies the nutrition equivalent to approximately five pounds of solid produce. Juicing, therefore, is one of the best ways you have of ensuring that your body is supplied with all of the minerals it needs each day.

Enzymes

Enzymes, which we discussed in Chapter 1, are a special class of biochemicals that act as catalysts in the body, triggering many functions, including the maintenance and regeneration of your body's fluids, cells, tissues, and organs. Scientists have identified approximately 1,000 enzymes, which are a part of all living things, including all plant foods in their raw, uncooked state. In fact, enzymes within fruits and vegetables are essential for them to grow and ripen, including, in some cases, changing color, such as green tomatoes turning red. Raw meats, poultry, and fish also contain enzymes. Without enzymes, none of your body's other biochemicals would be able to carry out their intended functions, nor would the other nutrients you receive from foods be able to operate within you.

One of the most important roles that certain enzymes play in the body is the proper digestion of food, followed by the assimilation of the nutrients that food contains. The human body manufactures over twenty digestive enzymes in order to properly digest and assimilate proteins, carbohydrates, fats, and sugars. Ideally, however, you also supply your body with enough enzymes each day by consuming a sufficient amount of raw or slightly cooked fruits and vegetables. (Plant foods that are overcooked have their enzyme content destroyed by heat.) By doing so, you enable your body to conserve its own enzyme supply, making them more available for other biological functions. Increasingly, however, most people fail to consume enough raw or slightly cooked vegetables each day, making it necessary for the body to rely on its own enzyme supply, in some cases to the point of depletion.

There are four primary categories of digestive enzymes. Amylase digests carbohydrates; cellulase digests fiber; lipase digests fats; and protease digests proteins. Nature has supplied the foods we eat with the enzymes that are needed to digest and assimilate the food elements they contain. For example, carbohydrate-rich foods, such as bananas and potatoes, are rich in amylase, while raw butter, which is high in fat, contains an abundant supply of lipase enzymes. However, when foods are cooked, much, if not all, of this enzyme content is destroyed.

Since following a primarily raw foods diet is not convenient for most people (and in some cases can be contraindicated due to an inability to properly digest the fiber), juicing provides a healthy alternative method for ensuring that you receive the enzymes your body needs. In addition, regularly drinking fresh fruit and vegetable juices can aid your body in preventing and recovering from a wide variety of other health problems that are caused or exacerbated by a lack of enzymes. According to Lita Lee, PhD, a leading expert in the use of enzyme therapy, a wide range of health problems can be resolved once adequate enzyme intake is established. Among the health problems she reports enzymes can resolve are allergies, arthritis pain, candidiasis (systemic yeast overgrowth), gastrointestinal disorders, inflammatory conditions, respiratory conditions, and conditions caused by toxicity in the colon, including constipation.

Chlorophyll

By regularly drinking juices made from fresh-squeezed green vegetables, you will be supplying your body with an abundant supply of chlorophyll, a green pigment contained in various plant foods, especially those that are predominantly green in color. Chlorophyll has been called the "blood" of vegetables because its chemical makeup and molecular structure so closely resembles hemoglobin, a prime component of human blood. Hemoglobin is rich in iron, as well as oxygen, hydrogen, carbon, and nitrogen, and plays an important role in delivering oxygen to your body's cells and tissues. Chlorophyll is composed of all of these same elements, except that it contains magnesium instead of iron. While most people have enough iron in their bodies, growing research indicates that nearly all of us are deficient in magnesium stores, making chlorophyll-rich vegetables a wise food choice.

The more chlorophyll-rich vegetables that you consume each day, the more you will boost your body's ability to transport oxygen to all of your cells and tissues due to their hemoglobin-like properties. In addition, chlorophyll also helps your body's organs, especially the liver, to eliminate toxins by enhancing the processes of cellular and organ detoxification, and increasing your body's production of red blood cells. Chlorophyll also has anticancer properties due to its ability to prevent carcinogens (cancer-causing agents) from binding to DNA in your body's cells. It also helps to protect against the buildup of calcium stones in the kidneys, as well as aiding in their breakdown and elimination. Finally, chlorophyll-rich vegetables help your body to maintain proper acid-alkaline balance, a factor that is of increasing importance in today's world, where over-acidity is so common in our bodies' internal environment.

Juicing is perhaps the easiest way to ensure that you are receiving a bountiful supply of chlorophyll. Juice dark, leafy green vegetables, such as chard, collard greens, romaine lettuce, kale, parsley, and wheatgrass. Other chlorophyll-rich vegetables you can juice include cabbage, celery, cucumbers, green peppers, spinach, turnip greens, and watercress, all of which can be combined with other vegetables to make delicious, energizing drinks.

NUTRITION THE WAY NATURE INTENDED

In the last few decades, increasing numbers of Americans have learned about the importance of vitamins and other nutrients for good health. As a result, the vitamin market has grown significantly in recent years. In the 1980s, Americans spent an estimated $2 billion on nutritional supplements. Today, that figure is approaching $30 billion.

While we certainly recognize the role that vitamin and other nutritional supplements can play in restoring and maintaining health, at the same time we also recognize that nutritional supplements are often unable to positively impact health in the way that nutrients obtained from a healthy, natural diet can. Ironically, a clue as to why this is so can be found in the meaning of the word *vitamins* itself, a term coined by Casimar Funk, a Polish-American biochemist and scientist who is credited with first formulating the concept of vitamins in the early twentieth century.

Funk's research was built on the work of other scientists and physicians of his time, including Christiaan Eijkman of Holland, and Sir Frederick Gowland Hopkins of England, both of whom were awarded the Nobel Prize in Physiology in 1929. In 1897, Eijkman proved that a substance in the hull of brown and other unpolished rice was essential to proper functioning of the body's nervous system as well as the proper metabolizing of carbohydrates. Eijkman also proved that when dietary deficiencies of this as yet unnamed substance occurred, they resulted in beriberi and other diseases. Hopkins, meanwhile, conducted research that eventually provided the scientific basis that proved that there were other nutritional factors besides proteins, carbohydrates, fats, and sodium that were necessary to sustain life. His work pioneered the study of vitamins and other nutrients, and eventually led to his discovery of the amino acid L-tryptophane and the essential role it plays in many body functions.

Influenced by the work of Eijkman and Hopkins, Funk devoted himself to trying to isolate the substance Eijkman had written about. He succeeded in 1911, when he discovered what today is known as vitamin B_1, also known as thiamine. Upon further study of the substance's chemical properties, Funk found that it contained amines, a class of chemicals containing a mixture of hydrogen, carbon, and nitrogen atoms. Because of this, he coined the phrase *vital amine* or *vitamine*, which literally means "union of vitality," and which today is known as *vitamin*. Funk was eventually awarded the Nobel Prize in Physiology for his discovery.

"Union of vitality," the intended meaning given by Funk to describe the class of nutrients he discovered, suggests that he realized that the nutritional components of the foods we eat are meant to act in concert with each other to create their multiple health effects. Ironically, the union of nutrients that Funk was referring to is often not found in the nutritional supplements people rely upon to help stay healthy. As we discussed in Chapter 1, fruits and vegetables and the juices that can be prepared from them contain nearly all of the nutrients that we need to ensure good health. Just as importantly, all of these nutrients work together to provide synergistic health benefits that are not possible when each nutrient is taken separately, as is so often the case with nutritional supplements. Many forms of vitamin C supplements, for example, do not contain the wide array of bioflavonoids that are necessary for vitamin C to act most effectively in the body.

By contrast, a wealth of bioflavonoids, as well as many other "co-factor" nutrients, are contained in fruits and vegetables that are high in vitamin C. It is for this reason that Casimar Funk, along with Dr. Albert Szent-Gyorgi, who was awarded the Nobel Prize in 1937 for his discovery of vitamin C, advised the public at the time to meet their bodies' nutritional needs primarily from a healthy diet, not from supplements. Dr. Szent-Gyorgi also stated that the concentrated whole foods he used in his research were far more effective than isolated vitamin C for preventing and reversing scurvy, which is caused by vitamin C deficiency.

Further compounding this problem is the fact that the vast majority of vitamin products in today's marketplace are synthetic, meaning that they are created in laboratories and meant to mimic their natural counterparts found in nature. This trend toward synthetic supplements is not surprising,

Potency and Juices

Most of us have had the experience of biting into a dark red strawberry and being surprised and disappointed by its complete lack of flavor. We may also have experienced making a favorite dish, following the seasoning directions explicitly, and finding it much spicier than we remember or like. This is due to many factors that can influence the flavors and properties of our foods, herbs, and spices. Some of these factors include the quality of the soil (organic or conventional); the time of and ripeness at harvest; the conditions of the growing season (how much sun, water, or rain); the variety of the plant; and for herbs, how they were processed or dried upon harvest.

This is an important consideration when adding foods and herbs to your juice recipes. Onions, garlic, ginger, turmeric, and cayenne pepper can be very potent foods, and too much of any one of these may result in a juice that doesn't taste good, or is too strong and can burn your stomach or intestines, cause perspiration, or have other unpleasant qualities. Each of us has individualized tastes and it is recommended that you be conservative when adding these foods to your juice recipes. For example, start with one clove of garlic; if it doesn't already taste too strong, try two or three. Similar guidelines for ginger, turmeric, onions, and cayenne should be followed.

In Europe, herbs are assayed for their constituents and properties. This allows for a standardization of herbal preparations, which are given a drug status and used in the conventional medical system. Cayenne will be assayed for both chemical content and thermal properties or BTUs (British Thermal Units). Typically the brighter red cayenne powders are hotter, with browning occurring over time (oxidation) or through excessive drying temperatures.

Different varieties of vegetables and herbs also exhibit different properties and tastes. The very large elephant garlic is much milder than the standard garlic and a large clove of this garlic will be milder than a single smaller clove of standard garlic. Walla Walla onions are very mild, Bermuda and yellow onions are intermediate, and white onions are typically the hottest. Know your produce, and unless you always order the spiciest foods at restaurants, start with smaller portions in your juices and work up to the maximum recommended amount as you choose, always considering taste and individual tolerance.

considering the fact that every major nutritional company in the United States is now a subsidiary of pharmaceutical companies. Employing the same pharmaceutical approach that is used to manufacture pharmaceutical drugs, most manufacturers of vitamin and mineral products today emphasize the isolation of so-called "active ingredients" at the expense of the equally important co-factor nutrients found in raw, unprocessed food. The end result of this process is that the synthetic forms of these nutrients are less effective than the natural forms found in food.

There are two main reasons why most vitamin and many other nutritional supplements do not provide the same range of benefits that nutrients obtained from food do. The first reason has to do with the fact that unnatural ingredients derived from man-made chemical processes make up over 90 percent of the supplements' composition. This means that such supplements do not possess the same "aliveness" that nutrients in raw, unprocessed foods do. As a result, synthetic nutritional supplements cannot be utilized by the human body to the same extent that the body is able to use naturally derived nutrients. Moreover, synthetic nutrients are far less absorbable than naturally-derived nutrients, further diminishing their effectiveness in the body.

Another concern with regard to synthetic nutritional supplements is that, when used long-term, they may be harmful in some instances. According to health writer and researcher Stephen Blauer, "Prolonged use or misuse of vitamin and minerals supplements may actually hurt us more than help us. By taking too much of one supplement, we initiate a negative chain reaction that destroys the balance of all other chemical levels in our body."

In *The Juicing Book,* Blauer further explains this point by writing about what happens over time when a person takes a synthetic iron supplement to treat anemia due to iron deficiency. He states:

> Adrenal glands are stimulated by the introduction of excess inorganic iron. As a reaction, sodium levels rise. Rising sodium levels cause magnesium levels to plunge. This signals calcium levels to sink, which in turn causes the potassium level to jump; which in turn decreases levels of copper and zinc. The net result is a chemical imbalance capable of producing a host of symptoms from headaches to heart palpitations. Most significant, however, this chemical balancing act depletes iron further, leaving the body more anemic than when it [supplementation] began.

As Blauer also points out in his book, these problems would not have occurred if, instead of supplementing with iron, the same person had chosen to make iron-rich foods a part of his or her daily food intake. Then, Blauer says, "the body would have absorbed all the organic iron it needed and excreted the excess. The body knows when to say 'no' to iron in its natural, organic form; it can't always tell when to stop with a continuing barrage of synthetic supplements."

Juicing organic fruits and vegetables, even more than eating them, avoids all of the potential shortcomings and problems associated with synthetic nutritional supplements. On average, your body requires two or more hours to properly digest fruits and vegetables when they are eaten in solid form. Only after this digestion process is completed are the nutrients that such foods contain fully absorbed by your body and then delivered to your cells, tissues, organs, bones, and muscles via the bloodstream. By contrast, when you juice fruits and vegetables, the nutrients they contain are available for your body to use almost immediately because of how such juices predigest themselves. In addition, because you can comfortably consume much more fruits and vegetables when they are juiced compared to when they are eaten, the amount of nutrition you receive from juicing is also far greater. In short, juicing is the easiest and most convenient method that we know of for providing your body with all of its nutritional needs in the way that nature intended.

OTHER HEALTH BENEFITS OF JUICING

As you will discover in Part Two, juicing is an effective self-care method anyone can use to help prevent and reverse a wide variety of disease conditions. This is because of the many health benefits fresh-squeezed fruit and vegetable juices provide. What follows is an overview of the most important of these benefits.

Acid-Alkaline Balance

For your body to be healthy, it needs to remain in a state of acid-alkaline balance, which is essential for the proper functioning of all of your body's self-regulating mechanisms, or homeostasis. Acid-alkaline levels are measured according to your body's pH levels. The term pH refers to the concentration of hydrogen ions in solutions such as blood, saliva, or urine. In an optimal state of health, your body's blood pH values should be at or near 7.365 on a scale of 1.0 to 14.0, with 7.0 being neutral. Levels below 7.0 indicate a condition of over-acidity, while levels above 7.4 indicate over-alkalinity.

Because most people today predominantly eat foods that are acid-forming once they are digested, the majority of Americans suffer from chronic over-acidity. Chronic over-acidity as a major contributing factor to poor health has become increasingly recognized by health practitioners in recent years, and has been written about for decades. In 1933, William Howard Hay, MD, introduced the common health problems associated with a highly acidic diet in his book, *A New Health Era*.

Dr. Hay's warning has been proved by subsequent research, which shows that chronic acid-alkaline imbalances cause cell function to become impaired. This, in turn, disrupts homeostasis, making it easier for disease to strike the body. Overly acidic conditions also increase your body's susceptibility to harmful microorganisms, such as bacteria, viruses, and fungi. Acid-alkaline imbalances have also been shown to contribute to various other health conditions, including allergies, blood sugar imbalances, fatigue, mood swings, and unhealthy weight gain.

Most fruit and vegetable juices counteract over-acidity because of their highly alkalizing effects. Just like the fruits and vegetables from which they are produced, such juices, once they are consumed, help to shift pH levels back to normal levels. Therefore, by drinking juices regularly, you can easily and conveniently help your body to maintain a healthy acid-alkaline balance.

Antioxidant Effects

Regularly drinking fresh fruit and vegetable juices will provide your body with a rich supply of antioxidant vitamins, minerals, enzymes, and other nutrients. Antioxidants are extremely important when it comes to good health because of how they protect against oxidative stress caused by free radical damage. An excess of free radicals in the body has also been shown to be a primary cause of premature aging.

Free radicals are molecules which, unlike normal molecules in the body, possess a free electron, causing them to attach to cell membranes, as well as fats, proteins, and various enzymes in the body, attacking them and causing them to become impaired. When free radical buildup in the body becomes too great, a host of health problems can arise, including impaired protein synthesis and enzymatic function, damage to cellular DNA, impaired tissue and muscle regeneration, lowered immunity, and the buildup of toxic wastes inside the body. Free radical damage is also considered to be one of the causes of cancer because of the cellular mutations that can occur when cellular DNA is damaged. All of the health-impairing effects caused by free radicals are known as oxidative stress.

Antioxidants help to prevent and reverse oxidative stress due to their ability to bind to free radicals, literally quenching their ability to cause further damage. In addition, antioxidants protect against the many causes of free radical buildup. In addition to poor diet, these include various food additives, pesticides, and preservatives, as well as external factors, such as environmental pollution and exposure to chemicals, including those found in many common household products. Drinking one to two 8-ounce glasses of fresh-squeezed juices every day will provide your body with the antioxidants it needs to neutralize existing free radicals and prevent their buildup in the future.

Protecting Against Alzheimer's Disease

New scientific evidence now shows that drinking fresh fruit and vegetable juices helps protect the brain from free-radical damage and can even help prevent Alzheimer's disease. In a study published in the *American Journal of Medicine* that tracked nearly 2,000 participants for up to ten years, U.S. researchers discovered that people who drank fresh fruit and vegetable juices at least three times a week reduced their risk of developing Alzheimer's by 76 percent.

Alzheimer's has been linked to the accumulation in the brain of a harmful type of protein known as beta-amyloid. Scientists believe that the buildup of beta-amyloid protein in the brain is due to damage caused by free radicals. In addition to the other antioxidants that fruit and vegetable juices contain, juices are also rich in a special class of antioxidants known as polyphenols, which scientists believe play a significant role in helping to prevent free-radical damage in the brain.

In addition to protecting against free-radical damage, juices help prevent Alzheimer's in another important way. Scientists now know that a contributing factor for Alzheimer's is diminished blood flow to the brain, which results in the deprivation of sufficient amounts of nutrients and oxygen. Both fruit and vegetable juices contain a wide variety of nutrients that help to keep blood vessels in good working order and maintain healthy blood pressure levels. The health-promoting actions of juices, therefore, help to ensure that the brain receives adequate supplies of blood and the nutrients and oxygen it contains.

Detoxification Benefits

All of us are exposed daily to a wide range of toxins, both from our environment and, in many cases, from the foods we eat. As a result, our bodies struggle under the burden of the ongoing buildup of toxins that lodge themselves in our cells, tissues, and organs, where they wreck havoc. Though your body is designed to eliminate toxins as part of its self-regulatory mechanisms collectively known as homeostasis, doing so becomes increasingly difficult as your exposure to toxins continues.

The primary internal organ of detoxification is the liver, which is also responsible for well over 1,000 other functions each and every day. As toxins build up in your body, all of these functions become impaired as the liver becomes increasingly overwhelmed. Fortunately, regular juicing, in tandem with other healthy lifestyle choices, can improve your body's ability to detoxify itself. Juicing aids in this task because of the abundance of nutrients that have potent detoxification properties. By minimizing your exposure to environmental toxins; following a diet of organic, whole foods free of additives, pesticides, preservatives, and other chemicals; and drinking at least one glass of fresh, organic juice each day, you can quickly begin to reverse whatever toxic burden your body is struggling with. (To enhance your body's ability to detoxify, you may also consider a juice fast. For more information about fasting on juices, see Chapter 7.)

Improved Digestion and Gastrointestinal Function

One of the truly amazing aspects of life is that virtually all organisms, including humans, possess the ability to digest their own cells. In the fruit and vegetable kingdoms, self-digesting enzymes are contained within each cell. During the juicing process, these enzymes are immediately released into the juice itself. Since these enzymes are specific to each of the nutrient classes the fruits and vegetables contain (proteins, carbohydrates, etc.), they are actually more efficient than the human body's own digestive enzymes when it comes to digesting and assimilating these nutrients.

As we have already mentioned, fresh-squeezed juices are absorbable almost immediately, once they are consumed, whereas solid foods take much longer to be digested. Overall, your body requires two hours to properly digest carbohydrates from solid foods, four hours to digest fats, and six hours to digest proteins. By making juicing a part of your daily health routine, not only will you be flooding your body with an almost immediate supply of the many nutrients fresh juices contain, you will also be supporting and enhancing your body's ability to digest solid foods. As a result, your body will be able to conserve the energy it would otherwise expend to digest foods, making that energy available for other uses.

This benefit is of particular importance for people suffering from pre-existing digestive problems. Such conditions make it difficult for the body to obtain all of the nutrients it requires to reverse such conditions, since poor digestion inevitably results in poor nutrient assimilation. Moreover, food that is not completely digested in the stomach passes on to the intestinal tract, where it can contribute to a buildup of toxins in the gut, as well as in the liver and, eventually, various other parts of the body as the toxins pass through the intestinal wall to enter the bloodstream. Left unchecked, poor digestion can result in an array of health problems, ranging from flatulence, bloating, and heartburn, to chronic fatigue, unhealthy weight gain, candidiasis, and various inflammatory conditions.

The abundant supply of digestive enzymes, along with the many other nutrients that fresh-squeezed juices contain, act to prevent and reverse such problems. In addition to improving digestion, juices also help to improve elimination, making them an excellent remedy for constipation. The end result is better digestion and assimilation of nutrients, improved energy, and overall improved health. Certain foods and herbs, however, that are ingredients in juice recipes, can be very potent. Some people may have digestive sensitivites to foods such as onions and garlic. See the inset on page 43 for a discussion of potency and juices.

Protection Against Inflammation

Physicians have long linked chronic inflammation in the body with certain health conditions, such as arthritis, edema, and inflammatory bowel disease. In recent years, however, scientists have come to understand that inflammation is a major contributing factor to a wide range of other health problems, including diabetes, heart disease, and certain types of cancer. Although there are times when inflammation is necessary in the body, such as in response to cuts, bruises, and other wounds, or during times of exposure to infectious microorganisms, typically these types of inflammation are acute, meaning that they are only temporary and will subside once the situations that trigger the body's inflammatory response are resolved. Chronic inflammation, however, is ongoing and, if left unchecked, can cause or exacerbate a variety of health problems.

One of the primary lifestyle causes of chronic inflammation is an unhealthy diet, especially one that is high in sugar and processed foods, as well as foods that are fried, barbequed, or overly browned (such as toast). Such foods, when consumed, unleash what are known as advanced glycation end products, or AGEs, into the bloodstream. AGEs are formed by an unnatural binding of sugars with proteins and fats. In addition to triggering inflammation in the body, they also generate free radicals, and have been linked to a number of diseases, including Alzheimer's disease, atherosclerosis (hardening of the arteries), cataracts, dementia, diabetes, high blood pressure, joint pain and stiffness, and kidney disease.

By following a diet that is high in fresh, organic fruits and vegetables, whole grains, and lean, healthy meats, fish, and poultry, and by avoiding unhealthy cooking methods, you can minimize your risk of developing chronic inflammation due to AGEs. Juicing can further diminish your risk, due to the potent anti-inflammatory properties that fresh-squeezed juice contains. In addition, as we discussed above, regularly drinking juice can neutralize free radicals that can trigger inflammation, and improve your body's ability to rid itself of toxins, another cause of inflammation.

CONCLUSION

Having read this far, you now have a better understanding of why we consider juicing to be such an important self-care tool for creating and maintaining good health. Simply put, there is no better way for you to so quickly and easily obtain the wide range of nutritional and other health benefits that juicing provides. Now that you are aware of these benefits, it's time to learn how you can design your own personal juicing program. We provide you with that information in the next chapter.

4

How to Juice

n this chapter, we will provide you with guidelines for getting started on creating your own personalized juicing program. If you are new to juicing, it is always best to go slow and to experiment with various juice combinations in order to note how you feel after drinking them. As you discover the juice combinations that work best for you, you can then start to make them a part of your daily health regimen. In order to achieve the best results, you need to know how to select the best fruits and vegetables for juicing and how to choose a juicer that is best suited to your budget, yet still capable of yielding high-quality juice. These and other important points will be explored in this chapter.

SELECTING A JUICER

To most effectively prepare fresh fruit and vegetable juices for yourself, it is best to purchase your own juicer. Juicers are designed to separate the liquids of fruits and vegetables from their fibrous pulp. This is a different process from blenders, which are more commonly found in most households, and which work by liquefying foods through a high-speed chopping process, creating a mushy mixture of fluids and pulp. Although blenders can be used to create certain types of juices, such as watermelon, overall they are not suited for preparing most types of fruit and vegetable juices, either alone or in combination with each other. This is why we recommend buying a juicer even if you already own a high-quality blender.

Types of Juicers

There are two basic types of high-speed juicers: centrifugal juicers and masticating juicers.

Centrifugal Juicers

Centrifugal juicers separate the juice of fruits and vegetables from their pulp as they are pressed down onto a spinning blade. With some types of centrifugal juicers, the pulp remains inside a plastic or stainless steel bucket until it is removed. Other types of centrifugal juicers come with a pulp ejector that ejects pulp into a side container during the juicing process.

Centrifugal juicers with pulp ejectors typically make it possible to produce a larger quantity of juice at one time, without having to stop and remove pulp in order to continue. Juicers in this category range in price from $50 to $400, depending on their features. If you intend to do a lot of juicing, we recommend models that come with a pulp extractor.

Masticating Juicers

Masticating juicers chop, or masticate, fruits and vegetables at high speeds, creating a paste of pulp and juice. The juice is then squeezed out from the paste through a screen. Some types of masticating juicers come with a built-in hydraulic press that makes separating juice from the paste easier.

In addition to juicing, certain brands of masticating juicers can be used to grind nuts, seeds, and sprouted grains, making it easy to produce fresh breads and butters. These models can also be used as a blender. One of the most well-known masticating juicers is the Norwalk Juice Press, which was developed by the late Norman W. Walker, one of the best-known juicing experts of the twentieth century. It is capable of producing some of the highest quality juice due to how efficiently it extracts juices from fruits and vegetables. Given their price tag, however (approximately $2,100), Norwalk juicers are most often used by juice bar owners, health food stores, and health food restaurants that need to produce large volumes of juice on a daily basis. Other models of masticating juicers typically range in price from $250 to $500.

CENTRIFUGAL AND MASTICATING JUICER MODELS

In general, centrifugal juicers are faster, more likely to have pulp ejectors, and easier to clean up than the masticating models. Masticating juicers, operating at a slower speed than centrifugal juicers, heat the juices less and tend to provide a greater juice output. There are, of course, variations found within both types of juicers, depending on their brand, model, and price range.

What follows is a listing of some of the most popular centrifugal and masticating juicers according to their model, type, and cost (all prices listed are the manufacturer's suggested retail price, or MSRP).

Model	Type	Price
LEAST EXPENSIVE ($40–$130)		
Juiceman Jr.	Centrifugal	$55.00
Jack LaLanne's Power Juicer	Centrifugal	$99.95
Juiceman Jr. Elite Pro	Centrifugal	$99.99
Panasonic MJ-66PR	Centrifugal	$106.00
Braun MP-80	Centrifugal	$115.00
L'Equip Mini Model 110.5	Centrifugal	$129.99
Omega 2	Centrifugal	$129.99
LOWER PRICE RANGE ($130–$300)		
Juiceman II Elite	Centrifugal	$169.99
NutriSource 1000	Centrifugal	$169.99
Breville Juice Fountain JE900	Centrifugal	$199.99
Breville Juice Fountain 95XL	Centrifugal	$199.99
Moline American Classic 101	Centrifugal	$229.00
Moline American Classic Pulp Ejection 104	Centrifugal	$279.99
Acme 5001	Centrifugal	$229.99
L'Equip Model 221	Centrifugal	$249.99
Champion	Masticating	$299.99
Omega 1000	Centrifugal	$249.99
Omega 4000	Centrifugal	$299.99
Omega 8003	Centrifugal	$299.99
Omega 8005	Centrifugal	$299.99
Omega 9000	Centrifugal	$299.99
SoloStar II	Masticating	$299.99
MID RANGE ($300–$1,000)		
Champion Commercial	Masticating	$350.00
Acme 6001	Centrifugal	$369.99
Green Star GS 1000	Masticating	$479.99
Green Star GS 2000	Masticating	$499.99
Green Star GS 3000	Masticating	$549.99

Green Power Gold	Masticating	$650.00
Wheetena Marvel Red	Masticating	$499.95
Wheetena Workhorse II	Masticating	$999.95
TOP OF THE LINE ($1,000–$2,500)*		
Miracle Pro	Centrifugal	$1,999.95
Miracle Pro MJ800	Centrifugal	$2,299.95
Norwalk 270 (Oak)	Masticating	$2,195.00
Norwalk 270 (Stainless Steel)	Masticating	$2,295.00
Nutrifaster N450	Centrifugal	$2,499.95

* Juicers in this price range are the most rugged of all juicers and designed to meet high volume. They are most commonly used in health resorts and juice bars due to their durability, yet are also suitable for personal use, particularly for those who produce a high volume of juice on a daily basis.

Where To Buy Juicers

Today it is easier to purchase juicers than ever before. Many major department store chains now carry various juicer models, as do many health food stores. Most manufacturers also make their juicers and related products available online, directly from their websites. Various online shopping sites, such as Amazon.com, also carry a wide selection of both centrifugal and masticating juicers.

Either type of juicer mentioned above can meet your daily juicing needs. Therefore, when it comes to making your purchase, you should make your choice according to your specific requirements and budget. If you enjoy making your own breads and butters, then a masticating juicer may be the most appropriate choice. If, on the other hand, you simply want to be able to prepare your own fresh juice combinations, a centrifugal juicer is probably all that you need. To further help you make your decision, be sure to compare the warranties that are offered by juicer manufacturers. In the table starting on page 52 you will find a listing of the most dependable brands of both centrifugal and masticating juicers, as well as their manufacturers' suggested retail prices.

CHOOSING FRUITS AND VEGETABLES TO JUICE

Once you've purchased a juicer, you will be ready to begin your daily juicing program. In order to do so, of course, you will need a supply of fresh fruits and vegetables. Selecting the produce you use to create the juices you

Supporting Your Local Farms

Given that diet is one of the primary foundations upon which to build good health, there is no excuse for not eating the healthiest foods available. In recent years, this has become easier to do, thanks to the growth of the organic farm/food markets, which has resulted in even large grocery chains today featuring organic food sections. Local farmers' markets are another way of obtaining quality foods. A third option is the movement towards community supported agriculture (CSA). CSA is designed to help you find local farmers who will sell their produce directly to individuals. We strongly encourage you to get involved with CSA if you can. Not only will this enable you to find quality foods at very reasonable prices, but you will also help local, small farms sustain themselves in the face of ever-increasing competition from the commercial, industrial farms that dominate America's food market. To help you get started, here are some websites you can use to find out more about CSA farms and where to locate them in your local area.

www.biodynamics.com/csa.html

www.buylocalfood.com/

www.eatlocal.net/

www.eatwellguide.org/

www.ecotrust.org/foodfarms/

www.foodroutes.org/

www.localharvest.org/farms/M9006

www.localharvest.org/csa/

newfarm.org/farmlocator/index.php

www.newfarm.org/features/0803/
localfoodchall.shtml

www.organicconsumers.org/

www.wilson.edu/wilson/asp/content.a
sp?id=804

drink is an important part of your juicing program. Ideally, you should always use organically grown produce. The availability of organic fruits and vegetables continues to increase all across the United States, so finding such produce should not be a problem.

In addition to organic fruits and vegetables now being carried by many grocery store chains nationwide, they are also commonly available at many health food stores, as well. An even better option is to seek out local farms in your community that raise their crops organically. Many such farms are willing to sell you their products on a weekly basis. In recent years, a movement known as community supported agriculture (CSA) has emerged that makes it easier for people to locate local farmers willing to sell their produce directly to individuals. (For more information about CSA, see "Supporting Your Local Farms" above.) Another option is to visit local farmers' markets and produce stands in your area.

By choosing to use organic fruits and vegetables whenever possible, you will be ensuring that the juices you prepare contain the most abundant supply of vital nutrients, since non-organic farming methods have been shown to result in produce that is deficient in such nutrients compared to organically raised crops. Just as importantly, by using organic produce, you will spare yourself from the many harmful chemicals that non-organic food crops typically contain, due to commercial farming methods that rely on the use of artificial fertilizers, pesticides, fungicides, and other man-made chemical products.

Tips for Preparing Fruits and Vegetables for Juicing

The following guidelines can help you to obtain the most benefits from your juicing program.

■ **Wash All Produce Thoroughly Before Juicing.** Even if you are using only organically grown fruits and vegetables, it's always a good idea to wash them thoroughly before you juice them in order to remove all dirt and other residues. A vegetable brush is excellent for scrubbing the skins of root crops like beets, burdock roots, and even larger carrots. This will often remove bitter qualities and make a better tasting juice without sacrificing the nutrition of the skins. Also inspect for bruises, molds, or other damage to the skin and remove such areas from the produce you intend to juice.

■ **Use the Leaves and Stems.** In addition to juicing the main portion of fruits and vegetables, be sure to also juice their leaves and stems, which are usually rich in nutrients. One exception to this rule is carrot greens, which should not be used because they contain substances that can act as toxins in the body.

■ **Avoid Juicing Pits.** When juicing fruits that contain pits, such as peaches and plums, always be sure to remove the pits before the fruits are placed in the juicer. Otherwise, you can quickly damage your juicer.

■ **Don't Juice the Outer Skins of Citrus Fruits.** The outer skin, or rinds, of citrus fruits (grapefruits, lemons, limes, oranges, tangerines, etc.) should not be juiced or only juiced sparingly because of their bitter taste. Therefore, be sure to peel such fruits. However, do make use of the white undercoating of the rinds of such fruits, as it is rich in vitamin C, quercetin, and other antioxidants.

■ **Cut and Dice Fruits and Vegetables Before Juicing.** Once you are ready to begin juicing, be sure that the portions of the fruits and vegetables you use fit easily into the opening of your juicer. To this end, you may need to cut or dice them first. In addition, don't attempt to juice too much produce at once. Never overstuff the opening of the juicer, attempting to force the process. Doing so can produce unnecessary wear and tear on the juicer's blade and motor that could result in damage.

■ **Avoid Using Overripe Produce.** Produce that is overripe should be avoided when juicing because it can result in the production of too much pulp, which can cause your juicer to become clogged. In addition, overripe fruits and vegetables contain less nutrient content than properly ripened produce.

■ **Running Your Juicer.** Before you start juicing, let your juicer run for ten to thirty seconds so that the blade is already at full speed before you add fruits and vegetables. When you finish juicing, let your unit continue to run for a minute or more. This will ensure that all juice that has been extracted runs off into your juice container. Also be sure to allow your juicer to come to a complete stop before you begin to disassemble it for cleaning.

DRINKING AND STORING JUICES

Ideally, it is best to drink fresh-squeezed juices within twenty minutes after they are prepared. In addition, since juices contain such a potent mixture of predigested nutrients, it is best to drink them slowly, allowing your body time to savor and assimilate them. So avoid gulping down the juices you prepare, choosing instead to fully enjoy each sip.

We also recommend that you drink juices at least twenty to thirty minutes before meals or one hour or more after eating. The reason for this has to do again with the fact that juices are predigested. Mixing juices with food, which your body has to digest, can result in unhealthy fermentation within your body's digestive tract, creating stomach upset and other discomforts.

As a general rule, we recommend making only as much juice as you intend to drink at one time. However, if you wish to prepare greater quantities of juice, you can do so as long as you take care to store the excess properly. Here are some guidelines for best doing so.

It is ideal to drink juice the same day that it is extracted. Once juice is stored in a refrigerator, there is nutritional loss every minute or hour. Nonetheless, juice that is properly stored and consumed within the first day is a source of excellent nutrition, including vitamins and enzymes. The maximum shelf life in the refrigerator for fresh-squeezed juices is forty-eight hours. Beyond that time, virtually none of the nutritional benefits of juice remain, beyond calories and some mineral content.

Glass is always the best material in which to store juices. Amber, blue, and green glasses are preferred by some health experts, but since storage is typically away from ultraviolet light, clear glass is fine. High-grade ceramic containers are also suitable, although the primary limitation to ceramic when it comes to storage is the ability to achieve air-tight containment. It is ideal to fill the juice to the top of such containers so that there is very little oxygen in the bottle.

Plastic containers are the least desirable storage or serving material for juices, as well as for other foods and beverages, including bottled water. Even though the plastics industry is continuously trying to make safer forms of plastics, recent research about the bisphenols and other materials used in plastics have been shown to promote cancers, hormone imbalances and other hormonal abnormalities, as well as various other health problems. These substances contained in plastic are released with heat and exposure to ultraviolet light (sunlight), as well as during normal oxidative breakdown. A general rule of thumb is that the softer and more flexible the plastic, the higher the level of toxins that are released, though this is not an absolute principle. For these reasons, we recommend that you use glass or ceramic containers whenever possible.

One other fact to be aware of when storing juices is how much a juice is heated and oxidized during the juicing process. Both of these factors determine how long juice remains vital and nutritious. Juice that is macerated

Suggested Juice Combinations to Get You Started

Once you are ready to start juicing, here are some juice recipes you can try, which we have chosen according to their delicious taste and nutritional benefits.

- **Dr. Bailey's Mainstay Juice Recipe:** Juice equal amounts (4 ounces or more of each vegetable) of carrot, beet, and celery. Dr. Bailey recommends adding a clove or two of garlic for additional health benefits.

- **A Norman W. Walker Favorite:** One of famed juice expert Norman W. Walker's favorite juice recipes was equal parts (4–8 ounces of each) of carrot and apple.

- **Juice Drinks of the Stars:** This juice combination is a big hit among Hollywood celebrities who consult with juice expert Bo Rinaldi: Juice one apple, one medium size cucumber, and two stalks of celery. Another favorite juice combination used by Bo is: one apple, one medium size beet, and 4 ounces of pineapple.

and expressed from masticating juicers generally remains fresher longer, compared to juice that is extracted from high-speed centrifugal juicers.

CLEANING UP AFTER YOU JUICE

After you have finished juicing and have enjoyed the juice you prepared, be sure to clean your juicer, instead of leaving this task for later. Doing so will help to ensure that your juicer continues to work as intended, as well as preventing opportunistic microorganisms from settling on the pulpy remains of the fruits and vegetables you've juiced.

Fortunately, the cleanup process for more juicers, especially the centrifugal models, is easy to perform. All you need to do is disassemble your juicer's parts, rinse them of pulp, and then wash them as you would any other plate, pan, or food utensil. The only part you won't need to wash is the main housing of the juicer, which contains the motor (although you may need to wipe it clean with a napkin).

Uses for Juice Pulp

The pulpy remains that result from juicing can be thrown out if you so choose. However, you might also consider using the pulp for other purposes. Here are a few ideas for you to consider.

Using Juice Pulp in Soups, Stews, and Other Dishes

Vegetable pulp can be added to soups and stews to add additional flavor and as a natural thickening agent. It can also be used as an addition to quiche and omelets, as well as in casseroles. Some people even use vegetable pulp to add taste and texture to lasagna and meat loaf.

Fruit pulp can be used in smoothies (see Chapter 6), as well as in breads and muffins. Fruit pulp added to fruit pies is another tasty option, as is adding fruit pulp to oatmeal or pancake mixes. Be sure to cook or blend fruit pulp first, before you use it for these purposes.

Using Pulp for Gardening

If you grow your own fruits and vegetables, juice pulp can serve as an excellent fertilizing agent that you can either apply directly to the soil, or add to your compost heap.

Using Pulp as a Beauty Mask

Certain pulp, especially cucumber, can be used as a natural beauty mask. For more on this subject, see Chapter 8.

CONCLUSION

By following the guidelines contained in this chapter, you will soon be ready to make juicing a part of your daily health routine. As with any other new endeavor, proceed at your own pace and by all means experiment with the juice combinations you prepare. A good rule of thumb is to proceed slowly but surely, noticing how much juice you are comfortable drinking at one time, which combinations most appeal to you, and which juices leave you feeling most energized. As you continue to explore the many health benefits that juicing can provide, you will before long become your own juice expert, knowing which juices you most enjoy and feel healthy drinking. Be sure to have fun as you do so, for the more that you enjoy juicing, the more likely you will make juicing an ongoing daily part of your health routine.

Now that you know how to get started juicing, let's take a look at some basic principles for healthy eating, which will make your juicing program most beneficial. You will find this topic discussed in the next chapter.

5

Juicing and Healthy Eating

While regularly drinking fresh-squeezed fruit and vegetables can provide you with a variety of health benefits (see Chapters 1 and 3), juicing in and of itself is not intended to replace healthy eating habits, which are essential for achieving and maintaining optimal levels of wellness. Following a healthy and nutritious diet will greatly enhance the benefits you receive from juicing. However, if you do not regularly eat healthy meals, at best, juicing will only serve to compensate for the loss of proper nutrition that results from consuming unhealthy foods. In this chapter, we are going to share with you basic healthy eating guidelines that are easy to follow so that you receive the most from your daily juicing program.

DIET: ONE SIZE DOES *NOT* FIT ALL

Though various authors of diet books claim otherwise, there is no universal diet that is most appropriate for all people. The reason a "one size fits all" diet does not exist should be obvious: Each of us is a unique individual with specific traits and needs, including specific requirements for various foods and the nutrients they contain.

This medical fact has been known and espoused by practitioners of various healing traditions throughout the ages. For example, it is a central tenet in the healing traditions of China (traditional Chinese medicine, or TCM) and India (Ayurvedic medicine), both of which are estimated to be 5,000 years old. Practitioners of TCM tailor dietary recommendations for their patients based on a system of health assessment known as the Five Element Theory, which has to do with the degree in which an individual expresses the energies of the elements of air, fire, metal, water, and wood in relation to life-force energy known as *Qi*, and its twin aspects of *yin* and *yang*. Similarly, Ayurvedic practitioners prescribe their patients' diets according to each person's constitutional body type, or *dosha*. Doshas are also said to be associated with various elements of nature. There are three primary doshas: *Vata*, which is associated with air; *Pitta*, which is associated with fire and water; and *Kapha*, which is associated with earth and water.

Ancient Western healing traditions also recognized the relationship between a person's body type and the foods he or she ate. These principles can be found in the writings of Hippocrates, Galen, and many other physicians who practiced medicine during the golden ages of Greece and Rome. Both Hippocrates and Galen wrote that individual foods could produce diametrically opposed results in different people, due to what they termed *humors*, which were also based on various natural elements in relation to an individual's specific constitution, as well as their age and life style. As a result, Hippocrates and Galen taught that diet and all other medicinal recommendations needed to be based on a deep understanding of each person's specific makeup.

In 1930, a pioneering biochemist and researcher named Roger Williams, PhD, published his book, *Nutrition Against Disease,* which was based on his years of research investigating diet and nutrition in relationship to the health of animals and humans. Dr. Williams coined the phrase "biochemical individuality" to describe his findings that dietary and nutritional needs are based on a person's unique genetics, as well as the quality, quantity, and ratio of the foods eaten. Among his many findings, Williams discovered that the need for specific nutrients could vary by as much as 600 percent from person to person, depending on their biochemical individuality.

The concept of biochemical individuality has influenced a number of health practitioners and researchers who followed in Dr. Williams's footsteps. One of them was William Donald Kelley, DDS. Diagnosed with metastatic pancreatic cancer, which is considered by conventional oncologists to be fatal in virtually all cases, Kelley successfully cured himself and lived for over forty more years by developing a program of nutrition, detoxification, and pancreatic enzymes that was tailored to his own unique metabolic type. Once he succeeded in curing himself, Kelley continued his research, adding much to our understanding of metabolic body types in relation to diet, nutrition, and health. Echoing the writings of ancient healers such as Galen and Hippocrates, Kelley declared, "The person who has the disease should be treated, not the disease that has the person." Guided by this principle, Kelley was able to reverse many other cases of cancer, and today his research and treatment protocols are being continued by Nicholas Gonzalez, MD, a well-known integrative physician who specializes in cancer care.

More recently, the concept of metabolic types has been popularized by naturopathic physician Peter D'Adamo through his popular *Eat Right 4 Your Type* book series, which is largely based on the research conducted by his father, who is also a naturopathic physician. D'Adamo's work is based on a person's specific blood type and holds that certain foods are optimal for each blood type, while other foods, even those that are normally considered healthy, can produce ill-health effects for people of a particular blood type.

William Walcott, who helped Dr. Kelley carry out his research during Kelley's later years, is another recent author who has stressed the importance of a person's metabolic type to diet and overall health. In addition to blood type, Walcott has found that various other metabolic factors deter-

Tips for Eating Right

Eat Raw Foods First: We recommend that you eat salads and other raw foods at the start of your meals. Doing so aids in digestion and supports proper immune relationships with your foods. In general you should emphasize raw and minimally cooked foods in your diet. Aiming for 50–60 percent raw and soaked is considered a good target for the average person.

Avoid Eating When You Are Upset: It is very important that you don't eat when you are upset or agitated. Such states of emotional distress cause your body to release adrenaline. Adrenaline depletes the digestive system of adequate blood and energy necessary for efficient digestion. During times of emotional upset, you should only consume juice and perhaps some soup, but definitely not a full, complex meal.

Give Thanks For the Foods You Eat: The concept of taking a moment to express your gratitude for the foods you are about to eat is common to all spiritual traditions, and is also known as "saying Grace." Such a practice helps to "quiet" the body and mind, which in turn helps to optimize digestion. It is never too early or too late to share this concept of giving thanks for our food with children and friends. It will not only help them to be more appreciative of the foods they eat, but will also extend into other important areas of character.

Take Time To Savor Your Food: It is important that you enjoy the taste of your foods. Pleasurable tastes stimulate the production of digestive enzymes and also aid the immune processes involved in efficient digestion. Noticing and appreciating the flavorful foods you eat also makes it easier for you to express your gratitude for the meals you eat.

mine a person's optimum diet. These factors include the rate at which one converts food into energy (oxidation rate), the dominance of either the sympathetic or parasympathetic function of the autonomic nervous system, the rate at which a person metabolizes glucose, and body temperature. Together, they are used to determine what Walcott calls *The Metabolic Typing Diet.*

Despite the preponderance of scientific research illustrating the relationship between a person's biochemistry, metabolic type, diet, and nutrition, little consideration is given to such findings by many conventional medical practitioners, and even many dieticians. It is beyond the scope of this book to provide detailed information on the foods you should eat based on such factors. Fortunately, however, there are certain principles of diet and healthy eating that *are* beneficial to everyone. The remainder of this chapter provides an outline of what they are.

THE IMPORTANCE OF EATING ORGANIC FOODS

Although government agencies and certain scientific groups continue to insist that organically raised foods are not inherently healthier and more nutritious than non-organic foods, their arguments are hollow and without merit. In this section, we will explain why. To begin, we must define what the term *organic* actually means.

Simply put, organic foods is the term used to describe foods that are grown and harvested without the use of manmade fertilizers, pesticides, fungicides, preservatives, and other harmful chemicals. In the United States, foods can be designated as organic if they are grown in soil that has been free of synthetic chemicals for at least five years. (Some farms which have shifted to the production of organic foods but have not been free of synthetic chemicals for five years are known as transitional organic farms, since chemical residues can usually still be found in their croplands, and therefore in the fruits and vegetables that are grown in it.)

This definition of *organic* is inherently limited, however, since it fails to recognize that foods that are truly organic are far more than foods that are free of manmade chemicals. Rather, they are foods that supply a more complete balance of nutrients as nature intended. As a result, they are healthier for you, compared to non-organic foods, as well as tastier.

Yet none of these factors are truly considered by federal regulatory agencies such as the U.S. Department of Agriculture (USDA) and the Food and Drug Administration (FDA), which are primarily concerned only with the presence or absence of synthetic chemical residues and not with evaluating the nutritional quality of organic and non-organic foods. In fact, both the USDA and FDA claim organic and non-organic foods are nutritionally equivalent, yet neither agency takes into account the differences that exist in the mineral and trace mineral content of organic and non-organic produce. Crop soil loaded with synthetic chemicals is noticeably deficient in minerals and trace minerals compared to soil unburdened by such chemicals. Since the overall mineral content in soil directly affects the overall nutrient content of crops that are grown in it, this means that organic crop soil yields produce that is more abundant in minerals and trace minerals, as well as vitamins, enzymes, phytonutrients, and other important nutritional factors.

Further distinguishing organic foods from non-organic foods is the alarming impact that non-organic, commercial farming methods have on crop soil itself, compared to croplands that are farmed organically. Organic farm methods not only maintain topsoil, but in many cases they actually increase it, resulting in healthier and more nutritious produce. By contrast, non-organic farming methods result in a loss of topsoil, further devitalizing the foods grown in such soil. In addition, chemical fertilizers, fungicides, and pesticides severely damage organisms in crop soil that are essential for the absorption of soil nutrients by plants. This negatively impacts the health of plants grown in such soil, as well as reduces the plants' nutrient content.

Non-organic farming methods pose threats to our health, as well. In addition to reducing the amount and variety of nutrients found in the produce, they also expose us to the chemical residues such food crops contain. Once such foods are consumed, the residues they contain find their way to fatty tissues and the fat cells of our bodies, where they are stored, causing a variety of toxic side effects. For example, there is now overwhelming evidence that pesticides stored in human tissues trigger increased rates of hormone-related cancers such as breast and prostate cancer, due to their ability to disrupt normal functioning of the body's endocrine system, which is in charge of hormone regulation.

A more recent health threat posed by non-organic farming methods has to do with produce that has been genetically modified due to the inclusion of genetically modified organisms (GMOs). Just as the USDA and FDA continue to insist that there is no discernible difference between organic and non-organic food groups, both agencies also maintain that GMO foods are identical to, and as safe as, natural foods. But this claim has never been fully established by thorough scientific investigation. In addition, according to a survey of field-tested GMO food crops conducted by research of the Union of Concerned Scientists, 93 percent of the genetic changes made to food crops are not made in order to produce nutrient content or taste, but merely to increase the profitability of commercial agriculture companies by making food production easier and less expensive. In fact, despite ongoing pressure by the United States to change their stance, the health and agricultural ministries of many countries within the European Union currently are resisting introducing GMOs into their nations' food chain because of the many unanswered questions regarding GMOs and health and safety.

There have already been identified risks associated with GMO foods. While the FDA does not require independent safety tests to be conducted, even with animals, on the GMO foods, there have been animal and human findings that are alarming. The first GMO tomato underwent animal studies by its developer. Ironically the rats in the study would not eat the tomatoes. They ended up force-feeding the rats, resulting in the rats having a 35 percent incidence of gastroenteritis and a 17 percent fatality rate. The FDA still approved this tomato for humans. Other animals have been observed refusing to eat GMO corn and in Norway, extensive research on rats fed GMO foods revealed the presence of new genes in all organs. Similar identification of GMO genes entering gut bacterium has been shown in the normal flora of humans.

Dr. Bailey has personally visited facilities that conduct genetic engineering to interview genetic scientists involved in GMO research. He has also spoken to FDA officials about GMO technology. He came away unimpressed with any of the arguments made by scientists and regulatory officials in support of GMO foods. As he wrote in his book, *The Fasting Diet*, "The discussions have been of such limited scope that true evaluation of [the] impact [of GMOs] is beyond their review and beyond their current knowledge."

To avoid including GMO foods in your diet, choose to buy only organic foods. In addition, beware of using canned foods, even if they claim to be organic. Corn is one of the primary ingredients found in most canned foods and, unfortunately, due to the clout of chemical giants such as Monsanto, our federal government has allowed GMO corn to be widely introduced into our nation's farmlands. As a result, today an estimated 95 percent of all corn grown in the United States contains GMOs. Many people working within the food industry will tell you that there are no GMO foods used in their product; unfortunately, only letters of certification can be trusted.

SELECTING HEALTHY MEATS, FISH, AND POULTRY

Depending on your biochemical makeup and metabolic type, regularly eating meats, fish, and poultry may be a healthy food choice. Choosing healthy servings of such animal foods can be problematic, however, due to many of the same environmental and food production factors that affect plant food crops.

Healthy Guidelines for Meat and Poultry Consumption

Commercially raised animals from which meat and poultry are derived are raised in extremely unhealthy conditions. Many chickens, for instance, are kept immobile in small cages, with their feet nailed together into boards. To prevent them from becoming sick due to the fact that they are forced to exist next to their own excrement, they are laced with antibiotics, residues of which can be found in chicken food products. Today, the use of antibiotics is so prevalent among commercially raised livestock and poultry that more than 40 percent of all antibiotics in the United States are used for this purpose.

Commercially raised cattle are subjected to similar unhealthy practices. In addition, they are fed grains, especially corn, which usually contains GMOs, instead of grasses, which cattle normally eat in a natural setting. Many cattle are also shot up with synthetic, genetically engineered growth hormone (BGH), residues of which have been shown to increase the risk of various cancers in people who eat commercial meats. Because of such unhealthy and unsanitary practices, if you choose to eat animal foods, we recommend that you eat only free-range meats and poultry that are free of antibiotics, synthetic hormones, and other unnatural substances.

Another type of meat that you should always avoid is meat that has been processed. Processed meats include meat that has been cured or smoked, bacon, sausage, hot dogs, salami, and ham. As this chapter was being written, the *Journal of the National Cancer Institute* published a scientific review of more than forty years' worth of scientific studies related to cancer and the consumption of processed meats. According to the review, processed meat consumption is directly related to a significant increase in stomach cancer. Overall, scientific studies from around the world have clearly established that heavy consumption of red meats is a risk factor for many types of cancer.

Further compounding the health risks posed by meat consumption is the way meats are prepared. Meats that are fried, barbecued, or broiled contain cancer-causing chemicals that are formed because of such cooking methods. Such chemicals are known as mutagens. Research has shown that they increase cancer risk because of how they damage cellular DNA. To reduce your risk of consuming mutagens, avoid these types of cooking methods, and also be sure not to overcook meats to the point where they are "well-done."

Healthy Guidelines for Fish Consumption

Due to environmental pollution, many types of fish, especially fresh water fish, are contaminated with high levels of unhealthy chemicals, including heavy metals (especially mercury), pesticides, and polychlorinated biphenyls (PCBs). So-called "farm-raised" fish are also unhealthy choices, due to the high amounts of antibiotics and food dyes that are used on such fish farms. By and large, it is no longer safe to regularly consume fresh water fish (fish found in lakes, rivers, and streams) because of the high levels of unhealthy contaminants they contain.

Many forms of seafood are also no longer healthy to eat, even though certain seafood, such as salmon, swordfish, and tuna, are naturally high in omega-3 fatty acids, which play an important role in helping to prevent inflammation and other health problems. If you enjoy eating salmon, be sure to avoid salmon that is farm-raised. Instead, choose wild-caught salmon, ideally from Alaska, which has been shown to have some of the lowest contaminants. Sardines are another healthy choice of fish and are also rich in omega-3 oils. If you eat tuna, avoid white tuna, which typically contains higher amounts of mercury than non-white tuna. Overall, you should only eat tuna sparingly, however. As a general rule of thumb, when you choose to eat fish, select fish that are deep-water ocean fish (except for shark and swordfish), since they are less apt to contain as many contaminants as fish that naturally occur nearer to shore, where environmental pollutants are found in higher concentrations.

AVOID FOODS TO WHICH YOU ARE ALLERGIC OR SENSITIVE

Food allergies and sensitivities are among the most common health problems in our nation today. Yet many health care practitioners fail to screen their patients for them. Ironically, people who do suffer from food allergies and sensitivities usually tend to crave the foods that cause them problems. In many cases, they may even be addicted to such foods, and will exhibit withdrawal-like symptoms when they don't eat them. These symptoms can be reduced with proper medical attention.

One of the reasons that food allergies often go undetected is because they can create a variety of health symptoms that mimic other disease conditions. Common symptoms of food allergies and sensitivities include constipation, diarrhea, chronic fatigue, fluid retention, gastrointestinal problems, headaches, hives, joint and muscle pain, rashes, respiratory problems, and unexplained weight gain. Food allergies and sensitivities can also often cause emotional, mental, and cognition problems.

Almost any food can potentially cause food allergies or sensitivities, especially if it is consumed on a regular basis. For this reason, some of the most common food offenders in this category are corn, chocolate, milk and other dairy products, egg whites, tomatoes, peanuts, shellfish and other types of seafood, soybeans and soy products, and wheat and wheat by-products. Processed foods can also trigger food allergies due to the various synthetic chemicals they contain.

Testing for Food Allergies

If you suspect that you may be affected by food allergies or sensitivities, the best thing to do is to consult with a health care practitioner trained in this area. Most conventional allergy screening tests are incapable of fully screening for food allergies since they do not test for IgG, the antibody most often produced by the body in response to food allergies and sensitivities. Instead, conventional allergy tests screen for IgE, the antibody most common produced by the body in response to environmental allergies. To be sure that your health care practitioner properly screens you, ask for the IgG ELISA (enzyme-linked immunoserological assay) Blood Test, which involves laboratory testing of a small sample of blood within 72 hours after it is drawn.

Self-Testing for Food Allergies

Though not as definitive as the IgG ELISA Blood Test, there is a simple home test you can perform to help determine if you suffer from food allergies or sensitivities. Known as the Pulse Test, it is performed by taking your resting pulse for one minute prior to eating. After you've taken your pulse, eat a bit of the food to which you suspect you may be allergic or sensitive. Then take your pulse again twenty minutes later. If your second pulse reading is more than ten points higher, you may be allergic or sensitive to the food you ate.

When performing the Pulse Test, be sure that you are relaxed. In addition, only eat one food at a time. For more accurate results, you may wish to test the same food on consecutive days to see if your pulse readings remain consistent.

Another effective method for determining food allergies is known as the Elimination Diet. It involves eliminating all suspected foods and beverages from your diet for four to seven days. After this time period, reintroduce the offending foods one at a time, and note any unhealthy changes that you feel that occur within 24 to 96 hours (because certain allergic reactions can take as long as four days to occur, you should wait four days to reintroduce an additional food). If you do experience negative reactions, more than likely you are allergic or sensitive to the foods you reintroduced, in which case you should eliminate them permanently from your diet. If you have developed a sensitivity due to poor digestion, it may be possible to improve your digestive function and later safely reintroduce the food.

EAT A WIDE VARIETY OF FOODS

Most Americans eat no more than twenty types of foods throughout their lives. Not only does eating such a limited variety of foods significantly increase the likelihood of developing food allergies and sensitivities, it usually also results in a failure to obtain the full range of nutrients that our bodies need on a daily basis in order to optimally function and stay healthy. To ensure that you are getting the most benefits from your diet, we encourage you to eat a wide range of foods and try to avoid eating the same foods less than three to four days apart.

Eating in this manner is sometimes referred to as a Rotation Diet. This eating approach is one of the simplest, yet most effective ways of providing your body with the nutrients it needs, while at the same time avoiding the problems caused by food allergies. By and large, today's standard American diet consists of a regular intake of dairy and wheat products, along with meats, poultry, and, to a lesser extent, fish. Lacking in such a diet is an adequate supply of fresh fruits and vegetables, along with nuts, seeds, and other nutrient-rich foods. You want to avoid such limited dietary routines. We encourage you to expand the range of healthy foods that you eat. Be especially sure to include plenty of fruits and vegetables in your meals each day, as well as other healthy foods that you normally do not eat.

In addition, vary the types of foods you eat in each food category. For example, if you tend to eat wheat products on a regular basis (breads, pastas, etc.), try substituting with whole grains such as brown rice, millet, couscous, amaranth, and quinoa, all of which contain plentiful supplies of vitamins, minerals, and other nutrients. Many people, when they start to expand the range of foods they eat, as well as limit their intake of each food to no less than every three to four days, soon start to notice improvements in their health, including greater levels of energy and improved mental and emotional well-being.

MAINTAIN ACID-ALKALINE BALANCE

Although the concept of acid-alkaline (see *Quick Definitions* on page 71) balance is common in modern medicine, where the maintenance of a precise blood pH is of life-and-death importance in emergency and critical care medicine, overall the mainstream medical establishment has overlooked the existence of low-grade pH imbalances, especially those caused by diet, until recently. Fortunately, today the acidifying and alkalizing influences of the foods we eat are becoming more widely recognized by physicians and the public alike. As a result, more and more health care practitioners are emphasizing and encouraging patients to monitor their urine pH as a way to maintain health and combat disease.

The link between acid-alkaline imbalance and disease is not new, having been written about by physicians since the early twentieth century. For example, in his book, *A New Health Era,* published in 1933, Dr. William Howard Hay wrote:

> [We] depart from health in just the proportion to which we have allowed our alkalis [reserves of alkaline-forming substances] to be dissipated by introduction of acid-forming food in too great amounts.... It may seem strange to say that all disease is the same thing, no matter what its myriad modes of expression, but it is verily so.

Today, every medical physiology textbook discusses the extreme and

Quick Definitions

Acid. Any substance in the body that gives off hydrogen ions when it is dissolved in water. Such substances have a pH value of less than 7.0.

Acid-Alkaline Balance. A necessary element of health created by a balanced state of acidic and alkaline substances in the body's fluids and tissues.

Acidic. Having a pH value less than 7.0.

Acidifying. Producing an acidic state.

Acidosis. A buildup of acid, and a state of excessive acidity in the body's fluids and tissues. Also known as *over-acidity*.

Alkali. Any substance that accepts hydrogen ions when dissolved in water. Such substances have a pH value of more than 7.0. Also known as a *base*.

Alkaline. Having a pH value greater than 7.0.

Alkalizing. Producing an alkaline state.

pH. Literally meaning "potential for hydrogen," pH is a measure of the acidity or alkalinity of a solution. The pH scale runs from 0 to 14, with 7.0 considered neutral. pH values below 7.0 are considered acidic, and pH values above 7.0 are considered alkaline.

life-threatening forms of acid-base imbalance. One of those books is *The Textbook of Medical Physiology,* an essential reference text in medical schools, written by Arthur C. Guyton, MD, who is known worldwide as an authority on human physiology. In it, Dr. Guyton writes, "[T]he regulation of hydrogen ion concentration is one of the most important aspects of homeostasis." (*Homeostasis* is the term given to describe the body's innate self-regulating mechanisms for maintaining balance within the body's various systems.)

The importance of eating primarily alkalizing foods was known well before the twentieth century, however. Thousands of years ago, Hippocrates, Pythagoras, and Galen, for example, advocated dietary practices that resulted in an alkalizing effect on the body, although they did not use terms such as *pH, acid,* and *alkaline.* Based on their teachings, such dietary practices were recommended by natural healers through the centuries. And even today, the traditional diets of people living in undeveloped countries are alkalizing. As a result, among such peoples, the rates and severity of chronic, degenerative diseases are much lower than they are in the United States and other developed nations.

During the mid-twentieth century, Edgar Cayce, known as the "Sleeping Prophet" because of the highly accurate medical and other types of information he was able to bring forth while in a state of trance, was a strong advocate of a diet that was alkalizing in nature. In order to maintain health and harmony in our bodies, he recommended eating meals that consisted of 80 percent alkalizing foods and only 20 percent acidifying foods. Cayce referred to this 80/20 ratio of alkalizing to acidifying foods as the "normal diet." Unfortunately, today's standard American diet (SAD) is highly acidic and one of the primary factors contributing to our nation's continually increasing health crisis.

Creating Healthy Meals
That Maintain Acid-Alkaline Balance

All foods have an inherent pH value. When it comes to good health, however, it is not a food's inherent pH value that is important, but whether or not the food creates an acidic or alkaline effect in the body after it has been digested and metabolized. To maintain your health, you should seek to achieve a pH level in your body that remains slightly alkaline (7.1–7.2). However, even if your body is mildly acidic (a pH of 6.5), generally you will still be relatively healthy. People who routinely eat the standard American diet usually are in a state of chronic over-acidity known as *acidosis.* In measuring the pH values of such people in his clinical practice, Dr. Bailey has found that they typically have pH readings of between 5.0–5.5. Such ongoing states of acidosis create chronic inflammation and other health imbalances, which have been linked to chronic fatigue, impaired cardiovascular function, headache, immune dysfunction, irritability, muscular tension and inflammation, and a wide array of other health symptoms.

To help you better understand why chronic acidity causes so many health problems, let's use baseball as a metaphor for hydrogen, which is given off by acidifying foods and accepted by alkalizing foods once they are digested. If there are only a few baseballs (acidifying foods) in the air (bloodstream) and a lot of available gloves (alkalizing foods) to catch them, it is easy for the balls to be caught, which equates to maintaining a safe and healthy environment inside the body. If, however, there are too many balls in the air (overconsumption of acidifying foods) and not enough gloves (health-promoting alkalizing foods), then many of the balls will go uncaught, dropping and bouncing everywhere to do a great deal of damage.

Based on this analogy, you can see that, just as there needs to be nine gloves on a baseball field and only one ball in play, so too does your body require 80 percent of the foods you eat at each meal to be alkalizing foods (gloves). Eating in this manner helps your body to significantly reduce inflammation and minimize the risk of chronic disease. Here are some guidelines to help you do so.

■ **Make Every Meal an Alkalizing Meal.** The 80/20 ratio between alkalizing and acidifying foods should be followed for all of your meals, instead of trying to eat all of your alkalizing foods at one or two meals, and acidifying foods at other meals. This helps to ensure that your body has what it needs to neutralize the acid residues of acidifying foods, preventing acid buildup in your body.

■ **Eat Plenty of Fresh Vegetables at Every Meal.** Vegetables are among the most alkalizing foods you can eat, and should therefore make up a generous portion of every meal. Vegetables are best eaten raw or lightly steamed to preserve their abundant nutrient content, which gets destroyed during other cooking methods.

■ **Don't Eliminate Acidifying Foods Altogether.** All of us require a certain amount of acidifying foods on a daily basis, regardless of whether or not our bodies are in a state of over-acidity. This is because many acidifying foods contain protein, which your body needs in order to function properly. Therefore, don't be tempted to completely eliminate acidifying foods, as doing so can cause your body to become too alkaline (greater than 8.5), which is unhealthy.

■ **Drink Water, Juices, and Other Beverages Away From Your Meals.**
Although most people commonly wash down the foods they eat with a beverage, doing so is not wise. This is because drinking while you eat interferes
with your body's ability to properly digest food by diluting the various
digestive substances that your body produces during eating. For this reason, we recommend that you drink water, juices, and other healthy beverages at least twenty to thirty minutes before eating.

■ **Avoid Drinking Alcohol, Coffee, Soda, and Tap Water.** All of these beverages are unhealthy and acidifying. We recommend that you avoid them
altogether, especially soda and tap water. If you choose to continue drinking coffee and alcohol, limit your coffee intake to no more than two cups a
day, and limit your alcohol to no more than one to two glasses of wine or
beer each day. All other forms of alcoholic beverages should be eliminated.

Acidifying Foods

Generally speaking, acidifying foods include breads, chocolate, milk and
dairy products, most grains and legumes, fish, meats, poultry, and most
nuts and seeds. The foods in the above categories do contain a variety of
health-promoting properties, however, and should be included in your
meal plans. For best results, limit them to no more than 40 percent of every
meal, and ideally only 20 percent. Ketchup, mustard, mayonnaise, and most
other commercial types of condiments are also acid-producing and
unhealthy overall, and should therefore be avoided, as should all forms of
sugar and artificial sweeteners. Yeast products should also be consumed
only sparingly.

Alkalizing Foods

Raw and lightly steamed vegetables are some of the most potent alkalizing
foods. We recommend that you include abundant servings of them at every
meal. Certain vegetables, such as potatoes and yams, both of which are
excellent alkalizing foods, can be cooked instead of steamed so long as they
are not overdone.

Fruits are also alkalizing, and rich in essential nutrients and fiber. However, because fruits are also high in natural sugars, they should only be
eaten sparingly during the day, ideally as snacks away from meals. The
exceptions to this rule are avocados, bananas, grapefruit, lemons, limes, and
tomatoes, all of which are highly alkalizing and can be eaten more often.
Other alkalizing foods include sprouted grains and legumes, seaweeds
(dulse, hijiki, kelp, wakame, etc.), certain grains (millet, quinoa, wild rice),

and certain nuts and seeds, which should always be soaked to maximize digestion (almonds, Brazil nuts, cashews, chestnuts, flaxseeds, macadamia nuts, pumpkin seeds, sesame seeds, and sunflower seeds). Most organic, cold-pressed oils, such as borage, canola, evening primrose, flax, grape seed, and olive oil, are also alkalizing, as are most herbs and spices (including Celtic unprocessed sea salts). With the exception of fruits, which should be eaten separately, see that at least 60 percent—and ideally 80 percent—of every meal you eat consists of foods from these categories, especially vegetables.

KNOW YOUR FATS AND OILS

Perhaps no other area of nutrition is fraught with so much misinformation and confusion as there exists in the discussion of fats and oils. This problem is compounded by the wide range of claims that the intake of dietary fat is strongly related to the development of many chronic disease conditions or to their prevention. Only when these seemingly contradictory claims are closely examined does the truth about fats and oils begin to emerge.

Simply put, certain fats and oils are not only healthy, but are also absolutely essential for the proper functioning of our bodies, and other fats and oils are unhealthy. This point was brilliantly made by Udo Erasmus in his books *Fats and Oils* and *Fats That Heal, Fats That Kill*. Most fats, including the two essential fats for humans, are produced within the plant kingdom during photosynthesis and are extremely sensitive to heat and ultraviolet (UV) light. This means that they can easily be damaged and destroyed by heat and prolonged exposure to UV light, as well as when they are extracted using heat and when they are overcooked. When such damage and destruction takes place, the result is toxic fat by-products known as trans fatty acids, which are the "fats that kill."

Trans fatty acids, which are commonly found in hydrogenated and partially hydrogenated oils (unsaturated oils to which hydrogen atoms are synthetically added), are known to play a causative role in both cancer and heart disease, as well as other health conditions. In addition, scientific research suggests that they may also be involved in various degenerative neurological diseases, including Alzheimer's and multiple sclerosis. This makes sense since the body's neurological system is comprised of tissues that are high in fat and depend on essential fatty acids to function properly. Essential fats also are found in every cell wall membrane and assist in absorption and elimination of all cells, as well as communication between cells.

When trans fatty acids enter the body through diet and improper cooking methods, they compete with essential fatty acids for a place within the body's tissues. Once they gain a foothold, the body is forced to expend more time and energy as it tries to eliminate trans fatty acids from tissues and the bloodstream. This is a difficult task, and is made even more so by the presence of other toxins within the body, including heavy metals, which bind with trans fatty acids. As a result, both the toxins and the trans fatty acids become more difficult for the body to eliminate.

To better understand why it is so difficult for your body to eliminate trans fatty acids, consider what happens when you fry foods with polyunsaturated oils, such as canola, corn, or safflower. During the frying process, as oil splatters in the frying pan, it forms into a hard, resinous substance that is difficult to remove. This is one of the reasons why we recommend that you don't fry foods. By doing so, you will literally be producing trans fatty acids on your stove. When you cook with olive oil (a mono-saturated fat) or saturated fats, these same splatters remain soft.

Based on the above information, it should be obvious that certain fats and oils pose serious threats to your health. Not all fats and oils act in this manner, however. In fact, all of us require a certain amount on a daily basis because of the many important roles such fats and oils have in maintaining health. The benefits of such fats and oils include supplying the body with energy reserves, maintaining proper body temperature and acting as the body's primary form of insulation, protecting against unhealthy inflammation, nourishing the skin and nerves, helping to transport oxygen to cells and tissues, and helping to metabolize and absorb fat-soluble vitamins. A significant key to health, therefore, is not to eliminate fats and oils from your diet, but to know which ones to include and which ones to avoid.

Choosing Healthy Fats and Oils

Healthy fats are called essential fatty acids (EFAs), meaning that they are required for life and cannot be manufactured within the human body. The two widely accepted EFAs are linoleic and linolenic acids, which have their first double bonds on the third and sixth carbons of the molecule. Thus, these are called omega-3 and omega-6 fats. We need approximately 5 percent of our total calories to be EFAs, yet the standard American diet rarely reaches this minimum goal. It is also often imbalanced with even less of the anti-inflammatory omega-3 fats. EFAs are used for a wide array of cellular and humoral (bodily fluid) functions, including their conversion into prostaglandins, which regulate your body's inflammatory response, strengthen cell walls and provide cellular energy, as well as enhance overall immune function.

Excellent sources of EFAs are organic, cold-pressed oils (oils that are extracted without the excessive use of heat or chemicals), such as borage, canola, evening primrose, flax, and grape seed oils. Oils high in EFAs and other polyunsaturated fats should never be used for cooking. Olive oil, which contains approximately 96 percent mono-saturated fats, is considered the best food oil for cooking, as it will not form trans-fats when heated. The other oils can be added to foods such as salads after they have been prepared. Various foods are also excellent sources of omega-3 EFAs. Especially good food sources of omega-3s are pumpkin seeds, walnuts, and wild-caught salmon and sardines.

Although there are many warnings to be found concerning the intake of saturated fats (fats that naturally contain a full quota of hydrogen atoms), your body needs a certain amount of saturated fats to ensure that its cells remain healthy and free of disease. Saturated fats include animal fats and tropical oils such as coconut and palm oil. Coconut oil is another saturated fat that is also safe to use for cooking.

All of the above fats and oils can be included in your daily diet, so long as they comprise no more than 30 percent (preferably 20–25 percent) of your overall food intake. The fats and oils you want to avoid are primarily hydrogenated and partially hydrogenated oils and trans fatty acids. These types of fats and oils are commonly used to prolong the shelf life of commercial food products, such as baked goods, cereals and other packaged foods, and most types of commercial salad dressings. Mayonnaise and margarine are other types of unhealthy fats and oils, as are cooking oils such as corn and safflower oils. All of these foods products should be avoided, which is easy to do if your diet is already based on fresh, organic, non-packaged, and non-processed foods. One of the single worst oils, found predominately in processed foods like chips, pretzels, and candy, is cottonseed oil, which is regulated by the USDA as a non-human crop. Cottonseed-containing products should be avoided.

DRINK PLENTY OF PURE, FILTERED WATER DAILY

One of the most overlooked and underutilized healing substances is water, which, next to air, is the most essential substance for the maintenance of life. The traditional medical systems of China, India, Greece, and Egypt all speak of creation and life as consisting of the elements Earth, Air, Water, and Fire. Approximately 70 percent of our bodies are made up of water (80 percent in infants), and water is the medium through which all of our body functions occur. Water is essential for:

■ Healthy brain function and conduction of nerve impulses

■ Proper metabolism and digestion (dehydration in the body can result in both constipation and diarrhea)

■ Delivery of oxygen into the bloodstream

■ Proper kidney and urinary function (lack of water can result in kidney stones and urinary tract infections)

■ Proper regulation of body temperature via perspiration

■ Joint lubrication and muscle function

■ Healthy respiratory function (lack of water in the body can result in diminished resistance to infection and sinus congestion)

■ Proper function of the lymphatic system and the elimination of waste products via the urine

When we fail to drink enough water each day, over time, many health problems can arise. These include:

■ Reduced brain size, leading to impaired neuromuscular coordination and mental function

■ Diminished oxygen supply in the bloodstream, resulting in lack of oxygen and nutrients to all body organs and muscles

■ Excess body fat

■ Poor muscle tone and muscle size

■ Buildup of toxins in body cells, tissues, and organs

■ Musculo-skeletal pain and related health conditions

■ Edema (water retention)

■ Impaired metabolism

■ Constipation and diarrhea

■ Blood thickening, which can increase risk of heart attack and hypertension

Based on the above, it's easy to see why water is so essential to our health. Yet, according to the late Dr. Batmanghelidj, the world's foremost authority on the relationship of water to health, most people are chronically dehydrated and aren't even aware of it. On average, each of us, under normal conditions, eliminates two and a half quarts of water each day through exhalation, perspiration, and urination. Exercise and exposure to heat, especially if you live in a dry climate, further increase water loss. That is why it is so important for you to make a conscious effort to replenish the water you lose each day by drinking water throughout the day.

Though you may not think you are dehydrated, chances are that you are. Most people equate dehydration with feeling thirsty but, according to Dr. Batmanghelidj, the body's most recognizable thirst signal, "dry mouth," is "the *last* outward sign of extreme *dehydration.*" Other signs of dehydration are fatigue, respiratory problems, and the various symptoms listed above. There are many health problems that are often associated with inadequate water consumption and the associated toxic accumulations related to chronic, low-grade dehydration. These include arthritis, constipation, depression, headaches, nausea, and skin problems, all of which are often profoundly improved by consuming adequate amounts of water.

Many health practitioners now recommend that you drink six to eight glasses of water a day, but in actuality the amount of water each person should drink is sometimes quite variable. The easiest indicator is to check how concentrated your urine is on a daily basis. Other than the rising urine, which reflects the clearing of wastes during our long sleep, your urine should be clear to light yellow. This, in turn, is influenced by how much fluid is in your foods, how much you exercise and perspire, and what other beverages you drink. Drinking coffee, soft drinks, commercial teas, milk, processed juices, or alcohol not only serve to further *increase* dehydration, they also can significantly impair your body's healthy acid-alkaline balance.

By contrast, even though most waters have a pH around 5.5 (with rain water more acidic at 5.0 and some filtrated water being neutral at 7.0), they exhibit a general alkalizing influence on the body. A healthy rule of thumb for ensuring adequate water intake is to daily consume 1 quart of water for every 70 pounds of weight, or 2–3 quarts of water daily. The more you drink, the less acidic you will be, as your body will be better able to eliminate stored acidic wastes.

Just as it is better to breathe in fresh air, as opposed to the polluted air of cities or industrial sites, it is better to drink high-quality water whenever possible, rather than tap or unfiltered water. Be sure the water you drink is pure and filtered (not chlorinated and free of fluoride). Distilled water is not recommended, since it is devoid of necessary minerals and can leach them from your body. Spring water is acceptable, but only after it is first tested for heavy metals, organo-chemicals and microbes. Initially, as you increase your water intake, you may experience a more frequent need to go to the bathroom. This will not last for more than a few days, after which your body adjusts to the increase.

An exciting and newly patented source of water is being extracted from organic plants via the freeze-drying process. This "new water," also called "living water," comes from the research of Ed Alstat, ND, RPh, and will soon be available nationwide with water extracts from strawberries, bananas, apples, and cranberries. With just an essence of these fruit flavors, it is an excellent water to introduce to children, as well as to include in your own diet. (See the Resource List on page 254 for more information about this water product.)

To get in the habit of drinking enough water, drink it throughout the day, but don't drink more than four 8-ounce glasses in any one-hour period. It's also best to drink one or two glasses of water upon arising, at least thirty minutes before breakfast. As a general rule, also drink at least thirty minutes before or after meals, because drinking a lot of water while you eat can interfere with digestion.

CONCLUSION

Now that you have read this chapter, we hope that you have a better understanding of how and why healthy dietary habits are so important to your health. When Hippocrates stated that our food should be our medicine, and our medicine our food, he revealed one of the most basic, yet essential, foundations for achieving and maintaining optimal health. Unfortunately, the wisdom contained in his famous adage is all too often ignored in our society. Yet the consequences of doing so can be deadly, a fact that is borne out by research that shows that over a third of all cases of cancers in this country could have been prevented if the cancer patients had only eaten more sensibly.

Don't make the same mistake. Your food intake is one of the most powerful aspects of your health that you can control. By following the guidelines we've shared with you above, you can do much to improve and maintain your health simply and easily.

In the next chapter, you will learn about Dr. Bailey's recipes for delicious, healthy alternatives to juices in the form of fruit smoothies and herbal tonics.

6

Healthy Smoothies and Tonics

ow that you have read this far, it is our hope that you have a better
understanding of the many health benefits juicing can provide. Ideally, you are also putting the information we have shared to the test
by making fresh, organic fruit and vegetable juices a part of your regular
healthy lifestyle. Some readers, however, may still be resistant to the thought
of preparing and drinking juices. This is especially the case with many children and teenagers, particularly if they are used to today's standard American diet of fast, processed, and nutritionally lacking foods and beverages.

For this reason, in this chapter we are sharing with you Dr. Bailey's
recipes for delicious and nutritious alternatives to juices in the form of fruit
smoothies, green smoothies, and herbal tonics. In addition, you will learn
how to prepare Dr. Bailey's Power Smoothie and discover a remarkable
health-enhancing smoothie based on the Gospel of Thomas from the Nag
Hammadi Library. Finally, we will share with you information that will
enable you and your loved ones to "drink the fruits of the rainbow," using
specific smoothies and meditations for each day of the week that will leave
you feeling more energized, content, and at peace. Let's get started by
exploring the various fruits, nuts, seeds, and super foods that you can use
to prepare the smoothies and tonics that follow.

HEALTHY FRUITS AND SUPER FOODS

What follows is an overview of various fruits, herbs, and concentrated nutrient-rich super foods that you can use to prepare the smoothies and tonics
that you will read about later in this chapter. In choosing the foods you want
to use, remember that although variety is a cornerstone of a healthy diet and
lifestyle, you needn't feel obliged to eat foods you don't enjoy just because
someone says they are good for you. On the other hand, you should not be
afraid to experiment and try foods that are unfamiliar to you. As when juic-

Understanding ORAC—
A New Measure of Nutritional Power

Oxygen Radical Absorbance Capacity, or ORAC, measures a food's antioxidant activity, and therefore the degree to which the food inhibits the action of harmful substances known as free radicals. Since free radical damage has been implicated in everything from aging and diabetes to heart disease and cancer, the ORAC Scale represents a powerful tool when choosing ingredients for a healthful diet. ORAC was developed by Dr. Guohua Cao in the early 1990s, and is accepted by the USDA, the food industry, and the research community as a reliable standardized measurement. The higher the ORAC value, the higher the food's antioxidant level.

Experts recommend consumption of 5,000 ORAC units daily, although the intake of five fruits and vegetables suggested by the government typically provides only around 1,750 units. Hence, people eating the standard American diet can experience significant benefits by eating high-ORAC foods such as blueberries and prunes. Be aware, though, that at this time, the ORAC tests only a food's action against one free radical—peroxyl. An expanded "total ORAC"—which would add the measurements for hydroxyl, peroxynitrite, singlet oxygen, and superoxide anion—will eventually be available.

It's important to understand that the ORAC Scale measures just a food's antioxidant activity—not all the other nutrients it contains. Scientific research has revealed that most plant cells contain over 5,000 chemical compounds, making it impractical and nearly impossible to quantify. It is sufficient to realize that plants offer us tremendous nutritional benefits. Use of the ORAC Scale can help you make high-antioxidant selections, but you need to seek a varied diet that includes as many types of organic whole foods as your tastes and resources allow. And don't be misled by processed foods that claim to be "pure," but that in actuality contain additives such as green tea extract or even unlabeled preservatives to boost their ORAC score. For the most nutrients, including antioxidants, stick with whole foods and prepare your smoothies and tonics in your own kitchen.

The following table presents ORAC values for selected super foods, as well as some foods common to the American diet. Note that these values represent only the food's action against the free radical peroxyl. The foods are presented in descending order of ORAC values, with higher-ORAC choices listed first, followed by lower-ORAC choices. Each ORAC value is for a serving of 3.5 ounces.

ORAC Values of Selected Foods

SUPER FOODS AND FUNCTIONAL FOODS

Food	ORAC Value Per 3.5-Ounce Serving	Food	ORAC Value Per 3.5-Ounce Serving
Maqui Berries	30,000 units	Goji Berries	25,300 units
Noni Fruit	29,000 units	Dark Chocolate	13,120 units
Raw Cacao	28,000 units	Blackstrap Molasses	8,860 units
Acai Berries	26,000 units	Red Wine	5,693 units
Barley Grass	25,500 units	Mangosteen	3,400 units

COMMON FRUITS

Food	ORAC Value Per 3.5-Ounce Serving	Food	ORAC Value Per 3.5-Ounce Serving
Cranberries	9,584 units	Strawberries	1,540 units
Prunes	5,770 units	Raspberries	1,220 units
Pomegranates	3,307 units	Prunes	949 units
Raisins	2,830 units	Oranges	750 units
Blueberries	2,400 units	Apples	218 units
Blackberries	2,036 units	Bananas	210 units

COMMON VEGETABLES

Food	ORAC Value Per 3.5-Ounce Serving	Food	ORAC Value Per 3.5-Ounce Serving
Kale	1,770 units	Corn	400 units
Spinach	1,260 units	Potatoes	300 units
Brussels Sprouts	980 units	Sweet Potatoes	295 units
Alfalfa Sprouts	930 units	Carrots	210 units
Broccoli	880 units	String Beans	201 units
Beets	840 units	Tomatoes	195 units
Avocados	782 units	Cucumbers	60 units

ing, one of the keys to fully benefiting from the smoothies and tonics in this chapter is to prepare them from the foods that most appeal to you, but with an eye on health as well. The list of foods below will help guide your selection by providing general information about the benefits of each ingredient, including its ORAC value—a measurement that shows the food's all-important antioxidant capacity, and therefore its ability to prevent certain health disorders. (To learn more about ORAC, see the inset on pages 82 to 83.)

Acai Berry (*Eutherpe oleracea*)

Acai is a deep purple berry of the Brazilian Acaiziero palm tree. Its pulp contains a remarkably high level of antioxidants, making acai's ORAC score significantly higher than that of red wine, which is touted as offering the powerful antioxidant known as resveratrol. The berries also contain omega-3 and omega-6 essential fatty acids, vitamins C and E, beta-carotene, minerals, and fiber. Early research has indicated that acai enhances immune system and cardiovascular health; improves energy, stamina, and exercise endurance; may have thermogenic (fat-burning) properties; and may improve sexual health in men. You will probably not be able to find fresh acai berries in your local store. Instead, contact Sambazon, which sells acai purées (see page 254 of the Resource List), or look for flash pasteurized liquid extracts.

Acerola Cherry (*Malpighiaceae emarginata*)

Found mostly in natural vitamin C formulations, the acerola cherry grows in both the Caribbean and the Middle East. It is one of the five foods recommended for health in the Gospel of Thomas (see page 98), and is the single highest source of edible vitamin C. Rich in beta-carotenes and other antioxidants, acerola cherries score high on the ORAC Scale, with a value of about 26,000 units. While tart, these cherries nonetheless have a very pleasant taste and add much to tonics and smoothies in terms of flavor and nutrition. Although acerola cherries themselves are difficult to find in the produce section of local stores, they are readily available as an organic powder, and Sambazon offers an acerola purée. (See page 254 of the Resource List.)

Bee Pollen

Containing all the essential amino acids, bee pollen is nature's own protein powder and provides a wide variety of health benefits, including greater energy. It can also be effective in reducing hay fever and other allergic conditions and their symptoms. Bee pollen is available in a granular form in bulk, and is sometimes also found in capsule form.

Black Cherry (*Prunus serotina*)

Known for its ability to reduce the uric acid levels associated with gout, black cherry—which grows throughout North America—is also a gentle but highly effective aid for constipation. For both these purposes, a pasteurized organic concentrate or juice is quite effective and tastes better than prunes, which have the same properties. The ORAC value for black cherries is high—over 2,000.

Cacao (*Theobroma cacao*)

In recent years, research on cacao—the key ingredient in cocoa and chocolate—has demonstrated that it is a "functional" (health-enhancing) food. The chemical compounds found in the seeds of the tropical plant appear to both relax arterial walls through the production of nitric oxide, and, like aspirin, reduce platelet aggregation (clumping or clotting). As a result, cacao is believed to lower blood pressure, improve cerebral blood flow, and decrease the incidence and mortality of heart attacks. One constituent is also thought to protect against the development of breast cancer. In a relatively low-fat form, cacao can make a tasty addition to your super food smoothies and tonics. For the lowest fat and highest nutrients—including the highest ORAC value—use raw organic cacao powder. Organic dark chocolate that is either plain or contains whole foods is also good. Just be sure to avoid highly processed chocolate that contains a multitude of unhealthy ingredients, such as corn syrup, milk solids, emulsifiers, and other stabilizers.

Carob (*Ceratonia siliqua*)

Carob beans are found in the pods of the carob tree. In biblical times, this tree was known as the "locust bush," and many believe the bean to be the locust of John the Baptist's diet of locusts and honey. Today, it is best known as a low-fat, low-stimulant substitute for chocolate.

Carob is rich in antioxidant substances, tannins, fiber, and vitamins and minerals, including calcium, potassium, magnesium, and iron. The fiber in carob has demonstrated an ability to lower cholesterol, and, in conjunction with tannins and other compounds, has proven an effective treatment for diarrhea. Research has shown that the leaves have a strong sedative action, similar to that of Valium. Since fruits typically contain agents similar to those found in the leaves of the same plant, carob beans probably have a mildly relaxing or sedative effect as well. Moreover, the flavonoid compounds in the beans may help prevent cancer. For all of these reasons, including its chocolate-like flavor, carob would make a good addition to the Saint Thomas Smoothie presented on page 99.

Cinnamon (*Cinnamomum zeylanicum*)

Taken from the bark of an evergreen tree, cinnamon has long been a popular spice. Medicinally, cinnamon has a long history of use as well, dating back to ancient China, Egypt, and Greece. The Greek physician Galen advocated the use of cinnamon in his writings. Cinnamon is helpful in treating gastrointestinal problems, dysentery, and respiratory conditions such as bronchitis and tuberculosis. Research shows that it may also improve circulation, lower cholesterol, and have strong antibacterial, antifungal, and antiyeast properties. Although cinnamon bark has an amazing ORAC value of 103,448, it's important to remember that this would require an intake of 3.5 ounces, which is not a practical expectation. However, you can add to your daily ORAC consumption by using cinnamon as a flavoring and taking powdered cinnamon supplements in capsule form. If you take three 1,000-milligram capsules daily, as many people do to lower their cholesterol, you will consume about 3,000 ORAC units through supplements alone.

Coconut (*Cocos nucifera*)

One of the five foods recommended for health in the Gospel of Thomas, coconuts can enhance the flavor of any health drink. Although coconuts are not a high-ORAC food, they contain ample amounts of calcium and magnesium for strong bones and muscles, and are one of the only plant-based sources of vitamin D—an important nutrient that helps protect against many cancers, bone loss, and depression. Vitamin D has been found to be lacking in many people, and the fatty acids found in coconut oil are ideally structured to aid production of this vitamin through exposure to the sun. Coconut is also believed to have antifungal properties and to be an aid in digestive health. In addition to using the fruit itself, you can use convenient products such as coconut milk, powder, and oil in your diet.

Cranberry (*Vaccinium macrocarpon*)

The tart, bright red berry known as the cranberry has long been recommended by both herbalists and physicians for its ability to treat and prevent urinary tract infections. This is thought to be the result of the bacterial anti-adhesion properties of certain compounds found in the fruit. Historically, the cranberry has also been used to help prevent kidney stones, and as a purifier of toxins in the blood. With its high level of benzoic acid, a natural preservative, and its flavonoids and other antioxidants, the cranberry has one of the highest ORAC values of any common food—9,584 units. Cranberries, cranberry extract, and cranberry powder all make healthful additions to smoothies and tonics.

Garlic (*Allium sativum*)

Few foods have had such a wide medical use throughout history as garlic. Famed for its antifungal and antimicrobial properties, garlic also reduces the inflammatory prostaglandins that contribute to cardiovascular disease and other inflammatory disorders. Garlic is helpful in the management of cholesterol, and is one of the most effective foods for maintaining a healthy liver. Although a 3.5-ounce serving has an ORAC value of 1,939, garlic is usually not consumed in that quantity, making garlic supplements a good choice.

Ginger (*Zingiber officinale*)

Ginger is remarkable for its ability to ease or eliminate nausea and vomiting. It is also helpful in the prevention and treatment of vertigo and motion sickness. Ginger is excellent for stopping both external and internal bleeding. In addition, when added to apple juice, it becomes a traditional postpartum drink that is valued in both midwifery and naturopathic obstetric practices. Ground ginger has an ORAC value of 28,811 for a 3.5-ounce serving—which is far more ginger than you are likely to consume in powder form. Ground ginger maintains most of the plant's therapeutic properties, but when making juices and smoothies, Dr. Bailey uses the fresh root whenever possible.

Goji Berry (*Lycium barbarum*)

Grown on an evergreen shrub in China and the Himalayas, goji berries are also known as lycii and wolfberries. This fruit contains more beta-carotene than carrots, provides powerful antioxidants, and is particularly recommended as a protective food for the eyes. It rates very high on the ORAC Scale (over 25,000), and its potent polysaccharides and carotenes have been linked to energy production, weight control, sexual enhancement, anti-inflammatory action, and general "anti-aging." Goji berries are commonly found in health food stores in dried form.

Green Powders

Available in health food stores, green powders concentrate the many wonderful nutrients provided by fruits and vegetables. There are many quality green powder products on the market, all of which can add a potent boost of nutrition to your health drinks.

Hawthorn Berry (*Crataegus*)

Found on the common hawthorn tree, the hawthorn berry is used in an herbal tonic throughout China. Hawthorn extract is recognized by German Commission E as a natural drug for high blood pressure and heart disease, and is indicated for chronic lung problems, as well. A flavonoid-rich berry,

Hawthorn has a moderately high ORAC value, similar to that of strawberries and raspberries—over 1,000 units per serving. Hawthorn is typically available as dried berries, bulk powder, or capsules.

Job's Tears (*Coix lacryma-jobi*)

Also known as Asian pearl barley or Hata Mogi, Job's tears is a barley-like grain that is a traditional source of Japanese fermented miso. Like all seeds, nuts, and beans, this grain should be soaked for at least twelve hours in order to activate its many enzymes for easy digestion. Job's tears is an excellent but often overlooked source of quality carbohydrates. Whether soaked and used raw in a smoothie or cooked in multigrain cereals or soups, it deserves a place on your weekly shopping list.

Mangosteen (*Garcinia mangostana*)

Known as the "Queen of Fruits" in Southeast Asia, the super food mangosteen has finally made its way to the American market. The mangosteen rates high in ORAC values and has high levels of xanthones—potent antioxidants that are believed to decrease inflammation, promote immune health, reduce free-radical damage, improve mood, and enhance energy and stamina. Among the substances found in this fruit are antioxidant flavonoids, amino acids, and vitamins and minerals, including zinc, iron, copper, calcium, and germanium. The mangosteen has a pleasant taste and makes a wonderful addition to smoothies and tonics. Presently, it is primarily available as a juice, extract, and encapsulated powder. Dr. Bailey uses the whole berry extract when making smoothies.

Maqui Berry (*Aristotelia chilensis*)

Grown in Patagonia, the southernmost region of South America, the maqui berry has an exceptionally high ORAC value, exceeding those of noni, mangosteen, and acai. This nutrient-dense food has shown the ability to help relieve pain, decrease oxidative stress and inflammation, and boost immune function. This super food is available as a juice and as a whole berry juice extract or concentrate.

Noni (*Morinda citrifolia*)

While noni is fairly new to Westerners, in Polynesian cultures, it has been recognized as a powerful health food for centuries. Now also grown in the Caribbean, noni could be called a detergent for its actions on liver function and the liberation of fat-loving toxins. Dr. Bailey discovered this for himself during one fast. (For more on the health benefits of fasting, see Chapter 7.) Noni also has one of the highest ORAC values of any food.

Beginning with the work of Dr. Ralph Heinicke in the 1950s, research has shown that noni contains many phytochemicals of remarkable benefit to both humans and animals. One of the fruit's many important chemical constituents is an alkaloid called *xeronine,* which activates both enzymes and proteins in the human body. Noni triggers the release of endorphins, making it effective as both a pain reliever and a mood elevator; and is rich in caprylic acid, which is a potent antifungal nutrient that also exhibits antibacterial properties. The list of noni's chemical constituents—which show promise in fighting cancer, hepatitis, and viral infections; in reducing blood pressure; in controlling parasites; and in improving overall health—continues to grow, but will never tell the whole story of what this remarkable plant can do when added to the diet. There are many noni products available today, but not all of them live up to their health claims, due to how they are produced. For a supplier of noni products that meet the highest production standards, see page 254 of the Resource List.

Papaya (*Carica papaya*)

Long utilized as digestive support due to its abundant supply of the protein-digesting enzymes bromelain and papain, papaya is also one of the five fruits of the Gospel of Thomas. In addition, the papaya is naturally rich in protein. We know this because in nature, enzymes are always coupled with the chemicals or nutrients they digest. The papaya is an excellent source of vitamin C, folic acid, and lycopene, and has an abundance of antioxidant compounds that give it an average ORAC of about 1,000 units per serving. The riper the fruit, the higher the ORAC value. Including the skin also boosts the ORAC level.

Pomegranate (*Punica granatum*)

Researchers are only beginning to recognize the health benefits of pomegranate, a fruit that was highly revered in biblical times. The pomegranate is mentioned repeatedly in the Bible, where it serves as a metaphor for spiritual elevation. It has a long history in Ayurvedic and Egyptian medicine, and was deemed one of China's three blessed fruits. Galen and Hippocrates considered the pomegranate a natural medicine for nausea, vomiting, and ulcers, when used with barley. In naturopathic medicine, the pomegranate is employed to expel parasites such as tapeworms, due in part to the alkaloid *peperidine* found in its root. Scientific research shows that the compounds in this fruit offer significant benefits for cardiovascular health, and have anti-cancer and antimicrobial properties, as well. With an ORAC value of over 3,000 units, the pomegranate would make a healthful addition to the Saint Thomas Smoothie (see page 99), as well as other smoothies and tonics.

Probiotics

Probiotics—literally, "pro life"—include the beneficial bacteria found in a healthy digestive tract. While most people have heard of acidophilus, the most popular probiotic supplement, there are many other varieties of healthy bacteria, and the best probiotic products usually contain eight or more of them. Probiotic supplements are widely available in health food stores, and are also found in cultured products such as kefir, lassi, and yogurt.

Seeds and Nuts

The following seeds and nuts can be soaked overnight and then placed in a blender along with other smoothie ingredients.

Almonds (Prunus amygdalus)

Soaked and peeled, almonds are a rich source of nutrients, and in traditional healing, are recommended to help prevent cancer and various other chronic diseases.

Flaxseeds (Linum)

Flaxseeds contain omega-6 essential fatty acids, and are even richer in omega-3 essential fats. Organic flaxseed oil is an excellent natural remedy that supports and enhances immunity and cardiovascular health, and provides many other general health benefits, as well. These benefits are increased when flaxseed is added to quality sunflower oil. Flaxseed can also be ground and sprinkled on soups and salads and blended in juices and smoothies.

Lotus Seeds (Nelumbo nucifera)

Always soaked before they are consumed, lotus seeds have a slightly bitter taste. They are held in the highest esteem in Eastern spiritual and healing traditions, and are often used in ceremonies and rites. Lotus seeds have been employed in traditional Chinese medicine to aid weak digestion; nourish, support, and strengthen the spleen; and support the kidneys. They are also a good source of protein, including the protein L-isoaspartyl methyltransferase, which helps rebuild and repair other proteins in the body. This makes lotus seeds a good anti-aging food. In addition, lotus seeds contain the powerful antioxidant quercetin, and are believed to have antifungal and antibiotic properties.

Pine Nuts (Pinus)

Pine nuts are high in protein, high in fiber, rich in antioxidants, and a good source of essential fatty acids. They are known to normalize and improve reproductive health and hormonal balance.

Sunflower Seeds (Helianthus annuus)

When soaked, sunflower seeds are a rich source of omega-6 fatty acids. As a cold-pressed oil, sunflower oil acts as a super nutrient that can relieve many types of inflammatory disease.

Turmeric (*Curcuma longa*)

The use of turmeric has a rich cultural history. In Thailand, turmeric is rubbed on the mother's skin immediately after she gives birth, and in India, it is rubbed on the bride's skin before the marriage ceremony. Hindu proverbs instruct you to rub turmeric on your skin to keep crocodiles away when you enter the Ganges, India's sacred river.

In the United States, turmeric became recognized at the start of the AIDS crisis, when it proved to be an excellent aid to lung and respiratory health. It is also known to reduce inflammation, and is used in many products to alleviate the pain and swelling of arthritis and muscular inflammation. Dr. Bailey's favorite form of turmeric is the fresh root. Since this is not always available, it is fortunate that ground turmeric provides many of the benefits of the fresh plant and is readily available. For the most healthful product, try to find organic sources.

HEALTHY SMOOTHIES

Some fruits are too dense or pulpy to process through standard juicing machines. Common examples are bananas, papayas, mangos, and coconuts. However, by blending these fruits and adding them to fresh fruit juices, you can enjoy their many benefits in the form of delicious, healthy smoothies.

Smooth, pulpy fruit drinks date back thousands of years. In Peru, a native beverage made from mashed passion fruit and water is an example of a traditional smoothie. Here in the United States, smoothies have been around since the first electric blender was introduced. Now these beverages are served at most juice bars, in many health food and grocery stores, and in many restaurants, as well.

Because of their rich taste and thick consistency, smoothies provide a natural vehicle for super-food additives such as bee pollen, lecithin, protein powders, green powders, flaxseed oil, and other concentrated foods. Because they are so creamy and delicious, they are loved by young and old alike, making them an excellent means of weaning children and adults off of high-sugar drinks and processed foods. What follows are smoothie recipes personally chosen by Dr. Bailey for their nutritional value and ease of preparation.

Drinking the Rainbow

In his book *The Rainbow Diet,* Dr. Gabriel Cousens documents the importance of eating a wide range of fruits and vegetables of many colors, so as to receive a "rainbow" spectrum of nutrients. By making juices and smoothies a regular part of your diet, it is also possible to "drink the rainbow." In preparing this chapter, Dr. Bailey decided to create a weekly smoothie recipe plan that would make drinking the rainbow easy and fun. When he shared his plan with his young daughter, Shayla, she suggested that she and her friends do a taste test of the smoothies Dr. Bailey had selected, and Dr. Bailey agreed. The recipes below have all been "kid tested and approved." In addition to the ratings that Shayla and her friends provided, each recipe is accompanied by meditative practices you can explore each day that correspond to the energies and properties associated with the color of each smoothie. For example, the color green is associated with the heart chakra or energy, and represents the many expressions of love and loving kindness, as well as courage. Similarly colored super foods are included as add-ins that you can use to boost the nutritional value of each drink.

For best results, use organic fruits whenever possible. Each recipe yields approximately two cups, which is one serving for most children in the five- to ten-year-old range, but can be two servings, depending on size and appetite. The smoothies can be stored in the refrigerator for later consumption and will still be nutritious on the second day, although to a lesser degree.

Monday—The Color Red

Combine 1 cup of fresh organic strawberries with $1/2$ to 1 cup of cranberry juice. While fresh cranberry juice is preferred, you can use bottled organic cranberry juice, as well as a splash of organic white grape juice. Blend until smooth. As an option, you can add 1 cup of pomegranate juice to this mixture. Makes one to two servings.

Kids' Rating: "The Best"

Add-ins: cinnamon, wolfberries, hawthorn berries

Meditative Practice: long walks, gardening, planting

Tuesday—The Color Orange

Mix 1 cup of peaches and 1 cup of papaya with $1/2$ to 1 cup orange juice.

Blend until smooth. Mango can be substituted for papaya or included along with it. Makes one to two servings.

Kids' Rating: "Nearly the Best"

Add-ins: ginger, cardamom, and calendula flowers

Meditative Practice: nurturing activities with children, and self-care

Wednesday—The Color Yellow

Combine 1 banana, ½ cup pineapple, and ½ to 1 cup lemon juice sweetened with white grape juice or maple syrup. Blend until smooth. Other options include peaches, yellow grapes, and/or pineapple juice. Makes one to two servings.

Kids' Rating: "Good"

Add-ins: turmeric, dandelion flowers, flaxseeds

Meditative Practice: good works, forgiveness

Thursday—The Color Green

Combine 1 apple with 1 to 2 kiwis and blend with 1 cup of lime juice that has been sweetened with a little white or green grape juice or maple syrup. Another fruit you can use is green grapes. Makes one to two servings.

Kids' Rating: "Very Good"

Add-ins: green powders, mint leaves, wheatgrass juice (See the "Wheatgrass Juice" inset on page 146.)

Meditative Practice: walks in nature, practice acts of loving-kindness

Friday—The Color Blue

Combine 1 cup of blueberries with ½ to 1 cup blueberry, apple, or black cherry juice. Blend until smooth. Makes one to two servings.

Kids' Rating: "Nearly the Best"

Add-ins: hyssop, elderberries

Meditative Practice: singing, music, dancing

Saturday—The Color Purple

Combine 1 cup of blackberries with ½ to 1 cup pear or black cherry juice. Blend until smooth. Purple grapes, Marionberries, and prune juice are other options. Makes one to two servings.

Kids' Rating: "Very, very good"

Add-ins: noni juice, lavender blossoms, juniper berries

Meditative Practice: quiet meditation, yoga

Sunday—The Color White

Combine 1 banana with 2 tablespoons grated coconut, 2 tablespoons soaked almonds, and 6 soaked lotus seeds, and blend with 1 cup fresh coconut milk until smooth. Pears, white grapes, and almond milk can also be added to this recipe. Makes one to two servings.

Kids' Rating: "Okay" (Both the lotus seeds and whole almonds proved to be less tasty to the four- to nine-year-olds who participated in the taste test.)

Add-ins: maca powder, osha root, Job's tears (soaked)

Meditative Practice: gratitude, thankfulness, prayer, water therapies and activities

Other "Kid-Tested" Smoothie Recipes

As a doctor and a parent, Dr. Bailey knows that he has to provide foods that please the tastes and meet the needs of many different people, young and old. When creating tasty smoothies, juices, or tonics, it's a wonderful idea to let each person choose his or her own favorite ingredients. Putting his advice into practice, Dr. Bailey allowed each of the children who participated in the seven "rainbow" smoothies taste test to choose combinations of fruits, nuts, and juices for his or her own smoothie. The result was that all of the children thoroughly enjoyed their creations and gave them enthusiastic approval.

Each of the combinations that the children invented were highly nutritious because only healthy ingredients were made available to them. If you have children who are resistant to the idea of drinking healthy smoothies, be sure to involve them in the selection and preparation of nutrient-rich foods. This is a fun way to encourage them to give smoothies a try. What follows are the recipes for the smoothies that Shayla and her friends prepared. Each smoothie is named after the child who originally created it, and each serving is approximately one 8-ounce glass.

Kayce's Smoothie

Mix 1/4 cup each of strawberries, pineapple, kiwi, blackberries, blueberries, and kiwi. Combine with 1 cup cranberry juice. Makes one to two servings.

Leyla's Smoothie

Mix ¼ cup each of blueberries, strawberries, papaya, peaches, and pineapple. Combine with 1 cup cranberry juice. Makes one to two servings.

Sofia's Smoothie

Mix ¼ cup each of pineapple, strawberries, blueberries, raspberries, and papaya; ½ medium banana; and 9 soaked and peeled almonds. Combine with 1 cup cranberry juice. Makes two to three servings.

Y Yan's Smoothie

Mix ¼ cup each of pineapple, blueberries, strawberries, blackberries, and kiwi; and 9 peeled and soaked almonds. Combine with 1 cup cranberry juice. Makes one to two servings.

Julia's Smoothie

Mix ¼ cup each of strawberries, blackberries, pineapple, and kiwi. Combine with 1 cup cranberry juice. Makes one to two servings.

Isabella's Smoothie

Mix ¼ cup each of strawberries, blueberries, watermelon, blackberries, and kiwi. Combine with 1 cup apple juice. Makes one to two servings.

Y Lai's Smoothie

Mix ¼ cup each of blueberries, strawberries, pineapple, kiwi, peaches, and watermelon; 1 to 2 tablespoons of grated coconut; and 9 each of soaked and peeled almonds and soaked lotus seeds. Combine with 1 cup blueberry juice. Makes two to three servings.

Shayla's Smoothie

Mix ¼ cup each of blackberries, blueberries, wolfberries, pineapple, peaches, papaya, kiwi, and watermelon; 1 to 2 tablespoons grated coconut; and 9 soaked and peeled almonds. Combine with 1 cup lemon juice. Makes two to three servings.

Gabrielle's Smoothie

Mix ¼ cup each of watermelon, peaches, and pineapple; and 9 soaked and peeled almonds. Combine with 1 cup cranberry juice. Makes one to two servings.

Sawyer's Smoothie

Mix ¼ cup each of kiwi, blueberries, strawberries, papaya, blackberries, and watermelon. Combine with 1 cup apple-and-pear juice. Makes one to two servings.

Dr. Bailey's Power Smoothie

The following smoothie was initially developed by Dr. Bailey for his cancer and AIDS patients, many of whom were taking up to 150 supplements a day in capsule and tablet form. Despite this intensive regimen, most of these patients were unable to derive much benefit from the supplements they were taking because their bodies were unable to properly digest and assimilate them. Dr. Bailey's Power Smoothie solves this problem by providing an abundance of essential nutrients in a tasty drink that is easily digested and absorbed. By including vitamins, essential fats, proteins, and other nutrients in a delicious smoothie, it is easy to optimize your nutritional status.

Dr. Bailey's Power Smoothie

2–4 opened capsules of vitamin/enzyme complex (There are many cap-suled vitamins that contain abundant vitamins, broad minerals, and vegetable-based enzymes. See page 254 of the Resource List for more infor-mation.)

5 drops natural liquid beta-carotene

1 tablespoon organic, cold-pressed flaxseed or flaxseed/sunflower seed oil (borage, evening primrose, fish oil, or hemp can also be used)

1 teaspoon lecithin granules or powder

1 tablespoon soy-free vegetable protein powder

Add various fruits and other super foods of your choice to the above ingre-dients and blend them all together.

While only supplying one meal's worth of calories, the Power Smoothie provides the same amount of micronutrients typically found in six healthy meals. The fresh fruits and juices, combined with the digestive enzymes, make the required digestive effort much less than that of a typical breakfast. As a result, people experience improved ener-gy and endurance when the Power Smoothie is consumed for at least five days a week. It is appropriate for both children and adults. For young children, however, reduce the amount of all of the above ingre-dients by one third.

A unique feature of Dr. Bailey's Power Smoothie is that the rich essential oils, lecithin, and proteins it contains act synergistically when combined with the body's naturally occurring serum cholesterol. Together, these four nutrients make up 95 percent of your body's cell wall membranes. The brain is composed of a higher level of cholesterol, lecithin, and essential fats. When these three ingredients are combined and absorbed with the Power Smoothie, they act synergistically to create new cells; repair cell membranes; and produce a fluid membrane that is more resistant to stress and free radical damage, and has greater membrane permeability, thus enhancing cellular energy and waste excretion. The result is literally a fountain-of-youth anti-aging effect at the cellular level.

Flaxseed oil is a rich source of omega-3 fatty acids and, to a lesser but still significant extent, omega-6 fatty acids, both of which protect against many chronic diseases and inflammatory states. Omega-3 and omega-6 oils are also the oils that plants utilize in photosynthesis, and are therefore highly sensitive to heat and sunlight, which is why flaxseed oil is not suitable for cooking. Sunflower oil is richer than flaxseed oil in omega-6 fats, and a blend of cold-pressed sunflower and flaxseed provides a better balance of both omega-3 and omega-6 fatty acids. Fish oils are even richer in omega-3s than either flaxseed or sunflower oil, and are therefore recommended for people suffering from inflammatory conditions that can cause degenerative diseases such as arteriosclerosis. Borage, evening primrose, and hemp oils are also rich in essential fats.

The natural liquid beta-carotene used to make the Power Smoothie is approximately three times more potent, in terms of being metabolically active and absorbable, than capsule or tablet forms of beta-carotene. Beta-carotene, along with zinc (which is included in the vitamin/enzyme complex), is a primary nutrient involved in genetic (DNA) transcription. By including both of them in the Power Smoothie, you can help your body experience faster cell regeneration and improved genetic activity.

Another health benefit of the Power Smoothie lies in its ability to improve both fat and protein digestion. While regularly drinking fresh, organic juices usually results in improved digestion and absorption overall, juices do not provide much benefit when it comes to digesting fats and proteins, making the Power Smoothie an excellent complementary beverage. In addition, the blend of protein powder and oil makes the Power Smoothie appropriate for people who suffer from candidiasis (systemic yeast overgrowth, also known as candida), and are unable to tolerate juices and other smoothies due to their naturally high sugar content.

The Saint Thomas Smoothie

The Saint Thomas Smoothie is derived from the Gospel of Thomas. (See the recipe on page 99, and the variation on page 100.) Within the written Gospel of Thomas, part of the Nag Hammadi Library, are found the following words attributed to Jesus: "For there are five trees for you in Paradise which remain undisturbed summer and winter and whose leaves do not fall. Whoever becomes acquainted with them will not experience death." There are many interpretations of this passage, starting with the surface meaning, or the discussion of the five trees and their fruits.

Many years ago, I was discussing the Gospel of Thomas with my cousin, Dr. Pat Hart. On mentioning this passage to him, he said that he had spent hours researching the trees that were growing in the Middle East at the time of Saint Thomas. He found only five that satisfy the conditions of this passage. They are the banana, coconut, papaya, lemon, and acerola cherry. All five of these trees bear fruit year round and do not lose their leaves. We then discussed what we knew of their nutritional properties, and found a remarkable completeness in terms of how all five fruits satisfy our basic human dietary needs. The Saint Thomas Smoothie consists of these five wonderful fruits, and the recipe yields approximately one to two servings. What follows is an overview of each fruit and the nutrients it provides.

Banana

The banana is a rich source of potassium, fiber, and high-quality glucose (a natural sugar and the primary energy source for both the body and the brain).

Coconut

A rich source of calcium, magnesium, and natural vitamin D, coconut also provides a naturally occurring water or milk that is highly nutritious.

Papaya

Rich in proteolytic enzymes, and therefore rich in proteins, papaya is also a good source of beta-carotene.

Lemon

Because of its highly alkalizing (antiacidic) properties, lemon is revered for its ability to move mucus out of the body. It is high in vitamin C, and even richer in bioflavonoids and OPCs (oligomeric proanthocyanidins), both of which act as potent antioxidants and anti-inflammatory agents in the body.

Acerola Cherry

The acerola cherry is the highest edible source of Vitamin C. (For more information on this fruit, see page 84.)

After learning about these five fruits from my cousin Pat, I decided to do a fast consisting only of smoothies made from these foods. To my pleasant surprise, I felt wonderful and satisfied—similar to the way I feel when undergoing a vegetable-juice or water fast. I experienced no hunger and enjoyed the fruit combination throughout weeks of fasting, during which time I drank as much of the smoothies as I desired and maintained normal if not improved digestive and eliminatory function. Breaking the fast and returning to a normal diet was easier than it usually is after liquid fasts. I have since repeated this fast with identical results.

Saint Thomas Smoothie

Blend:
2 bananas
1 papaya
$1/2$–1 cup coconut
with $1/2$ of the milk
of a whole coconut

Juice:
4 lemons
1 cup acerola cherries (if you have trouble finding
acerola cherries, substitute 2 tablespoons organic
acerola powder, and add enough water to make a
juice consistency)

Blend the banana, papaya, and coconut meat and milk, and set aside in the blender. Juice the lemons and cherries, add to the blender, re-blend, and enjoy. Makes one to two servings.

Although the Saint Thomas Smoothie is tried and true, you should feel free to change the formula as desired by substituting or adding other high-nutrient foods. Dr. James Duke, renowned botanist and authority on biblical plants, writes that three other evergreen fruits were grown in the Middle East at the time of the scripture's origin—the date, the pomegranate, and carob. Like the five fruits in the original smoothie, these foods have incredible nutritional properties and would make a healthful and delicious addition not only to this recipe, but to any smoothie.

Favorite Green Smoothie Recipes

Green smoothies are easy to make and provide an excellent source of chlorophyll, minerals, enzymes, and other nutrients found in leafy greens and herbs. Some of Dr. Bailey's fasters drink a one-quart green smoothie as breakfast, but you can simply add green smoothies to your normal diet and

A Variation on the Saint Thomas Smoothie

I developed the following smoothie recipe—which I named the Smoothie of Depth and Wisdom—after I found myself spontaneously composing a poem of the same name one evening as I sat beneath three redwood trees in my backyard. Normally, when I write songs or poetry, it is a deliberate process. In this instance, however, the words came to me in the form of a rap that began running through my mind. Very quickly, I wrote the following:

Smoothie of Depth and Wisdom

Where the Jew and the lotus do meet,
With Job's tears at the Buddha's feet.
Manna from heaven, Boswellia, and Frankincense are one,
Turmeric and ginger add to the fun.
St. Thomas, the Gospel everlasting reveals,
The bananas, lemon, and papaya, we must peel.
From the coconut come the meat,
With its milk brings the sweet.
And the cherry both sweet and tart,
Add lemon, the recipe opens the heart.
The door opens to the east, the home we all yearn,
For when brothers and sisters are one, to nature we return.

Based on the above poem, I developed the following recipe, which yields two servings.

Smoothie of Depth and Wisdom

1–2 bananas
1 tablespoon each of soaked Job's tears and lotus seeds
$\frac{1}{2}$ teaspoon each of turmeric, ginger, and boswellia
1 cup fresh coconut milk
$\frac{1}{4}$ cup fresh coconut
Juice of 3–4 lemons
2 tablespoons acerola cherry powder
Water as needed

Add all of the above to a blender, blend, and enjoy. Makes one to two servings.

enjoy the nutritional benefits. With the exception of the Tropical Green Smoothie and the Fall Smoothie, the following drinks are more alkaline than smoothies that contain only fruit, and have a more favorable glycemic index, so if you have blood sugar concerns, these beverages can help you meet your dietary and health needs. Remember that green smoothies are limited only by the produce you have at hand. There are no hard and fast rules to making green smoothies, so you should feel free to experiment to meet your own preferences and resources. You can also enhance these smoothies by adding one, two, or more of the super foods mentioned earlier in this chapter.

One last word needs to be said before we present the green smoothie recipes. While you can use any blender to prepare green smoothies, the ingredients will provide more resistance than your blender may be able to handle on a long-term basis. If you plan on making green smoothies part of your daily diet, we suggest you look into the Vita-Mix blender, which was designed for heavy-duty use. Visit the Vita-Mix website at www.vita-mix.com for more information.

Daily Tonic

$1/2$ bunch spinach
$1/2$ bunch Swiss chard (3–4 leaves)
$1/2$ bunch parsley
$1/2$ cucumber, peeled (remove seeds if desired)
1 pear or apple
1 cup apple or orange juice

Place all the ingredients in a blender, and blend until well liquefied. Makes one serving.

Erica's Favorite Green Smoothie

$1/2$ avocado
Handful each of spinach, sprouts, and salad greens
Small cucumber, peeled (remove seeds if desired)
One celery stalk, chopped
Cinnamon to taste
2 leaves stevia, or $1/8$ teaspoon stevia sweetener
1 tablespoon seaweed or to taste, soaked (optional)
Juice of one young Thai coconut
Juice of $1/2$ lime (optional)

Place all the ingredients in a blender, and blend until well liquefied. Makes one serving.

Detoxification Smoothie

$1/2$ bunch cilantro
Greens from 2 beets
$1/2$ cucumber, peeled (remove seeds if desired)

$^{1}/_{2}$ bunch parsley
1 apple
1–2 cloves garlic, diced
1 cup papaya juice

Place all the ingredients in the blender, and blend until well liquefied. Makes one serving.

Tropical Green Smoothie

1 banana
1 cup pineapple chunks
1 kiwi
$^{1}/_{4}$ cup fresh peppermint leaves
Small handful spinach leaves
2 cups fresh fruit juice, or
   1 cup bottled juice plus 1 cup water
$^{1}/_{2}$ cup orange juice
2 tablespoons blackstrap molasses

Place all the ingredients in a blender, and blend until well liquefied. Makes two to three servings.

Fall Smoothie

1 pear
1 apple
4 kale leaves
1 tablespoon lecithin granules
2 cups fresh fruit juice, or
   1 cup bottled juice plus 1 cup water
2 tablespoons lemon juice

Place all the ingredients in a blender, and blend until well liquefied. Makes two to three servings.

Healthy Heart Smoothie

$^{1}/_{2}$ cucumber, peeled (remove seeds if desired)
$^{1}/_{2}$ bunch parsley
4 leaves Swiss chard
1 apple
1 cup pomegranate juice

Piece of fresh turmeric root size of baby carrot, minced,
   or $1/2$ teaspoon turmeric powder

Place all the ingredients in a blender, and blend until well liquefied. Add additional water or juice if needed for consistency. If you're using turmeric root and you don't wish to mince it beforehand, place it in the blender first with a small amount of juice, and blend until well chopped. Then add the remaining ingredients and blend again. Makes one serving.

Women's Smoothie

1 cup blueberries
1 handful each of spinach, Swiss chard, and salad greens
1 teaspoon ground cinnamon or ginger,
   or 2 x 2-inch piece fresh ginger root, minced
1 cup well-steeped raspberry leaf tea
$1/2$ cup noni juice (see page 254 of Resource List)

Place all the ingredients in a blender, and blend until well liquefied. If you're using ginger root and you don't wish to mince it beforehand, place it in the blender first with a small amount of juice, and blend until well chopped. Then add the remaining ingredients and blend again. Makes one serving.

The Royal Green Smoothie

4 cups fresh fruit juice, or 2 cups bottled juice plus 2 cups water, divided
2 cucumbers, peeled (remove seeds if desired)
1 large pear
1 small bunch spinach
1 medium turmeric root, diced, or $1/2$ teaspoon turmeric powder
1 small bunch parsley
1 teaspoon Celtic or sea salt

Place 2 cups of the juice and all of the cucumber and pear in a blender. Blend until smooth and transfer to a shallow bowl. Place the remaining ingredients in the blender and blend until smooth. Pour the spinach mixture into the center of the bowl containing the juice mixture, and serve as is or garnished with olives. We have served this smoothie as a cold soup to guests who are new to a raw food diet, and it is always a big hit. Makes three to four servings.

If you find these green smoothies as wonderful and invigorating as we have, you might want to look into the writings of our friends Dr. Gabriel Cousens and Victoria Boutenko. They have led the way in the green smoothie movement.

HEALTHY TONICS

A tonic is an invigorating, refreshing, or restorative agent—a drink that stimulates or tonifies a part or system of the body. Typically, a tonic has a base of fruit juices, water, or naturally carbonated water to which herbs, spices, or teas are added. Often, the fruit juices are chosen for their taste and the tea is chosen for its action. Herbs can include ginger, cinnamon, cardamom, cloves, turmeric, and mint.

Tonics are typically tasty and, for many, provide an immediate energy boost and a feeling of well-being. They can also be used therapeuti-

An Example of the Therapeutic Benefits of Tonics

A few months before this book was written, a new patient came to Dr. Bailey's clinic suffering from severe health concerns. She had been vomiting constantly for two months, had lost thirty pounds, and had consulted twelve doctors and received three CAT scans. She was scheduled for more invasive procedures and visits with more specialists.

Dr. Bailey made a tentative diagnosis of chemical sensitivity during the first visit, which proved accurate. This condition had rapidly progressed from initial high stress that was further complicated by the effects of a course of antibiotics, exposure to chemical fumes, and finally, after moving into a new home, exposure to the toxic mold Stachybotrys. The first task at hand was to get her body to start accepting food. A simple tonic worked wonders.

The patient fully expected to throw up with each meal as her digestive tract had a "memory" of intolerance and vomiting, and she was in a highly stressed condition of fear. Dr. Bailey began with a tonic of ½ teaspoon of ginger in 6 ounces of apple juice. Whereas she had been throwing up water, this combination stayed down. When repeated, it continued to stay down most of the time.

The patient then graduated to broths and soft vegetable soups, followed by smoothies. Soon her vomiting was reduced from throwing up after every meal to vomiting every other day, and then every third day. As she began adding barley to her liquid intake, she became constipated and was very uncomfortable. At that time, the doctor had her take 1 tablespoon of Knudsen Family's Black Cherry Juice Concentrate in 6 ounces of water. By the third cherry tonic, she had regained normal bowel function. Within a few more weeks, she was able to return to eating all of her favorite foods, with the added benefit that, due to what she learned in working with Dr. Bailey, she was improving both her and her family's nutrition by preparing healthier meals and exploring the use of tonics, along with healthy juices and smoothies.

cally for a variety of health conditions. The following three tonics complement the smoothies already presented in the chapter because of their health-enhancing, disease-preventing qualities, and can serve you well as a regular part of a healthy lifestyle. As with juices and smoothies, the potential exists for a limitless number of tasty, healthy tonic combinations. Feel free to experiment to find the combinations that you and your family will most enjoy.

Tonic for Nausea and Vomiting

Combine $1/2$ to 1 teaspoon ground ginger with 6 to 8 ounces of apple juice, and drink as needed.

Tonic for Constipation

Combine 1 tablespoon Knudsen Family's Black Cherry Juice Concentrate in 6 to 8 ounces water, and drink as needed.

Trucker Joe's Tonic

Joe is a long retired long-haul truck driver. A student and sage of sorts, he decided to begin a new career in Portland, where he established an organic raw food restaurant aimed at serving the poor. Joe, who is healthy and hearty at nearly ninety years of age, makes everyone around him reconsider the saying, "You can't teach an old dog new tricks." Certainly he is constantly learning and expanding his horizons. During conversations with Joe, he shared the tonic that he would prepare and take on long drives. He feels that this tonic greatly helped him to stay healthy during his many cross-country travels.

Begin preparing the tonic by juicing the following: 1 apple, 1 peach, 1 pear, $1/2$ small pineapple, and 2 carrots. Blend the juice with 1 cup each of blueberries and cranberries, along with $1^1/2$ teaspoons ground ginger. When they are in season, you can also add 1 cup of black grapes or cherries. Blend all the ingredients until smooth, and enjoy.

CONCLUSION

As we hope this chapter has made clear, the benefits of drinking freshly prepared juices can be deliciously complemented with equally nutritious smoothies and tonics. The recipes in this chapter are a good place to begin your exploration of smoothies and tonics, but they are hardly the last word on the subject. We encourage you to experiment with other smoothie and tonic combinations, just as Shayla and her friends did in creating their own smoothies. By letting imagination and personal preference be your guide, you will soon discover that many other tasty drinks await you. Now let's return to the subject of juicing to explore the detoxification benefits of juice fasting.

7

The Juicing Fast

Given how incredibly polluted our environment has become, as well as the ever-increasing body of scientific research that directly links environmental toxins to a wide range of diseases, including cancer, the need for regular periods of detoxification of our bodies has never been greater. And when it comes to effective self-care approaches for detoxification and disease reversal, fasting has no equal. Not only are the many benefits of fasting observable and predictable, they also serve as a remarkable example of the healing power of the human body.

Both of us can attest to this fact due to the periodic fasts that we have undertaken, especially Dr. Bailey, who has engaged in fasting for nearly 40 years and regularly supervises juice fasts for his patients. Among the benefits we have both experienced during fasting are improved energy, enhanced sensory awareness, improved mood, increased mental clarity, and even heightened states of consciousness. Yet fasting, despite being recommended as a healing technique by various traditional healing systems for thousands of years, remains misunderstood and maligned by many health experts, as well as the general public.

Contrary to popular misconception, fasting is not a state of starvation and deprivation. Rather, it is an undertaking that can quickly improve your body's ability to heal, repair, and rejuvenate itself. The key to ensuring the various health benefits that fasting can provide lies in knowing how to fast properly, as well as how to prepare for fasting and how to appropriately reintroduce food once the fast is over. In this chapter, you will find guidelines for how to safely and effectively fast using juices based on Dr. Bailey's many years of extensive research on this subject.

Caution: Although Dr. Bailey has helped patients with virtually every major disease condition to successfully fast, if you suffer from such conditions you should not fast without appropriate medical supervision. Fasting is also contraindicated for pregnant and lactating women. People who have excessive fears about fasting should also forego undertaking a fast until their concerns are resolved.

THE BENEFITS OF JUICE FASTING

As we mentioned, never in human history has there been a more important need for the health benefits that fasting provides, due to how polluted our planet has become. Helping your body to eliminate environmental toxins stored in cells and tissues is essential.

In the many years that he has conducted supervised juice fasts with his patients, Dr. Bailey has witnessed a variety of health conditions resolved as a result of fasting. Among the most common benefits observed in his patients who fast are improved circulation, enhanced immune function, greater energy levels, improved moods, and the elimination of food allergies and sensitivities. Other disease conditions of Dr. Bailey's patients that have improved as a result of fasting include:

- arthritis and joint pain

- asthma

- attention deficit disorder (ADD)

- blood sugar problems (hypo- and hyperglycemia)

- candidiasis (systemic yeast overgrowth)

- cardiac arrhythmia (irregular heartbeat)

- chronic fatigue

- constipation, diarrhea, and other gastrointestinal problems, including colitis, Crohn's disease, diverticulosis, esophageal reflux, gastritis, and irritable bowel syndrome (IBS)

- fibrocystic breast disease (including one case in which the cysts were so painful that mastectomy was originally scheduled)

- fibromyalgia

- halitosis

- headaches and migraine

- heavy metal poisoning

- high blood pressure (hypertension)

■ nausea

■ obesity

■ premenstrual syndrome (PMS)

■ prostate problems

■ respiratory conditions

■ skin problems (dermatitis, eczema, hives, psoriasis)

■ urinary problems

■ vision problems

The above list of conditions is by no means definitive. "The conditions I have seen improve with fasting are an A to Z list of most diseases," Dr. Bailey reports. "All of these improvements are due to the many physiological benefits that occur during a fast."

HOW FASTING WORKS

Fasting, when properly undertaken, spares your body from expending the great deal of energy it requires to digest food and convert it into glycogen, a type of starch that the body uses to produce energy. During a fast, the body initially turns to the liver to create an alternate fuel source. The liver does this by converting stored sugars into glucose. By the third day of a fast, these stored sugars are usually used up, at which point the body begins to use stored fat as an energy source. As this process occurs, a variety of health benefits begin to accrue. These include:

■ the breakdown and elimination of toxins stored in fatty tissues

■ a reduction of inflammation within the digestive tract

■ blood thinning, which results in increased oxygen and white blood cells being delivered throughout the body via the bloodstream

■ increased energy made available for the body's systems of self-regulation, including proper cell growth, eliminatory functions, and immune function

■ increased ability of the body to recognize old and nonessential tissues for elimination, along with the recycling of the nutrients they contain for new cell production

All of these benefits help to explain how and why fasting can be so beneficial, both as an ideal means for maintaining health and preventing illness, and for helping to reverse a wide variety of disease conditions.

WATER VS. JUICE FASTS

The most common type of fast conducted throughout history is the water fast, which consists of drinking only water during the fasting period. In addition to being used as a therapeutic tool by health practitioners in many of the world's traditional healing systems, water fasts have long been used as a spiritual practice by many cultures and religions, serving as a rite of passage into a deeper understanding of spiritual truths. Water fasts are also unquestionably the most powerful of all fasting methods. However, it is precisely because of how powerful water fasts are that Dr. Bailey and many other fasting experts recommend juice fasts instead, at least until a person has successfully completed a number of juice fasts and is detoxified enough to engage in a water fast.

The reason for this has to do with the toxic burden all of us labor with due to the abundance of toxins in our environment. Until the body has had the opportunity to significantly eliminate such substances, water fasting can result in an accelerated release of toxins that, for most people, will be too strenuous and even harmful. This fact was confirmed by the late Evarts G. Loomis, MD, who was known as the modern-day founder of the concept of holistic medicine. At his famed Meadowlark health retreat in Hemet, California, Dr. Loomis spent more than a decade conducting supervised water fasts with patients. During that time, although his patients inevitably benefited from their fasts, he noticed that while they fasted they often suffered from intense fatigue and other symptoms. Dr. Loomis then visited two famous naturopathic clinics in Zurich, Switzerland—the Bircher-Benner Clinic and the Landhaus Nurpfli Retreat. There he was introduced to juice fasting, which proved to provide many of the same benefits as water fasting, without unpleasant side effects. Moreover, Dr. Loomis discovered, patients who underwent juice fasts, instead of water fasts, were also much more likely to adopt and continue healthy eating habits afterwards.

In general, Dr. Bailey recommends fasting on vegetable juices over fruit juice fasts. One reason for this is that when undiluted fruit juices are consumed during a fast, they can create swings in blood sugar that are similar to what occurs from eating refined sugar. If you choose to use fruit juices during a fast, dilute them with pure, filtered water in a 50/50 ratio. Doing so will help to prevent blood sugar fluctuations.

Another reason why vegetable juices are preferable to fruit juices during fasting is because vegetable juices produce alkalizing effects in the body, while most fruit juices tend to be acid-forming once they are consumed. (For more on acid-alkaline balance, see Chapter 5.) The acid-producing quality of fruit juices can negatively impact the body's many acidic-detoxification pathways, leading to reduced elimination of toxins and discomfort during the fast. Finally, vegetable juices contain a much broader base of nutrients, many of which aid directly in detoxification, liver support, and immune stimulation.

In most cases, Dr. Bailey recommends fasting solely on vegetable juices. If you wish to include fruit juices, consume 2 quarts (64 ounces) of fresh vegetable juices and 1 quart of fresh fruit juice (diluted with water) each day during a fast. This combination provides many health benefits while still allowing for a variety of juice options.

BASIC FASTING GUIDELINES

There are three aspects to a healthy fast: the pre-fast diet, the fast itself, and the reintroduction of food. In addition, during fasts of more than one day, it is important to aid the body in the elimination of wastes as they are broken down. There are a variety of ways that you can accomplish this, which we discuss later on in this chapter (see Intestinal Cleansing, page 118).

Based on his many years of personal and clinical experience with fasting, Dr. Bailey has found that certain guidelines can significantly enhance the fasting process. To begin with, be sure that your intent to fast is voluntary and that you have the knowledge you need to safely and effectively undergo a fast. If you are new to fasting, you should ideally seek out a health care practitioner who is familiar with fasting, who can supervise your progress.

Dr. Bailey finds that it also important not to tell others that you are fasting. When undertaken as a spiritual practice, people who fast are cautioned not to speak of it because fasting is intended to be a private, non-boastful act. According to Dr. Bailey, even when fasting for health reasons, not speaking about it is suggested since most people will interpret your fast with starvation or deprivation. As a result, they may fill you with fears that can sap your intent to successfully see your fast through to its proper end.

Other factors to consider when preparing to fast and during the fast itself are the quality of the produce you use to create your juices (see Chapters 4 and 5), the quality of your water (be sure it is either filtered or distilled), and the time of the fast (avoid undertaking fasts during heavy social activities and obligations, such as parties and weddings that you are expected to attend). You will also pay attention to your activities during the fast. For best results, avoid overwork or stressful activities, and be sure to engage in supportive healthful activities such as gentle forms of exercise (walking, stretching, yoga). During the fast, you might also wish to schedule one or more therapeutic massage sessions, as massage can help facilitate the elimination of toxins. Contemplative activities such as meditation, prayer, and affirmations can also significantly enhance your fasting experience.

GETTING STARTED: THE PRE-FAST DIET

Before beginning a multi-day fast (three to seven days or more), we recommend that you prepare yourself with a three-day pre-fast diet. The pre-fast diet has a number of objectives. These include:

- Cleansing the intestines with high-fiber foods and fiber supplements

- Eliminating most fat and protein from the intestines

- Optimizing liver and gallbladder function

- Reducing glycogen stores in the liver

By achieving each of these ends with the pre-fast diet, your body will be better prepared to undergo the fast itself and better able to breakdown and eliminate stored toxins.

The vast majority of patients that Dr. Bailey has supervised have achieved excellent results with the pre-fast diet over three days. Some people may require a longer time period in order to achieve similar results, however. This is especially true of people who are in the habit of eating processed foods and/or large quantities of meat and dairy products and small amounts of fresh fruits, vegetables, and whole grains. People who drink a lot of coffee may also find it useful to extend the pre-fast diet, since they will need to wean themselves of their coffee habit before fasting. If uncomfortable bloating or stomach cramping occurs during the first day of the pre-fast diet, it should also be extended, and the amount of high-fiber foods reduced. To determine how long you need to stay on the pre-fast diet, listen to your body and use your common sense. Refer to page 114 for the pre-fast diet routine, which begins with the liver-gallbladder flush.

The Liver-Gallbladder Flush

Each morning of the pre-fast diet begins with a tonic drink that is traditionally used by naturopaths and other natural healers to flush out toxins and stones from the liver and gallbladder. The tonic consists of 3 table-spoons of high-quality virgin or extra-virgin olive oil mixed with 1–2 minced cloves of garlic and combined with the juice of 1 lemon and the juice of 1 orange. The tonic should be taken on an empty stomach. (**Note:** If you have had your gallbladder removed, suffer from liver problems, or have difficulties digesting fatty foods, reduce the olive oil content to 2 table-spoons.)

Olive oil increases bile flow in the liver. The added ingredients of the liver/gallbladder tonic help to enhance the flow of bile. When the tonic, which is high in fat content, is consumed on an empty stomach, the body reacts as if further fat is on the way. This anticipation by the body causes the gallbladder to contract and the liver to produce additional bile to help digest and absorb the expected additional fat.

Triggering these responses by the liver and gallbladder each morning of the pre-fast diet creates a number of desired effects in the body that better prepare it for fasting. This occurs because of what happens when the liver produces and releases bile into the intestinal tract. Normally, when we eat fatty foods, the bile mixes with digested fats before being reabsorbed in the small intestine, where it aids in the transport of fat in the bloodstream. Most of the bile (90–95 percent) is then reabsorbed, with the dietary fats distributed to the body and the bile eventually stored in the gallbladder.

The degree to which bile is reabsorbed by the gallbladder is directly related to the amount of fiber in one's diet. The higher the dietary fiber, the smaller the percentage of bile that is reabsorbed. Since cholesterol and fatty acids make up this reconstituted bile (along with water, salts, and lecithin), this helps to explain why high-fiber diets have consistently been shown to lower cholesterol levels. It is for this reason that the liver/gallbladder tonic is followed thirty minutes later by a fiber supplement, such as psyllium husk powder, mixed with juice or water, along with a gentle herbal laxative tablet, before eating a low-fat fruit breakfast thirty minutes after that. At least thirty minutes before lunch and dinner, the fiber, water, and herbal laxative are repeated. Lunch and dinner consist entirely of vegetables eaten raw (in colder months, the vegetables can be steamed, but raw is preferable). This protocol helps to eliminate from the body a much higher percentage of reconstituted bile, along with the fats it contains. In addition, it also helps to lower the amount of reconstituted bile that is stored in the gallbladder.

Various other health benefits also occur during the pre-fast diet. The elevated bile production by the liver that is triggered by the tonic mixture helps to decongest liver tissues. As this happens, normal blood flow is

The Pre-Fast Diet Schedule

The following routine comprises the pre-fast diet and should be followed for at least three days prior to the fast itself.

At least one hour before breakfast and before drinking anything else, consume the liver/gallbladder tonic. To prepare the tonic, mix the following ingredients:

- 3 tablespoons high-quality virgin or extra-virgin olive oil (reduce to 2 tablespoons if your gallbladder has been removed, you have liver problems, or you have problems digesting fatty foods)
- 1–2 cloves diced or minced fresh, organic garlic
- juice of 1 lemon (organic)
- juice of 1 orange (organic)

Thirty minutes after the tonic is consumed take the first of three daily fiber supplements as follows:

- 1 teaspoon psyllium husk powder, mixed with
- 2–4 ounces pure, filtered water or fresh-squeezed vegetable juice
- 1 gentle herbal laxative tablet or capsule
- one to two 8-ounce glasses of pure, filtered water (the water and laxative are to be taken after the psyllium drink combination)

At least thirty minutes after the dietary fiber and laxatives have been consumed, eat an all-fruit breakfast consisting of fruits you most enjoy eating. Be sure the fruits are fresh and organic and eat them raw. Breakfast can be accompanied by herbal tea, pure water, or water and fresh-squeezed fruit juice, as you desire.

Later in the morning, you may find that you again feel hungry. This is fine. Feel free to snack on raw fruit or vegetables, as well as raw sunflower seeds. You can drink diluted juices between meals, as well.

At least thirty minutes before lunch and dinner, repeat the fiber, laxative, water protocol outlined above. For lunch and dinner, eat as many fresh, raw, organic vegetables as you wish. (In cold or winter months, the vegetables can be lightly steamed, although raw is still preferable.) The easiest way to do this is to prepare a large salad for both meals that consists of a wide variety of fresh vegetables. You can top your salad with extra-virgin olive oil, balsamic or apple cider vinegar, lemon juice, or a nondairy organic salad dressing of your choice. Herbs and raw sunflower seeds can also be added.

Fluid Intake Between Meals

Based on his many years of clinical experience guiding his patients through the pre-fast diet, Dr. Bailey recommends drinking at least 3 quarts of healthy fluids per day. This includes the one to two 8-ounce glasses of water that are consumed with the fiber and herbal laxative three times a day, which leaves 6–9 glasses of fluid left to drink throughout the rest of each day. Use pure, filtered water, mineral water, herbal teas, or diluted juices to meet this daily fluid quota.

increased, resulting in improved circulation. Greater oxygenation of the blood supply also occurs, resulting in more oxygen being delivered to the body's cells and tissues. Overall, liver function can be significantly enhanced by the pre-fast diet, making the fast that follows it more beneficial and easier to tolerate.

DR. BAILEY'S FIVE-DAY POWER FAST

Once you have completed the pre-fasting diet, you are ready to move directly into the fast itself. For most people, Dr. Bailey recommends the following five-day fast, which can be used twice a year to maintain your health and prevent and help reverse illness. Because of the many patients he has personally witnessed have their health dramatically improved by this fast, while maintaining excellent energy and a strong spiritual focus, he has named it the Power Fast.

The Power Fast consists of fresh, organic vegetable and fruit juices. Drink 2 quarts of vegetable juice each day, along with 1 quart of fruit juice. Dr. Bailey recommends that the first quart of vegetable juice consist of $1/2$–$2/3$ carrot juice and $1/3$–$1/2$ celery. The second quart of vegetable juice should consist of equal amounts of carrot, celery, and beet juice. For fruit juice, you can juice any combination of fruits according to taste, except for citrus fruits and tomato, which should not be used during the fast.

During each day of the fast, you should try to consume a total of 5–6 quarts of fluids. In addition to the amounts of juice recommended above, throughout the day you can also drink pure, filtered water, herbal tea, or additional juice to achieve this total intake of fluids. The additional juices that you make should also consist of vegetable combinations. For a variety of juice combinations you can try, see the juice recipes provided in Part Two. If you are dealing with any health conditions during the Power Fast, choose juice combinations according to the recipes that are listed there for each condition.

Supporting the Power Fast

In order to optimize your fasting experience, the following guidelines and activities are recommended.

Personal Hygiene

Fasting creates a condition of internal cleansing in the body. Equally important is external cleansing. Be sure to shower or bathe each morning and evening, but avoid extreme hot water temperatures, as well as overly long showers or baths, as they can be physically taxing. Before you shower or bathe, consider dry skin brushing, which consists of brushing your entire body with a bristle brush (available at most health food stores). Skin brushing not only helps get rid of old skin cells and tissues, it also stimulates the body's lymphatic system, aiding in the elimination of toxins.

You should also avoid the use of all cosmetics and commercial deodorants, as these products contain chemicals that enter the body through the skin. This counteracts the elimination of toxins that occur as a result of fasting. Mouthwash and toothpaste products should also be avoided. As a substitute for commercial mouthwash products, add 2 capfuls of hydrogen peroxide and a pinch of baking soda to a few ounces of water and gargle thoroughly. Baking soda and salt mixed with hydrogen peroxide also acts as an effective and nontoxic alternative to toothpaste.

Just as you want to keep your body clean inside and out during the Power Fast, also be sure that your home environment is clean. This is especially important with regard to your bedroom and kitchen. In your bedroom, sleep on clean sheets and make sure that there is proper ventilation. Ideally, it is recommended that you sleep with a bedroom window open to benefit from a supply of fresh air. As for your kitchen, be sure that your countertops are clean, as well as your refrigerator, and always be sure to promptly clean your juicer after each time that you use it.

Physical Activity

Most people do not experience any appreciable drop in their energy levels during the Power Fast. In fact, many experience increased energy as the fast progresses. Even so, you want to be sure that you do not overtax yourself while you are fasting. Pay attention to your body and rest and take naps as appropriate.

This doesn't mean that you should become sedentary, however. On the contrary, a certain amount of exercise and physical activity can be highly beneficial during the Power Fast. Gentle forms of exercise such as stretching, yoga, or Tai Chi are all recommended. Walking is also encouraged, especially walks in a natural setting. Being outdoors within nature will also enhance the contemplative nature of fasting, bringing you more in touch with your connection to all of life and your own divinity.

If at all possible, avoid activities (including personal interaction with others that are prone to upset you) that you find stressful while you fast, as they can significantly and adversely affect your fasting experience. Such activities can even include watching the news, with its daily barrage of negativity. In fact, we recommend that you abstain from watching television altogether during the Power Fast, as doing so will enhance your ability to turn within and reconnect with yourself.

Rest and Relaxation

Rest and relaxation are essential steps towards rejuvenation in body, mind, and spirit. This is particularly true during fasting. Therefore, be sure that you take time to rest and relax during each day of the Power Fast. This can include napping during the day, as appropriate, and engaging in activities that you enjoy and which relax you. Taking time to meditate is also recommended. If you are new to meditation, consider simply sitting still with your eyes closed for ten to twenty minutes each day as you gently notice your breath. Without seeking to direct it, allow yourself to connect to the rhythm of each inhalation and exhalation. Most people experience a sense of peace and calm after doing this simple exercise.

Finally, be sure that you get enough sleep each night. In addition, try to go to sleep early, and awake early as well. According to various natural systems of healing, such as the Ayurvedic system from India, sleep is deeper and more restorative the closer we adopt our sleeping patterns to the natural cycle of sunrise and sunset. While it isn't always possible to do so in today's modern world, we recommend that you try to get to bed no later than ten o'clock each night and arise by six or seven in the morning.

Spend Time in the Sun

Sunlight is vital to your general health, and spending time in the sun during the Power Fast can be especially so. Whereas for years we were warned against getting too much sunlight, now researchers are discovering that lack of sunlight exposure on a regular basis not only depletes our bodies' supply of vitamin D, it can also result in a variety of other health problems, including impaired mood and depression. Therefore, we recommend that you spend at least half an hour each day outside in the sun, not only during the Power Fast, but as a part of your normal daily health routine.

INTESTINAL CLEANSING

Although water fasts do not require supportive intestinal cleansing procedures such as enemas, fresh vegetable juice fasts, including the Power Fast,
do require such support. The reason for this is that vegetable juices contain
pulp that, once it is consumed, coats the lining of the large intestine (colon)
and blocks elimination in the intestinal tissues. As a result, without some
form of colon cleansing in addition to the fast itself, people often experience
a variety of uncomfortable symptoms, including fatigue, headaches, irritability, and sometimes minor depression. Two very effective self-care
approaches for cleansing the colon during fasts are enemas and the saltwater flush.

Enemas

Enemas have a long history of use in traditional healing systems around the
world because of their ability to eliminate stored and putrefying waste matter in the colon, or lower large intestine. Enemas are easy to perform and
can be self-administered. This makes them a convenient and useful method
for reducing the buildup of waste matter in the lower intestine that occurs
during vegetable juice fasts.

To perform an enema you will need to purchase an enema kit, which
you can find at your local drug store. The kit consists of a 2-quart enema
bag, an attached hose, a plastic hanger, and a rectal speculum. (Some enema
kits come with two speculums, one for the rectum and one for the vagina.
The vaginal speculum has multiple small holes and is wider than the rectal
speculum.) You will also need a natural ointment or lubrication cream such
as Vaseline or KY Jelly.

To get started, fill the enema bag with warm (not hot) water that is close
to body temperature. Avoid using water that is too cool or too hot. Cold
water can result in muscle contractions in the rectum and colon that make
it difficult to retain the water in the body long enough to achieve the desired
elimination of waste matter. Conversely, water that is too hot can cause too
long of an expulsion of waste matter due to the hot water's relaxation of the
colon muscles. Then add 1 tablespoon each of baking soda and salt to the
water, letting it dissolve.

Next, hang the enema bag to a towel rack in your bathroom so that it
hangs three to four feet above the floor. Lubricate the speculum and attach
it to the hose, then kneel comfortably on the floor, raising your buttocks in
the air and placing your head on the ground, inserting the speculum into
your rectum. Once this is done, release the clamp on the hose and allow the

water mixture to flow into you, taking in as much as is comfortable. (On the first day of the fast, you may not be able to comfortably take in all 2 quarts, but by the second or third day, you should be able to easily do so.)

Once you have taken in the water mixture, rest comfortably, gently massaging your lower abdomen over the colon area. Five to fifteen minutes later—or sooner, if necessary—sit on the toilet and void the solution. To help elimination, continue to massage your lower abdomen. You may find that you need to return to the bathroom more than once after the enema is performed. This is normal and nothing to be alarmed about. However, we recommend that you do not perform an enema during times when you know your schedule is tight. Many people find the most appropriate time is in the evening after the day's activities and responsibilities have been seen to. Perform the enema each day of your fast.

The reason why salt and baking soda is added to the enema water is because using water alone causes the water to be absorbed through the intestinal wall. The salt and baking soda prevents this from happening. You can also substitute finely minced garlic (3 cloves) and 2 tablespoons of Epsom salt to achieve a deeper purging. To do this, add the minced garlic to the water before you pour it into the enema bag and let it simmer for five minutes before straining the cloves out. Then add the Epsom salt and pour the water into the bag.

On the last day of the Power Fast, we recommend that you substitute acidophilus for the salt and baking soda. Doing so will help recolonize any healthy intestinal flora that may have been depleted by the enemas. Simply add 1/8 teaspoon of powdered acidophilus or the contents of 4–5 acidophilus capsules to the water and let it dissolve.

The Saltwater Flush

A safe and effective alternative to the daily enema during the Power Fast is a daily saltwater flush. Known in Ayurvedic medicine as *Shankhaprakshalana* or *Varisara Dhauti* (which translates as "washing of the intestines"), this method of colon detoxification has been used in India for thousands of years. It is also recommended by naturopathic physicians and many other natural healers.

The saltwater flush has a number of advantages compared to enemas. For one, it is easier to do and does not require the purchase of an enema kit. It can also be performed at any time, both during fasts and while eating solid food. In addition, unlike enemas, which primarily cleanse only the colon or lower intestine, the saltwater flush helps to move toxins and waste matter out of the entire gastrointestinal tract. Because of its convenience and effectiveness, many health-conscious individuals perform the saltwater flush on a weekly or monthly basis as a method of detoxification.

There are two basic versions of the saltwater flush, the Ayurvedic model and the naturopathic model. In the Ayurvedic version of the saltwater flush, 2 liters (just over 2 quarts) of salted water are to be consumed. Each liter contains 2 teaspoons of salt. Pure water is always consumed in at least an equal volume. In this version a number of yoga postures are then performed after the salt water has been consumed in order to stimulate the bowels, lymphatic system, and the body's purification energies. The naturopathic version of the saltwater flush is simpler and equally effective. In this version, 2 teaspoons of salt are added to 2 pints of warm to mildly hot water. After you drink the 2 pints, sit or walk comfortably for about five to ten minutes until you feel the urge to void.

In both versions of the saltwater flush, drink unsalted, pure filtered water in equal amounts to what you expel while sitting on the toilet. Continue to drink water until the liquid you are expelling is nearly clear. If you do not start voiding within fifteen minutes of drinking the saltwater solution, drink about 1 quart of warm water to trigger the eliminatory process. On day two and beyond of the Power Fast, it is only necessary to drink 1 pint of the salt solution to start elimination.

When doing this wash while eating a normal diet, it is recommended that you take a light, semi-liquid meal the night before. A vegetable soup is a good semi-liquid meal. Whole fruit can also be used. The 2-pint solution should be used when eating whole foods, just as on the first day of a juice fast. When eating normally, the first voiding is typically solid, but soon becomes liquid.

By following the juicing recommendations and taking care to support your body's elimination of wastes using enemas or the saltwater flush, most people have no difficulty following the five-day Power Fast. In addition, by the second or third days, the majority of people will also begin to notice improvements in their energy levels. Typically, their moods also improve, and they find themselves calmer and happier. Most people are also able to continue to carry out their daily activities.

BREAKING THE FAST AND RETURNING TO NORMAL EATING

The most important part of any type of fast is the appropriate reintroduction of food. The most common mistake first-time fasters make is to quickly resume normal meals. Doing so is a big mistake and can significantly interfere with the benefits achieved by fasting. Therefore, it is vitally important that you reintroduce foods gradually, starting with foods that are easily digested and then, over the course of a few days, slowly resuming the eating of more complex foods.

What follows are guidelines for successfully breaking your fast, based on Dr. Bailey's many years of guiding his patients through the entire fasting process. Be sure to abide by them. Otherwise, you will most likely experience uncomfortable abdominal bloating and cramping, as well as other potential gastrointestinal problems, such as constipation.

Reintroducing Foods in Their Proper Sequence

During the fasting process, every cell, tissue, and organ of your body's gastrointestinal tract shifts into a state of rest and repair, freed of the normal demands placed upon them by the process of eating, digesting, and assimilating foods and eliminating their waste products. Therefore, the first foods that you want to begin eating after you break your fast are those foods that require little effort by your body to digest. As your body begins to adjust to the process of eating again, you can then slowly start to introduce more complex foods.

Initially, begin with fruits and non-starchy vegetables (starchy vegetables include winter squash, pumpkins, yams, sweet potatoes) for at least a day, as these foods require the least amount of energy to digest. (The vegetables can be eaten raw or lightly steamed.) Then proceed to starchy vegetables, such as squash and yams, whole grains, and seeds, before moving on to legumes and fatty foods. Eventually, you can reintroduce protein foods, such as fish, poultry, meats, and nuts. Here is how such a reintroduction diet looks over the course of six days.

As you begin reintroducing foods, it is important to consider potential food allergies and sensitivities, which we first discussed in Chapter 5 (see Testing for Food Allergies on page 69). The first few days after a fast provide an ideal opportunity for you to determine if you have food allergies or sensitivities. In the guidelines that follow, we point out foods that commonly cause food allergies and sensitivities, directing you to eat them away from other foods, so that you can notice if they cause any unpleasant reactions. You can also use the Pulse Test that we shared with you in Chapter 5 (see page 69). By monitoring your reactions to foods as you reintroduce them, you will quickly begin to notice if any of the foods you eat cause a reaction, at which point you can avoid eating them in the future.

Day One

Begin the first day after your fast by drinking the liver/gallbladder tonic described on page 113. Unlike the pre-fast diet, however, this time around you are only to drink the tonic itself without following it with fiber supplements and herbal laxatives. The tonic is to be consumed only once. Its purpose is to prepare your body's digestive system, along with the liver and gallbladder, for the reintroduction of foods, including normal fats.

For the rest of day one, eat freely of organic fresh fruits and non-starchy vegetables. However, avoid all starchy vegetables, as well as foods that can potentially cause allergies or food sensitivities, such as citrus fruits, corn, potatoes, and tomatoes. Both the fruits and vegetables consumed on day one can be eaten raw or lightly steamed. They can also be made into homemade soups and salads, as well as fresh juices and smoothies. Be sure to thoroughly chew each bite of food you consume, both to make digestion easier and to stimulate the release of enzymes from the salivary glands in your mouth.

Day Two

On day two, in addition to the foods introduced on day one, you can add millet to your meals. Millet is an extremely nutritious cereal grain, and is also highly alkalizing, helping to maintain proper acid-alkaline balance. (For more about the importance of acid-alkaline balance, see pages 70–75.) Choose organic millet, if possible.

You can also eat organic tomatoes and organic, unflavored yogurt, but take care to eat these foods separately from each other and from other foods, at least one hour apart. The reason for this is that both foods are common food allergens and sensitivities. By eating them alone, you will be more apt to notice if they cause any reactions related to food allergies and sensitivities. If they do, avoid them from that point on, and also avoid any other foods to which you know or suspect you are allergic or sensitive.

Day Three

On the third day, you can add additional starchy vegetables to your diet. These can include barley, yams, winter squash, as well as potatoes. Citrus fruits can also be introduced at this time. If you choose to eat potatoes or citrus fruits, limit your servings to 1–2 tablespoons, at first, taken at least an hour away from other foods. Such a portion is enough to determine if you are allergic or sensitive to such foods. If you do not notice any uncomfortable reactions, most likely you can safely eat both foods.

Day Four

On day four, you can add legumes and rice to the foods you are eating, along with eggs. Eat the eggs separately, at least an hour away from other foods, to determine whether they cause an allergic reaction. Among legumes, peanuts and soy nuts are the foods most likely to cause such reactions, so eat them away from other foods as well and notice if any reactions occur.

Day Five

Day five is when wheat, one of the most common food allergens, is reintroduced to your diet. Because of how common wheat allergies and sensitivities are among the American populace, limit your wheat intake to one small serving initially, and also be sure to use only organic, whole-wheat products. If you experience unpleasant reactions, avoid the use of wheat and wheat by-products in your diet.

Other grains that you can add on day five include oats, rye, quinoa, and triticale. Assuming you had no adverse reactions when you reintroduced yogurt on day two, you can also begin introducing organic dairy products on day five, such as cheese. However, if you proved to be sensitive to yogurt, avoid dairy products altogether, or experiment with goat milk and feta cheese.

Day Six

Day six is when you add the foods that require the most energy from your body in order to be digested. Foods that you can begin eating on day six include fish, poultry, and meats. Be sure that you choose only organic, free-range meats and poultry and wild-caught, saltwater fish.

Various nuts, such as almonds, cashews, and walnuts can also be reintroduced on day six. If you use yeast products, such as baker's and brewer's yeast, this is the day that you can also begin using them. Be aware, however, that yeast products are another common food trigger of allergies and sensitivities.

By the end of day six, you will have successfully reintroduced all of the healthy food groups that you are normally used to eating. At this point, you should also have a better idea of which foods to avoid due to the allergic or sensitivity reactions they cause you. Also be sure to avoid all unhealthy foods, additives, and preservatives (see Chapter 5). If you were used to drinking coffee or alcohol prior to your fast, do so in moderation, if at all, limiting your coffee intake to no more than one to two cups a day, and your alcohol intake to one glass of beer or wine.

Finally, we of course encourage you to continue to make juicing a part of your daily diet, as well. After your fast, you will be more aware of the health benefits you are receiving with each serving of fresh juice you drink. Most likely, your sense of taste will have improved as well, making the juices you drink even more delicious.

CONCLUSION

As both of us can attest, as can Dr. Bailey's many patients, fasting can make a dramatic positive difference in your health and overall well-being. After reading this chapter, we hope that you will consider fasting once or twice a year to ensure that your body is better able to maintain itself in the face of the many environmental toxins all of us are exposed to on a regular basis. Periodic fasts, along with daily juicing and a healthy diet, are three of the most important self-care tools available to you for creating and maintaining vibrant health. In the next chapter, you will learn how juicing and healthy eating can also enhance your appearance.

8

Juicing and Beauty

Human beauty, as it is reflected from our appearance, is often said to be "only skin deep." Although this saying is intended to warn us against putting too much emphasis on how we and other people look, when it comes to matters of health it isn't true. Your skin, in terms of its tone, coloring, hydration, and other factors, reflects the overall health of your body's cells, tissues, and organs. By examining your skin, it's not uncommon for holistic health practitioners to make an accurate assessment of the health of organs such as your lungs, liver, and kidneys, as well as the functioning of your circulatory, digestive, immune, and other of your body's systems. Therefore, as far as your health is concerned, having healthy skin is far more important than many people realize.

In our culture, with its overemphasis on "youthful looking skin," too many of us succumb to the lure of easy skin care solutions in the form of topical creams, lotions, and moisturizers and, in some case, cosmetic surgery, failing to realize that achieving both healthy skin and beauty is truly an "inside job." After all, cosmetic surgery and the use of makeup, even skincare products that are organic or "all natural," are incapable of addressing the various underlying imbalances that can cause skin to become unhealthy and unattractive. Fortunately, there are many simple, healthy, and quite inexpensive alternatives to such measures, including juicing, and in this chapter we are going to share them with you. But before we do, let's take a closer look at what beauty actually means.

BEAUTY FROM THE INSIDE OUT

Ancient philosophers such as Plato equated beauty with truth, and with good reason. Life is full of natural beauty. A gorgeous sunset, a magnificent waterfall, the sight of an eagle soaring heavenward, the majesty of a lone oak tree within a field—scenes such as these leave us with warm, glowing feelings of happiness and peace, quieting restless thoughts and inspiring us to be more of all that we are and are capable of achieving. The beauty that is so abundant in nature also calls to us to live more closely in accordance with natural laws, leaving behind all thoughts and actions that create and perpetuate disharmony in ourselves and in others.

People who have consciously made a decision to live according to such principles, regardless of their physical appearance, can also have this affect on us. We have all had the experience of encountering people who, despite so-called "normal" or "plain" external features, radiate an inner beauty that attracts our gaze and admiration. Conversely, people who are born with naturally attractive features can seem unattractive and even ugly when they are not acting harmoniously. One of the primary keys to being and looking beautiful, therefore, is to cultivate mental, emotional, and spiritual growth, feeding our souls, as well as our bodies, with that which is nourishing and life-affirming.

In addition to the spiritual precepts common to all religious faiths and teachings, nature also provides us with clues as to how we can best live in ways that support our health in body, mind, and spirit. Consider animals and plants that are healthy and beautiful. They are free of "worry lines" and do not suffer from "bad hair days." Rather, they simply live fully in the moment, attending to what comes their way without stress and using the strengths and talents with which nature provided them. By appreciating your own unique strengths and talents, and focusing on the present instead of your past or future, you, too, are capable of living in such a manner, increasingly exhibiting your true beauty, which comes from within. In the process, you will find that you are freeing yourself from many of the stress factors that science has shown not only contributes to unhealthy and pre-maturely aged skin, but to poor health in general. Here are a few suggestions that you can use to create a more harmonious and healthier life that will leave you feeling and appearing more attractive.

■ **Spend time in nature.** By making it a point to spend time outdoors amidst a natural setting, you can better attune yourself to the harmonies of the natural world.

■ **Place plants in your home and workplace.** Plants not only brighten up your home and work environments, they can also help to buoy your spirits. In addition, many plants act as natural air purifiers, helping to keep your home and workplace free of indoor airborne irritants.

■ **Take time to meditate or engage in prayerful contemplation.** A large body of scientific studies proves that prayer and meditation can provide a host of physical health benefits. Just as importantly, by taking time to regularly engage in such contemplative practices, you will find that it becomes easier to attune yourself to life's inner rhythms and become better able to tap into greater levels of intuition and spiritual guidance.

■ **Laugh, smile, breathe, dance, and play.** No facial expression uses fewer muscles than smiling. While we have heard of smile wrinkles and they are normally of a pleasant accent, the worry lines and anger lines of many people are considered very unattractive. Playful activities such as dancing and laughing are not only helpful to our skin but support the production of healthful and youthful chemicals. Full natural breathing and its improved oxygenation are, with abundant pure water, perhaps the least expensive and most important beauty supplements that we can consume.

■ **Adopt a pet.** If it is appropriate and convenient for you to do so, consider bringing a pet into your home. Becoming responsible for the care of animals such as cats and dogs can deepen your connection to nature. Studies have shown that pets can significantly improve the mental and emotional well-being of the humans who care for them.

There are, of course, many other methods that you can use to create more harmony in your life. Find the ones that you are most comfortable with and commit to making them a regular part of your daily activities. It is up to each and every one of us to do what we can to move past the fast lane of modern society and renew our relationship with nature and what is best for our bodies, minds, and spirits. In the process of doing so, we become more attractive, not only to others, but, most importantly, to ourselves through the deepening self-acceptance that is a natural consequence of committing ourselves to living in harmony with ourselves and each other.

JUICING, DIET, AND PROPER SKIN CARE

To achieve and maintain healthy skin you need to understand how your skin, as your body's largest organ of elimination, is directly affected by the internal health of your body. The more toxins that are present in your cells, tissues, and organs, the more likely it is that the appearance of your skin will suffer, as well. Therefore, doing all that you can to eliminate toxins is essential if you want to look and feel your best. This fact is born out by Dr. Bailey's own clinical experience. Approximately 90 percent of all dermatological conditions that he has treated have significantly improved as he worked with his patients to improve their digestion and elimination. This includes cases of acne, eczema, hives, psoriasis, and seborrhea, which had previously proven to be intractable, despite his patients using a wide array of topical skin care products and, in certain cases, even antibiotics and steroids.

Juice Recipes for Healthy Skin

We've already discussed at length how juicing can help rid your body of toxins, improve digestion, and enhance your overall health (see Chapters 1, 3, and 5). And in Part Two, we also provide specific juice recipes you can use to help resolve specific skin conditions. Therapeutic juice fasts (see Chapter 7) are a very effective method you can use to improve the overall quality of your skin and appearance. When done correctly, juice fasts quickly result in noticeable improvements in skin texture and hue, as well as improved clarity of the eyes, and overall improvements in muscle tone due to the elimination of toxins that cling to fat cells. Many of Dr. Bailey's patients who undergo supervised fasts with him report that their family, friends, and co-workers comment on how good they look as a result of fasting on juices.

The positive changes in skin tone and appearance can last well beyond the fast itself, especially if you continue to drink one or more glasses of fresh-squeezed juice each day. Consuming 16–32 ounces of juice on a daily basis is an ideal skin maintenance program. What follows are two especially useful juice recipes for healthy skin.

■ Juice 3 carrots and 4 stalks of celery, or enough of each vegetable to produce 12 ounces. Drink twice daily.

■ Juice 3 carrots and 1 cucumber. Drink 12 ounces twice daily.

For best results, consider drinking the first juice combination in the morning, and the second combination later in the day. You can also add 1 beet and/or ½ bunch of spinach to either recipe.

Other juice combinations that promote healthy skin are:

■ Juice red grapes and black currants, using twice as many grapes as currants to produce 8 ounces of juice. Drink twice daily.

■ To the above fruit juice recipe, add 1 teaspoon noni juice and 1 teaspoon seabuckthorn for every 8 ounces of juice produced.

Cucumber is an especially useful vegetable that can be used to maintain your skin. In addition to including cucumber juice in the juice combinations you make, you can also apply cucumber juice directly to your skin with a washcloth, and you can make a facial mask using the extracted cucumber pulp. Placing sliced cucumbers over your eyes can also help reduce bags and inflammation. This technique is a well-known traditional skin care method that today is also used in many health spas.

Juicing, Healthy Skin, and Weight Loss

The health and appearance of your skin can also be improved by losing excess weight. The high nutritional value of vegetable juices make them an ideal "fuel" that can assist weight loss. Short-term vegetable juice fasts can further accelerate weight loss without lowering your metabolism and sparing you from the "yo-yo effect" that is common to so many fad diets. Ideal juice recipes for weight loss include:

■ Juice 3 carrots, 1/2 cucumber, 1/2 beet, 1 garlic clove, and 2 stalks burdock root. Makes approximately 14 ounces. Drink once or twice each day.

■ Juice 3 carrots, 2 celery stalks, 1/2 cucumber, and 1/2 bunch parsley. Makes approximately 16 ounces. Drink twice daily.

■ Juice 1 medium grapefruit, 1 medium orange, and 1 medium lemon. Makes approximately 16 ounces. Drink once or twice daily.

Healthy Eating

In addition to drinking fresh-squeezed juice on a daily basis, eating healthy foods is also essential for the health of your skin. Ideally, you should eat only organic foods, with your meals consisting of at least 20–30 percent of raw vegetables. One of the simplest ways to ensure that you eat enough raw fruits and vegetables each day is to include a large salad made up of a wide variety of fruits and vegetables with at least one of your meals each day. Eating such salads can also help you to lose weight if you need to do so, and to keep it off without the need for dieting. (For more information about how to eat healthily, see Chapter 5.)

Water and Your Skin

In addition to eating healthy foods and drinking juices each day, also be sure that you daily drink adequate amounts of pure, filtered water. As it is in the rest of your body, water is the most abundant ingredient in your skin. Drinking water regularly throughout the day is one of the easiest and most effective methods you can use to maintain healthy skin, as well as increase your energy level and improve your mood. Most of us do not consume enough water, however, resulting in chronic dehydration. Further compounding this problem, many of us regularly consume drinks that lead to even higher levels of dehydration, such as coffee, non-herbal teas, soda, and alcohol.

As a general rule of thumb, many health experts advise that we drink eight 8-ounce glasses of water each and every day. This is a good starting point, although the exact amount of water that you need to drink each day is best determined by your individual biochemistry, as well as other factors, such as how often and how strenuously your exercise (the more you exercise and the more active you are, the more water you need to drink each day).

Perhaps the greatest authority on the importance of water to overall health was the late Dr. F. Batmanghelidj, author of *Your Body's Many Cries for Water* and *Water for Health, for Healing, for Life: You're Not Sick, You're Thirsty*. Dr. Batman (as he liked to be called) spent more than thirty years exclusively researching the many roles that water plays in creating and maintaining good health. Based on his research, he determined that nearly everyone suffered from chronic dehydration. Many of the chronically ill patients that he worked with, including those who suffered from serious illnesses such as crippling arthritis, cancer, and heart disease, experienced complete recoveries from their health problems when they started drinking water according to Dr. Batman's recommendations. Dr. Batman's basic formula for water consumption was as follows: Divide your weight in half and drink as many ounces of water per day to equal the result. (For example, if you weight 150 pounds, drink 75 ounces of water each day.) For people who are very active, Dr. Batman suggested that they drink as many ounces of water as two-thirds of their body weight (using the same example above, you would then need to drink 100 ounces of water each day). He also suggested adding half a teaspoon of salt to one of the glasses of water you drink, in order to improve the absorption of water into your body's cells, and to prevent vital minerals from being flushed out of the body.

For more healthy eating tips, see Chapter 4.

EXERCISE AND HEALTHY SKIN

The other essential component for helping to maintain healthy skin is regular exercise. In addition to the many other health benefits exercise provides, it helps to maintain healthy skin tone by causing toxins to be eliminated through the skin by sweating. This is especially true of aerobic exercises, which include bicycling, jogging, running, and rebounding (bouncing on a mini-trampoline).

One of the other ways in which exercise helps to enhance healthy skin has to do with the increased respiration rates that often occur as a result of exercise and physical activity in general. Many people breathe inefficiently throughout the day, taking shallow breaths into the chest, and frequently pausing between inhalations and exhalation. This results in diminished levels of life-supporting oxygen being available to the body's cells, as well as a buildup of carbon dioxide and other toxins and waste products that are eliminated during exhalation.

Shallow breathing also interferes with the function of your body's lymphatic system, which acts as a filtration system, eliminating toxins and cellular wastes via the flow of lymph. Exercise stimulates respiration, causing deeper and fuller breathing. This, in turn, improves delivery of oxygen and increases the amount of toxins and waste by-products that are eliminated via exhalation, as well as through the lymphatic system. An end result of increased breathing rates is healthier skin.

In the second half of the twentieth century, perhaps no one did more to promote the importance of regular exercise than the fitness guru Jack

THE SKIN AND BEAUTY SECRET OF THE STARS

Many movie stars and other celebrities maintain healthy-looking skin by using the following technique, which you, too, can easily add to your skin care regimen.

Step 1: Fill a pot with water and bring it to a boil, adding aromatic herbs, such as mint or rosemary. Once the water comes to a full boil, turn off the burner and drape a large towel over your head, holding your face at a comfortable distance from the pot, exposing it to the rising steam for five minutes.

Step 2: Following steaming, immediately gently wash your face with a facial scrub. (A variety of organic facial scrubs are available at most local health food stores.) Then rinse and pat dry your face.

Step 3: Place ice cubes in a large bowl, then fill it with water. Immerse your face into the ice water, holding it underwater for as long as you can do so comfortably before having to come up for air. This will cause your facial skin to tighten and smoothen.

The above routine, if performed on a regular basis and used in conjunction with the rest of the skin care and beauty tips we've shared in this chapter, will leave your face and skin bright, clean, and healthy.

LaLanne, who became a famous TV personality. Today, LaLanne is in his 90s and still well-known and physically active, and continues to sing the praises of exercise, along with healthy diet and drinking fresh juices. In fact, in recent years, he's even developed his own brand of juicer (see Resource List on page 250). What few people know, however, is that LaLanne was a very sick child and might never have recovered had he not met naturopathic physician Paul Bragg. LaLanne credits his long life and good health to the health principles he was taught by Bragg, including the importance of diet, exercise, juicing, and fasting.

What is also not well known is the fact that juicing and fasting can actually enhance physical performance, including athletic achievement. This fact was illustrated by one of Dr. Bailey's patients who, at the time she consulted with him, was a varsity long-distance runner at her college. Based on Dr. Bailey's recommendation, she underwent a supervised seven-day juice fast. During this time, she continued to run, and set her personal best times in both the 5,000 and 10,000 meter runs while consuming nothing but fresh juices and water. Later in that same year, she went on to win the Portland, Oregon Marathon.

CONCLUSION

As we hope we've made clear in this chapter, beauty and healthy skin both start from the inside out, and can be significantly enhanced by making use of the recommendations we've provided above. We encourage you to try them out for yourselves, including our recommendations for cultivating your "inner beauty" and coming more into harmony with nature's laws and rhythms.

PART TWO

Juice Recipes
for Health Disorders

Introduction

I n this part of the book, you will find hundreds of juice combination recipes that you can use to prevent and help relieve the symptoms of more than 120 of our most common diseases. All of these juice remedies are based on their clinical use by Dr. Bailey as a means of helping his patients to recover from the disease conditions included in this section. We invite you to try these recipes for yourself to discover how they can benefit you, as well.

Tips for Preparing Fruits and Vegetables for Juicing

The following guidelines can help you to obtain the most benefits from your juicing program.

■ **Wash All Produce Thoroughly Before Juicing.** Even if you are using only organically grown fruits and vegetables, it's always a good idea to wash them thoroughly before you juice them in order to remove all dirt and other residues. A vegetable brush is excellent for scrubbing the skins of root crops like beets, burdock roots, and even larger carrots. This will often remove bitter qualities and make a better tasting juice without sacrificing the nutrition of the skins. Also inspect for bruises, molds, or other damage to the skin and remove such areas from the produce you intend to juice.

■ **Use the Leaves and Stems.** In addition to juicing the main portion of fruits and vegetables, be sure to also juice their leaves and stems, which are usually rich in nutrients. One exception to this rule is carrot greens, which should not be used because they contain substances that can act as toxins in the body.

■ **Avoid Juicing Pits.** When juicing fruits that contain pits, such as peaches and plums, always be sure to remove the pits before the fruits are placed in the juicer. Otherwise, you can quickly damage your juicer.

Before you do so, however, we suggest that you read the juicing tips below, so that the juices you prepare are of the best quality and most pleasing to your taste. In addition, be sure to augment your juicing program with a healthy diet based on the dietary principles we shared with you in Chapter 5. Bear in mind, as well, that the amount of fruits and vegetables called for in each recipe, as well as the total ounces of juice that they will produce, are general estimates that can vary. (For more on this subject, see the Juice Conversion Tables on page 243.) What is most important is that you try the recipes and stick with them long enough so that you are able to experience their full potential benefits. As you do so, please feel free to experiment, guided by your personal tastes and your intuition. The more that you personalize your daily juicing regimen, the more apt you will be to enjoy and continue it.

■ **Don't Juice the Outer Skins of Citrus Fruits.** The outer skin, or rinds, of citrus fruits (grapefruits, lemons, limes, oranges, tangerines, etc.) should not be juiced or only juiced sparingly because of their bitter taste. Therefore, be sure to peel such fruits. However, do make use of the white undercoating of the rinds of such fruits, as it is rich in vitamin C, quercetin, and other antioxidants.

■ **Cut and Dice Fruits and Vegetables Before Juicing.** Once you are ready to begin juicing, be sure that the portions of the fruits and vegetables you use fit easily into the opening of your juicer. To this end, you may need to cut or dice them first. In addition, don't attempt to juice too much produce at once. Never overstuff the opening of the juicer, attempting to force the process. Doing so can produce unnecessary wear and tear on the juicer's blade and motor that could result in damage.

■ **Avoid Using Overripe Produce.** Produce that is overripe should be avoided when juicing because it can result in the production of too much pulp, which can cause your juicer to become clogged. In addition, overripe fruits and vegetables contain less nutrient content than properly ripened produce.

■ **Running Your Juicer.** Before you start juicing, let your juicer run for ten to thirty seconds so that the blade is already at full speed before you add fruits and vegetables. When you finish juicing, let your unit continue to run for a minute or more. This will ensure that all juice that has been extracted runs off into your juice container. Also be sure to allow your juicer to come to a complete stop before you begin to disassemble it for cleaning.

Best Times to Drink Juice
for Maximum Benefits

Ideally, juice should be consumed at least thirty minutes before eating any solid food, or at least one to two hours after most meals. Following high-protein meals of average to large size, wait at least three hours before drinking fresh juice. This is because juice is immediately absorbed when consumed on an empty stomach, but when solid food is present, the juice cannot be absorbed until the stomach is clear. It is forced to "wait in line" behind the solid food. While starchy foods typically take only an hour to leave the stomach, protein foods can remain in the stomach and small intestine for a full six hours. This is why it is best to wait until any solid food has been largely digested before consuming fresh juice.

Finally, please be aware that the information contained in this section is not intended to take the place of medical advice from your physician or other health care practitioners. If you find that the health condition you are dealing with continues to persist, seek proper medical attention.

Part Two lists various health conditions in alphabetical order, complete with general information and the recommended juicing remedies. The serving amount and frequency of consumption is individualized and variable. Feel free to choose one or more of the suggested juicing recipes for each condition. Experiment and see which ones you enjoy. We are not suggesting that you must drink all the recipes each day at the amounts specified. In general, any serving amount will be beneficial and the more fresh-squeezed juices that you consume, the better and faster the positive results can be expected. If any recipe must be limited in intake, that is stated.

ABSCESS

Abscess is the name given to an accumulation of pus anywhere on the body. Typically, abscesses are caused by bacterial, viral, or fungal infections, but they can also be due to parasites. The most common areas of the body in which abscesses occur are the armpits, face, arms and legs, rectum, and the female breast, especially in women who are nursing and lactating.

Common symptoms of abscesses include swelling, tenderness, and/or heat in and around the infected site. Reddening of the skin can also occur, as can fever, chills, cellulites (inflammation of cellular tissues around the affected area), fatigue, and, in some cases, rupture of the affected area and blood infection.

Mild forms of abscess may resolve without the need for medical treatment. However, because of the potential seriousness of abscesses, professional medical care should be considered, as well as the use of antibiotics, if necessary.

JUICING RECIPES

• Juice 4 medium carrots, 1 medium beet, 4 celery stalks, and 2 cloves fresh garlic. **Makes 16 ounces. Consume once to twice daily.**

• Juice 3 medium carrots, $1/_2$–1 medium cucumber, 1–2 ounces wheatgrass juice, and $1/_2$ bunch spinach. **Makes 14 to 16 ounces. Consume once to twice daily.**

• Juice 3 medium carrots, 2 burdock roots, 2–3 garlic cloves, and 3 celery stalks. **Makes 12 ounces. Consume once daily.**

HEALTHY TWIST

🌰 Add 6–8 leaves of the herb yellow dock (5 percent of total juice) or 1–2 ounces of turmeric to any of the above recipes. **Consume once daily.**

ACNE

Acne is a skin condition caused by inflammation in the sebaceous glands, which are located below each hair follicle. When the sebaceous glands become clogged with the natural oils that your body produces, bacterial buildup can occur inside them, causing the inflamed, raised spots that are characteristic of acne. Acne spots can be red, black, (blackheads), or whitish in color.

In addition to adolescence, at which time the human body undergoes changes in hormone levels that can contribute to acne, acne can be caused by poor hygiene; poor diet; nutritional deficiencies; food allergies; allergic reactions to commercial soap, skin care, and shampoo products; stress; and other hormonal changes, such as those that occur during menstruation and pre-menstruation. Contraceptives can also be a factor.

JUICING RECIPES

- Juice 4 medium carrots, 1 medium beet, and 4 celery stalks.
Makes 16 ounces. Consume once daily.

- Juice 3 medium carrots, 1 medium cucumber, and $1/2$ bunch lettuce (not iceberg). Makes 14 ounces. Consume once to twice daily.

- Juice 3 medium carrots, $1/2$ medium beet, 3 celery stalks, and 2 garlic cloves. Makes 12 ounces. Consume once to twice daily.

- Juice 2 medium apples, 2 medium lemons, and add 1 tablespoon noni juice. Makes 10 ounces. Consume once daily.

- Juice 1 bunch spinach and 3 or more medium carrots.
Makes 12 ounces. Consume once daily.

ADDICTIONS

Addiction is a term used to describe a broad range of physical or psychological dependencies that negatively impact one's health and overall well-being. All forms of addictions are biochemical in nature, meaning that whatever substance a person becomes addicted to—whether it be the nicotine in cigarettes, alcohol, or the various chemical ingredients in drugs (including, in many cases, prescription drugs)—becomes a necessary ingredient for the body to feel well. When someone with addictive behavior is deprived of the addictive substance, he or she will usually experience withdrawal symptoms as the body cries out for the chemical influence that it has become used to. Such withdrawal symptoms often compel people back to their addictive behavior, perpetuating a cycle of self-destructive behavior.

Researchers now know that receptor sites in the brain are formed when a person uses substances that are addictive. The more such substances are used, the greater the number of brain receptor sites that are formed. Eventually, enough receptor sites form so that, when the chemical substances are not provided to "feed" them, the brain literally signals its craving for them. In essence, this is the biological basis for addiction, and explains why so many people struggle to break their addictions only to fail, despite the best of intentions. To effectively end addiction, a program that shuts down these receptor sites is often the best solution, especially in cases where all other means of intervention have failed. This can be accomplished by replenishing the body and the brain with the nutrients they require in order to function properly. Because of the immediate flood of essential nutrients that fresh-squeezed, organic juices provide, juicing is an excellent method for helping people to recover from addiction.

JUICING RECIPES

• A two to three week juice fast (see Chapter 7) can be effective for detoxifying the bloodstream from nicotine and to end the craving for cigarettes, as well as for helping the body to eliminate the craving for other addictive substances, including drugs and alcohol. The best juices for helping to end addiction are any combination of carrot, celery, and beets. Drink one to two 8–12 ounce glasses each day.

During the withdrawal phase, avoid acidifying juices (citrus, tomato), however, as these juices can be counter-productive. Orange and lemon juices, as well as bananas, can be used with good results during the post-withdrawal detoxification phase.

AGING (*See also* ANTI-AGING / LONGEVITY)

Fresh juices are good for all ages. However, as we age, they are even more powerful in their ability to improve health and increase energy. As we grow older, we often experience a decrease in our sense of taste, which directly decreases our digestive energy and function. Such decreases, in turn, can negatively affect our overall health. By regularly drinking fresh-squeezed juices, you can counteract this process, due to the rich nutritional benefits juicing provides. Almost all vegetable juices will provide significant nutritional gains. To get started, try one or more of the following juice combinations.

JUICING RECIPES

• Juice equal parts carrot and apple. Consume 8–16 ounces daily.

• Juice 3 medium carrots and 3 celery stalks.
Makes 12 ounces. Consume once daily.

• Juice 2 medium apples, 8 ounces blueberries, and 1 tablespoon noni juice.
Makes 10 ounces. Consume once daily.

AIDS (ACQUIRED IMMUNO-DEFICIENCY SYNDROME)

AIDS (Acquired Immuno-Deficiency Syndrome) is an immune disorder that can cause a wide range of other disease symptoms and opportunistic infections. When any of these opportunistic infections include a positive diagnosis of the HIV virus, a patient is said to have AIDS. AIDS is controversial, in this respect, because of how widely symptoms can vary, both in terms of how it manifests around the globe, and also how it affects different risk groups.

Common characteristics of AIDS include Kaposi's sarcoma (a type of cancer); pneumocystis pneumonia; candidiasis; and mycobacterial infections such as tuberculosis, toxoplasmosis (a disease caused by protozoa that damages the central nervous system, eyes, and internal organs), cytomegalovirus, and the herpes virus. Other symptoms often associated with AIDS include diarrhea, weight loss, night sweats, fevers, rashes, and swollen lymph glands.

Because of how AIDS compromises immune function, it is ideal that an immune-boosting protocol be part of every overall AIDS treatment plan. Juicing can help in this regard because of the many immune-enhancing nutrients juices contain. The following juice remedies are particularly effective.

JUICING RECIPES

• Juice 4 medium carrots, 3 celery stalks, $1/2$ medium beet, 2 garlic cloves, and $1/4$ ounce fresh turmeric. Makes 16 ounces. Consume 8 ounces twice daily.

• Juice 1 medium apple, 4 ounces pineapple, and add 1 tablespoon noni juice. Makes 6 ounces. Consume once to twice daily.

• Juice 3 medium carrots, 3 celery stalks, 2 burdock roots, and 2 garlic cloves. Makes 14 ounces. Consume once daily.

• Juice 2 medium apples, 2 medium lemons, and 1 ounce ginger. Makes 10 ounces. Consume twice daily.

ALCOHOLISM

Alcoholism is a specific form of addiction caused by the body's craving for alcohol. Without alcohol, alcoholics are unable to experience consistent levels of well-being and happiness. Like all other forms of addiction, alcoholism is due in large part to the buildup of receptor sites in the brain that form each time alcohol is consumed. Shutting down these alcohol-specific receptor sites is therefore a key to successfully ending one's addiction to alcohol.

As we explained in "Addictions" (see page 138), this can be accomplished by replenishing the body and the brain with the nutrients they require in order to function properly. Because of the immediate flood of essential nutrients that fresh-squeezed, organic juices provide, juicing is an excellent method for helping people to recover from alcoholism.

JUICING RECIPES

- Juice 4 medium carrots, 1 medium beet, $^1/_2$ medium black radish, 1 medium burdock root, 2 celery stalks, and 1–2 garlic cloves.
Makes 16 ounces. Consume once daily.

- Juice 3 medium carrots, $^1/_2$ bunch lettuce, 1 medium cucumber, and 1 garlic clove. Makes 14–16 ounces. Consume once daily.

- Juice 8 ounces pineapple, 2 medium oranges, and add 1 tablespoon noni juice. Makes 14 ounces. Consume once daily.

- Juice 8 ounces cantaloupe, 8 ounces blueberries, and add 1 teaspoon cinnamon. Makes 6–8 ounces. Consume once to twice daily.

ALLERGIES

Allergies are caused by adverse reactions by the body's immune system to one or more substances that normally are harmless. Allergens, the substances that trigger allergy symptoms, are proteins, or *haptons* (molecules that bind to proteins), that the body erroneously perceives to be foreign and dangerous. The body's abnormal reaction that follows exposure to these allergens is what causes an allergic response.

Common allergy symptoms include congestion and other breathing difficulties, bloodshot or itchy eyes, watery eyes and tearing, sneezing, coughing, itchy skin, puffiness in the face, reddening of the cheeks, dark circles under the eyes, runny nose, hives, vomiting, stomachache, and intestinal irritation or swelling. Serious allergic reactions can include anaphylactic shock, which can be fatal if not treated in time.

Allergies can be caused by substances in the environment, such as pollen, and by certain foods. Ironically, food allergies are often caused by the foods a person most enjoys eating, to the point that he or she craves them regularly.

Inflammation is a major component of allergic reactions. As we discussed in Chapter 3, one of the primary benefits that juicing provides is protection against unhealthy inflammation. This makes juicing an excellent self-care method for relieving allergy symptoms.

JUICING RECIPES

- Juice 3 medium carrots, $^1/_2$ medium beet, $^1/_2$ medium cucumber, and $^1/_4$–$^1/_2$ bunch parsley. Makes 12 ounces. Consume once daily or twice daily during acute stage.

- Juice 4 medium carrots and 3 celery stalks. Makes 14 ounces. Consume once daily.

- Juice 1 medium apple, 8 ounces blueberries, $^1/_3$ medium papaya, and add 1 tablespoon noni juice. Makes 8 ounces. Consume once to twice daily.

ALZHEIMER'S DISEASE / SENILE DEMENTIA

Alzheimer's disease and senile dementia are both associated with aging, and affect brain function. Alzheimer's, named after neurologist Alois Alzheimer, who identified it in 1907, is the most severe type of senile dementia. Both conditions are marked by progressive degeneration of a person's mental capacity caused by the way the conditions attack the brain. The primary symptoms of Alzheimer's and senile dementia are impaired memory and cognitive skills, impaired intellectual capacity, stunted emotional functioning, and, eventually, a complete breakdown of a person's ability to function mentally and physically.

In addition to the above symptoms, patients affected by either Alzheimer's disease or senile dementia typically experience depression, fatigue, and aggressive or paranoid behavior, along with short- and long-term memory loss and a breakdown in their ability to understand others' conversations and in their own ability to speak intelligibly. Repeating themselves and an inability to perform simple arithmetic, as well as spatial and time disorientation, are other symptoms of both conditions.

Although juicing is by no means a cure for either Alzheimer's disease or senile dementia, because of the beneficial supply of nutrients needed by the brain that juices supply, regularly drinking fresh-squeezed juices can do much to prevent the onset of these conditions and slow their progression.

JUICING RECIPES

- Juice 3 medium carrots, $^1/_2$ medium beet, and 3 celery stalks. Makes 12 ounces. Consume once daily.

- Juice 3 medium carrots, 2 celery stalks, 1 garlic clove, $^1/_2$ medium cucumber, and $^1/_4$ bunch cilantro. Makes 12 ounces. Consume once to twice daily.

- Juice 2 medium apples, 1 cup black cherries or prunes, and add 1 tablespoon noni juice. **Makes 12 ounces. Consume once daily.**

- Juice 4 medium carrots, 3 medium apples, add ginko as capsuled powder (1–2) or liquid extract (1 teaspoon).
Makes 22 ounces. Consume once daily.

HEALTHY TWIST

🍇 Lecithin, phosphatidyl choline, and phosphatidyl serine (2 caps of any of the three) are excellent supplements to these juices.

AMEBIASIS

Amebiasis is a disease caused by the parasitic infection of the ameba *Entiamoeba histolytica,* and similar strains, which can be ingested via contaminated food or beverages. Common symptoms of amebiasis include nausea, vomiting, diarrhea, abdominal pain, and general fatigue and weakness. In some cases, amebiasis can also lead to dysentery, and amebic hepatitis, an infection of the liver.

If you suspect you are suffering from amebiasis, seek immediate medical attention. The following juice remedies can help to relieve symptoms.

JUICING RECIPES

- Juice 4 medium carrots, 1 medium beet, 2–3 garlic cloves, 1 medium burdock root, and $1/8$ ounce basil. **Makes 12 ounces. Consume two to three times daily.**

- Juice 8 ounces papaya ($1/2$ medium papaya), 2 medium lemons, and add 1 tablespoon noni juice. **Consume once to twice daily.**

- Juice 3 medium carrots, 1 bunch cilantro, 3 celery stalks, and 2 garlic cloves. **Makes 14 ounces. Consume once daily.**

HEALTHY TWIST

🍇 Consider adding neem or wormwood (one 1,000 mg capsule of each) to any of the above combinations.

ANEMIA

Anemia is a condition that is characterized by chronic fatigue, as well as a variety of other potential symptoms. These include impaired memory and cognitive skills, dizziness, headaches, skin pallor (pale skin), and general weakness. Other possible symptoms include canker sores, irritability, impaired muscle control, sleep disorders, and weight loss.

Anemia commonly results from deficiencies of either red blood cells or hemoglobin, which is necessary to transport adequate supplies of oxygen to the cells. Both of these deficiencies can be due to a lack of essential nutrients, especially folic acid, iron, and vitamin B_{12}, which is also known as cobalamin. Therefore, it is important that people suffering from anemia have a blood test that screens for nutritional imbalances. It is also important to rule out bleeding disorders and genetic or metabolic causes of anemia. A complete blood count test (CBC) and other common blood tests can differentiate the causes of most anemias.

As part of an overall treatment program to recover from anemia, the following juice combinations are recommended.

JUICING RECIPES

- Juice 3 medium carrots, 1 medium beet, $1/2$ bunch spinach, and 1 burdock root. Makes 14 ounces. Consume once daily.

- Juice 1 medium apple, blend and add 1 medium banana and 4–6 medium figs. Makes 12 ounces. Consume once daily.

- Juice 3 medium carrots, 1 bunch spinach, 3 celery stalks, and add $1/2$ teaspoon cayenne pepper. Makes 16 ounces. Consume once to twice daily.

ANKYLOSING SPONDYLITIS

Ankylosing spondylitis is a musculo-skeletal condition that is characterized by extreme and progressive inflammation and stiffness of the spine and the joints along the sacrum, which is located at the base of the spine. As the condition progresses, people affected by it increasingly are forced to sit and walk in a "bent forward" posture.

In the initial stages of the disease, other symptoms include intermittent pain in the lower back, sciatic pain, and stiffness that is particularly pronounced in the morning, following sleep. As ankylosing spondylitis progresses, back pain can spread upward to the mid- and upper back, as well as into the neck. Pain in the arms and legs can also occur, as can anemia, increased muscle stiffness, and, in some cases, weight loss.

Although ankylosing spondylitis is thought to be due, at least in part, to genetics, it can also be related to impaired gastrointestinal functioning, food allergies, nutritional deficiencies (especially digestive enzymes), and infections caused by bacteria, fungi, viruses, or parasites (such as amebiasis). The following juice remedies can be helpful in slowing the progression of anklyosing spondylitis, and even, in some cases, helping to reverse it.

JUICING RECIPES

- Juice 3 medium carrots, 1/2 medium beet, 2 celery stalks, 1/2 bunch parsley, 1/2 medium potato, and 4 ounces alfalfa sprouts. Makes 16 ounces. Consume once daily.

- Juice 4 medium carrots, 1 medium cucumber, and 1 bunch watercress. Makes 16 ounces. Consume once to twice daily.

- Juice 1 medium papaya, 12 ounces coconut, and 4 medium lemons. Makes 12 ounces. Consume once to twice daily.

ANOXIA

Anoxia is a condition caused by an insufficient supply of oxygen in the body, such as what occurs when there is a lack of hemoglobin production. Since certain vegetables are high in chlorophyll, which mimics hemoglobin in the body once the vegetables are ingested, a variety of vegetable juice combinations can be helpful in reversing anoxia. Among them are the following.

JUICING RECIPES

- Juice 3 medium carrots, 1 medium beet, 1 medium cucumber, and then add 2 ounces wheatgrass juice. (See Wheatgrass Juice inset on page 146.) Makes 16 ounces. Consume once daily.

- Juice 3 medium carrots, 1 bunch spinach, 1 bunch parsley, and add 1 ounce turmeric root. Makes 16 ounces. Consume once to twice daily.

- Juice 4 medium lemons, 4 medium kiwi, 1 medium lime, and 2 medium apples. Makes 14 ounces. Consume twice daily.

ANTI-AGING / LONGEVITY (See also AGING)

Never before in history has science understood so much about the factors that cause us to age, as well as the factors that promote a long and healthy life. One of the keys to both anti-aging and longevity is optimum nutrition. Poor nutrition is a primary factor in premature aging, as well as the host of health conditions that are associated with age, while a daily supply of all of the nutrients your body needs to properly function (vitamins, minerals, enzymes, and various other nutritional co-factors) helps to promote good health and keep the ravages of age at bay. Juicing is one of the simplest and most powerful health solutions for improving your ability to live a long and healthy life because of the abundant supply of anti-aging nutrients fresh-squeezed juices provide. The following juice recipes are particularly helpful in this regard.

JUICING RECIPES

- Daily intake of fresh fruit and vegetable juices.
Consume 16–32 ounces daily.

- Drink wheatgrass juice. **Consume 2 ounces daily.** (See inset below.)

- Juice 3 medium carrots, $1/4$ head cabbage, 2 celery stalks, and 1–2 garlic cloves. **Makes 12 ounces. Consume once to twice daily.**

- Juice 4 medium carrots, 2 burdock roots, 1 ounce turmeric, and $1/2$ bunch parsley or spinach. **Makes 12–14 ounces. Consume once daily.**

WHEATGRASS JUICE

Nutrient-rich wheatgrass juice first became popular in the United States in the 1960s and 1970s, largely due to the late Dr. Ann Wigmore, founder of The Hippocrates Health Institute, which was later renamed The Ann Wigmore Foundation. After years of poor health, Dr. Wigmore discovered the health benefits of wheatgrass juice, which she consumed daily. She then spent the next thirty-five years of her life promoting natural healing methods, such as raw food diets and wheatgrass juicing, and became one of the leading voices in the natural health food movement.

Wheatgrass juice is derived from the grass grown from sprouted wheatberries. The juice is dark emerald green in color and has an extremely sweet, distinct taste. Wheatgrass juice contains a variety of potent antioxidant and anti-aging nutrients, including vitamin A, vitamin B complex, vitamin E, and an abundance of minerals, including calcium, iron, magnesium, and potassium. It is also rich in amino acids, which are necessary for the body's manufacture of essential proteins.

Perhaps the most important nutrient supplied by wheatgrass juice is chlorophyll, which is contained in the juice in rich supply. Chlorophyll is often called the "blood" of green plants because of how closely its chemical makeup and molecular structure resemble hemoglobin, a primary component of human blood. Like hemoglobin, chlorophyll delivers live-sustaining oxygen to the body's cells and tissues. It also aids the liver and other organs in eliminating toxins, and prevents carcinogenic (cancer-causing) agents from binding to the DNA of healthy cells.

Among the other benefits of wheatgrass juice is its ability to enhance the overall health and functioning of blood cells, muscles, bones, and teeth, as well as the kidneys, liver, and spleen. Wheatgrass juice also has potent hypotensive properties,

- Juice 2 medium apricots, 1 medium lemon, 1 medium lime, 1 medium papaya, 4 ounces pineapple, and 1 tablespoon noni juice.
Makes 16 ounces. Consume once daily.

ANXIETY

Anxiety is a fairly common psychological condition that is characterized by a sense of dread, fear, or chronic worry over present or future life situations. Anxiety can also be a factor in other psychological conditions, such as obsessive-compulsive disorder, phobias, and post-traumatic stress disorder (PTSD). In addition to its psychological symptoms, anxiety can also result in a variety of physical symptoms. These include breathing difficulties and/or shortness of breath, cold flashes, increased heart rate, perspiration,

which means it helps regulate and reduce high blood pressure. Regular consumption of wheatgrass juice can also help improve circulation and the body's metabolism. Because of its powerful detoxifying effects, initially, this juice should be taken in small amounts—one to two ounces per day—until your body becomes accustomed to it. After that, you can consume as much as desired.

Another positive feature of wheatgrass juice is that it does not contain gluten, so most wheat-sensitive individuals can drink it without experiencing negative side effects. However, anyone with wheat allergies, especially those with advanced sensitivities, should consider a challenge test before making wheatgrass a regular part of their diet.

Wheatgrass juice is prepared by grinding fresh wheatgrass. To grow wheatgrass, place wheatberries in a flat planting tray with high-quality soil. When the grass is about six inches high, it is ready to harvest. Use a wheatgrass juicer (or other high-quality masticating juicer) to grind the fresh grass. These juicers are available in many health food stores and online sites as both manual and electric models. (See the table on pages 52–54 for more information.)

Be aware, however, that growing wheatgrass is both time consuming (it takes about a week for the grass to grow) and space consuming (for daily juice, you will need window space for five to seven large growing trays). Unless you are willing and able to put in the time and effort to create your own daily wheatgrass supply, it is recommended that you purchase the juice at a health food store or health food co-op. A growing number of supermarkets also carry wheatgrass juice, and there are online websites that offer fresh-squeezed wheatgrass juice that is delivered daily right to your home.

and skin flushing. Gastrointestinal problems such as diarrhea can also occur as a result of anxiety attacks, as can dizziness, dry mouth, fatigue, irritability, impaired mental function, and sleep disorders such as insomnia.

Although anxiety is considered to be primarily a psychological condition, dietary and nutritional imbalances and deficiencies can also be contributing factors. Restoring proper nutritional balance should, therefore, always be considered as part of an overall treatment program for anxiety. Because of the rich supply of nutrients juices supply, juicing can be helpful in this regard, especially the following juice remedies.

JUICING RECIPES

• Juice 2 medium carrots, 2 celery stalks, $\frac{1}{2}$ bunch parsley, and $\frac{1}{2}$ head lettuce. Makes 12 ounces. Consume once daily.

• Juice 6 ounces cantaloupe, $\frac{1}{3}$ medium papaya, and add 1 tablespoon noni juice. Makes 6 ounces. Consume once to twice daily.

• Juice 2 medium apples, 12 ounces cantaloupe, 4 ounces blueberries, and add 2 capsules or $\frac{1}{2}$ dropper of passion flower extract.
Makes 12 ounces. Consume once to twice daily.

ARRHYTHMIA (IRREGULAR HEARTBEAT)

Arrhythmia is a heart condition that is characterized by irregularities in the rhythm of the heartbeat. In most cases, arrhythmia is caused by disturbances that interfere with the proper transmission of impulses through the conductive tissue of the heart that are caused by electrical impulses originating in the sinoatrial node, a specialized group of cells located in the heart's right atrium, or chamber. There are two main types of arrhythmia: bradycardia and tachycardia. Bradycardia is characterized by irregular heart rhythms that are too slow, while tachycardia, the most common form of arrhythmia, is characterized by heart rhythms that are too fast.

In addition to accelerated heartbeat, symptoms of tachycardia include chest pain or discomfort, weakness, fainting, sweating, shortness of breath, confusion, or dizziness. Symptoms of bradycardia include fatigue, lightheadedness, shortness of breath, and, in some cases, loss of consciousness. Although all of us experience arrhythmia at some time in our lives, such as when we feel as if our hearts "skipped a beat," usually such events are brief, nonrecurring, and harmless. Ongoing arrhythmia, on the other hand, can lead to more serious health challenges, including heart attack and stroke. If you suspect you suffer from chronic arrhythmia, seek immediate medical attention.

JUICING RECIPES

- Juice 2 medium carrots, $\frac{1}{2}$ medium cucumber, 1–2 celery stalks, 1 garlic clove, and when possible, $\frac{1}{4}$ cup hawthorn berries.
Makes 10 ounces. Consume once to twice daily.

- Juice 2 medium apples, 8 ounces pineapple, add 2 medium bananas, and blend. Makes 16 ounces. Consume once to twice daily.

- Juice 3 medium carrots, 1 bunch parsley, 1 bunch watercress, and 2 garlic cloves. Makes 12 ounces. Consume once to twice daily.

ARTERITIS

Arteritis is a general term that refers to conditions of inflammation in the arteries. There are two main types of arteritis. The first, and most common, type is known as giant cell arteritis (GCA), which can also be referred to as temporal arteritis. The second type is known as Takayasu's arteritis, which is named after the Japanese physician Dr. Mikoto Takayasu, who first described it in the medical literature in 1908. Both conditions are related to vasculitis, a condition characterized by inflammation in either the arteries or veins.

In cases of giant cell arteritis, inflammation primarily occurs in the carotid arteries, which run along the neck to the head and the sides of the face near the temples and are responsible for transporting blood and oxygen from the heart to the head and brain. GCA is an autoimmune condition, meaning that it is caused by the immune system reacting against and attacking itself. Symptoms of GCA include dull, throbbing pain in the neck and head area, particularly the sides of the face and the temples. Pain can also occur in and around the eyes and jaw, and also be mistaken for common headache symptoms. At times, the pain can become acute and be accompanied by burning, stabbing sensations. If left untreated, GCA can continue to progress and, in severe cases, result in irreversible blindness and partial blindness. Therefore, it is important that you seek prompt medical attention if you suspect you suffer from GCA.

Takayasu's arteritis is a relatively rare condition caused by inflammation to large- and medium-sized blood vessels, especially the branches of the aorta, the main blood vessel of the heart (typically, the aorta itself remains unaffected), and the arteries that supply blood and oxygen to the arms, legs, kidneys, intestines, and other blood vessels of the heart. In some cases of Takayasu's arteritis, inflammation can result in the weakening and/or stretching of the arteries, causing aneurysm, a condition characterized by bulging blood vessels. The disease can also cause arteries to narrow or become entirely blocked, leading to arterial occlusion (blocked arteries).

Symptoms of Takayasu's arteritis include anemia, arthritis-like symptoms, dizziness, fatigue, low-grade fever, muscle ache, night sweats, and swollen glands. The condition can also cause abdominal pain, especially after eating. In some cases, it can also lead to heart attack and stroke. Like GCA, Takayasu's arteritis requires professional medical attention.

Since, as we discussed in Chapter 3, one of the main benefits of juicing is a reduction in unhealthy inflammation, regularly drinking fresh-squeezed juices can help to relieve symptoms of both types of arteritis, as well as preventing their occurrence in the first place. The following juices, in particular, are especially useful.

JUICING RECIPES

• Juice 4 medium carrots, $\frac{1}{2}$ medium beet, 2 garlic cloves, 4 ounces alfalfa sprouts, and $\frac{1}{2}$ ounce turmeric or ginger root.
Makes 12 ounces. Consume once daily.

• Juice 3 medium carrots, 1 medium cucumber, 1 bunch parsley, and $\frac{1}{4}$ medium onion. Makes 16 ounces. Consume once daily.

• Juice 8 ounces blueberries, 8 ounces black cherries, 8 ounces pomegranate, and add 1 tablespoon noni juice.
Makes 10–12 ounces. Consume once daily.

ARTHRITIS (GOUT, OSTEOARTHRITIS, AND RHEUMATOID ARTHRITIS)

Arthritis is a general term used to describe inflammation, pain, and/or stiffness in the joints and the overall musculo-skeletal system, including cartilage, ligaments, and tendons, as well as the back, fingers, feet, knees, hips, neck, and shoulders. Symptoms range from mild pain and stiffness, to pain and stiffness that become so severe that persons become disabled and unable to participate in their normal, regular activities. According to the National Institutes of Health (NIH), 15 percent of all Americans (approximately 45 million people) suffer from arthritis to some degree. Despite the widespread incidence of arthritis in this and other Western nations, it is virtually non-existent in countries around the world whose people follow diets that primarily consist of whole, unprocessed grains and plenty of fresh fruits and vegetables.

Although over 100 types of arthritis have been identified, overall there are four main types of arthritis: osteoarthritis, rheumatoid arthritis, gout, and traumatic arthritis. Osteoarthritis is the most common form of arthritis. It is characterized by the breakdown of cartilage, a smooth tissue that is necessary to prevent the bones of your body from rubbing against each other. As osteoarthritis progresses, the degeneration of cartilage becomes so great that bones directly touch each other. This, in turn, leads to abnormal hardening of the bones, bone spurs, inflammation, and chronic joint pain. Osteoarthritis can also cause bones to become brittle and more susceptible to fracture.

Rheumatoid arthritis is more prevalent in women than in men. It is an autoimmune disease characterized by painful swelling and inflammation of the joints, and, in some cases, joint deformity. As rheumatoid arthritis progresses, the membrane that lines the joints, known as synovial tissue, is eaten away. Since the synovial tissue is responsible for secreting the lubricants that enable bones to move smoothly and painlessly against each other, the progression of rheumatoid arthritis can be increasingly painful and, at times, even crippling. Symptoms can occur gradually or spring up seemingly overnight and without warning. In some cases, they can also be accompanied by low-grade fever.

In ages past, gout was once referred to by Europeans as the disease of kings and noblemen, or "the rich man's disease," since the condition was rare among peasants, serfs, and others not born into the nobility. The reason gout was so common among the nobility while so rare among the common folk was because the former ate a diet high in animal proteins and other foods containing high amounts of the amino acid *purine*, while the latter could hardly afford regular meals of meat and poultry, subsisting on grains and vegetables instead. Animal proteins, and other high purine-containing foods, when consumed regularly and accompanied by a genetically linked inadequacy to metabolize purine, cause a buildup of uric acid to occur in the body. Once uric acid levels become too high, the body is unable to adequately eliminate the acid, causing it to form crystals in the cartilage and synovial tissue of the musculo-skeletal system. This, in turn, causes jabbing, needle-like pain in the joints, usually beginning in those of the big toes. As gout progresses, other symptoms can also occur, including loss of mobility, chills, and fever.

Traumatic arthritis is a form of inflammation and joint erosion that is caused by repetitive micro and macro injury to a joint or joints. This can result from repetitive use of a joint in work or from repeated accidents to a joint or area, as we see in athletic events and extreme sports.

Conventional treatment for these arthritis conditions varies as to which type of arthritis is involved. Rheumatoid arthritis is treated by a range of anti-inflammatory drugs ranging from over-the-counter products like aspirin and ibuprofen to steroidal prescriptions and sometimes even the discarded chemotherapy drug metho-trexate. Gouty arthritis can often be managed by diet alone but includes prescriptions that are targeted at the elimination of uric acid from the body. All forms of arthritis can be benefited by the right juice selections, and the consequences of the drug therapies can also be lessened with fresh juices.

JUICING RECIPES

• Juice 4–6 celery stalks during acute inflammation stage.
Makes 6–8 ounces. Consume once daily.

• Juice 3 medium carrots, 2–3 celery stalks, and 4 ounces cabbage.
Makes 12 ounces. Consume once daily.

• Juice 3 medium carrots, 1 medium beet, and $\frac{1}{2}$ medium cucumber.
Makes 12 ounces. Consume once daily.

• Juice 1 medium apple, $\frac{1}{3}$ medium papaya, 4 ounces blueberries, and add 1 tablespoon noni juice.
Makes 8 ounces. Consume once to twice daily.

• For gouty arthritis: Juice 8 ounces black cherries, 8 ounces prunes, and 1 medium apple. Makes 8–10 ounces. Consume one to three times daily.

ASTHMA

Asthma is a common respiratory condition that is characterized by spasms in the bronchi or bronchioles, both of which are smooth muscles that surround the airways of the lungs. Due to such spasms, during asthma attacks, the airways narrow, creating a sensation of being unable to breathe as well as other general breathing difficulties. In most cases of asthma, the buildup or secretion of mucus within the mucous membranes of the lungs also occurs.

There are two general classifications of asthma: acute and chronic. Acute asthma can strike suddenly and unexpectedly, causing severe breathing difficulties which, in some cases, can require immediate medical attention. In cases of chronic asthma, symptoms are similar to those of acute asthma, but usually less severe. Other symptoms, common to both types of asthma, include coughs, hay fever, heart palpitations and accelerated heart rate (often due to inhalant medicines), sleep problems, tightness in the chest, and wheezing.

JUICING RECIPES

● From Ralph Weiss, ND, DC, PhD, DD (Dr. Weiss, who contributed this recipe for this book, has seven doctorates and was Edger Cayce's doctor from 1938–1942.): Use 1 teaspoon horseradish, 1 teaspoon fresh lemon juice, and 1 $^1/_2$ teaspoons best virgin olive oil. Mix well. It's hot, so take small amounts slowly. Best taken after meals, when mucus develops.

● Juice 4 medium carrots, 2 garlic cloves, and 1 ounce fresh rosemary leaves. Makes 10 ounces. Consume once daily, or three times daily during acute stage.

● Juice 2 medium apples, 4 medium lemons, 1 medium orange, and add $^1/_2$ teaspoon cinnamon. Makes 16 ounces. Consume once to twice daily.

● Juice 4 medium carrots, 5 celery stalks, and 2 garlic cloves. Makes 16 ounces. Consume once daily.

HEALTHY TWIST

❦ Consider adding $^1/_2$ cup pitted hawthorn berries, 1–2 ounces turmeric, and $^1/_4$–$^1/_2$ bunch lettuce to above recipes.

❦ During acute episodes, inhaling rosemary leaves or oil as a vapor can often provide immediate relief.

BACK PAIN

Back pain is one of the most common of all health conditions. It is estimated to affect 80 percent of all Americans at some point in their lives. It is also the leading cause of disability in people below the age of 45.

There are two types of back pain: acute and chronic. Acute back pain flares up suddenly and without warning and is usually due to accidents, injury, heavy lifting, or sudden movements that causes misalignments in the spine and surrounding muscles. It may also occur in conjunction with sustained periods of high stress accompanied by muscle tension. Chronic back pain typically develops over time and in most cases is due to long-standing unhealthy habits, such as poor posture, lack of exercise, unhealthy weight gain, and chronic stress on the musculoskeletal system.

In addition to the pain in areas of the back, symptoms of back pain include diminished mobility, impaired gait, difficulty breathing, muscle spasms and muscle tension, and problems sleeping due to pain that flares up when lying down. Although the majority of cases of back pain are structural in nature, they can be exacerbated by lack of proper nutrition. Because of this, juicing can be helpful due to the ability of the nutrients juices contain to help improve muscle function, support proper bone health, and relax chronic tension.

JUICING RECIPES

- Juice 4 medium carrots, 2 garlic cloves, 3 celery stalks, and $\frac{1}{2}$ bunch lettuce. Makes 16 ounces. Consume once daily.

- Juice 1 medium pear, $\frac{1}{3}$ medium papaya, 4 ounces pineapple, and add 1 tablespoon noni juice. Makes 8 ounces. Consume once daily.

- Juice 8 ounces black cherries, $\frac{1}{2}$ medium papaya, 1 medium apple, and add 1 ounce ginger root. Makes 16 ounces. Consume twice daily.

BAD BREATH (HALITOSIS)

Bad breath is a health condition that affects most everyone at some point in their lives. It is characterized by unpleasant odors from the mouth. In most cases, the person with bad breath is unaware that he or she has it.

There are a number of factors that can cause or contribute to bad breath. These include poor diet and nutrition, digestive problems, gastrointestinal disorders, and problems with the gums, mouth, or teeth. The following juice remedies can often quickly improve bad breath problems.

JUICING RECIPES

- Juice 3 medium carrots, 2 celery stalks, $\frac{1}{2}$ bunch parsley, $\frac{1}{4}$ bunch spinach, 2 ounces watercress, 4 ounces alfalfa sprouts, and 4 ounces beet tops. Makes 16 ounces. Consume once daily.

- Drink wheatgrass juice. Consume 2 ounces daily. (See inset on page 146.)

- Green juices (any combination of green vegetables). Consume 8–16 ounces daily.

- Juice 3 medium carrots, $\frac{1}{4}$ bunch spinach, and $\frac{1}{2}$ medium cucumber. Makes 12 ounces. Consume once daily.

- Start each day with the juice of 1 medium lemon in 8 ounces of warm water.

- Juice 1 medium apple, 2 medium lemons, and 4 ounces pineapple. Makes 8 ounces. Consume once daily.

BED SORES

Bed sores are skin ulcers caused by extensive bed rest, such as from prolonged hospital stays or during convalescence at home from serious illness, which can necessitate a person being bedridden. When a person lies in bed for long periods of time (days), ongoing pressure is created on areas of the body, such as the buttocks, hips, pelvis, and shoulders. This can cause bed sores to form. Bed sores are usually reddish and, should they become ulcerated, very painful. To avoid bed sores, a patient should be moved regularly and his or her bed sheets should be frequently changed. Regular exposure to fresh air is also recommended, as is wearing comfortable bed clothes (pajamas, gowns, etc.).

Juices that are rich in vitamin A, beta-carotene, vitamin C, and other nutrients can help to prevent bed sores and also hasten recovery from them because of how such nutrients promote healthy skin. Juices that fall into this category include:

JUICING RECIPES

- Juice 4 medium carrots and $1/2$–1 medium beet.
Makes 12 ounces. Consume once to twice daily.

- Juice $1/3$ medium cantaloupe, 4 ounces currants, and 4 ounces red grapes. Makes 12 ounces. Consume once daily.

- Juice 3 medium carrots, 2 burdock roots, 3 celery stalks, 2 garlic cloves, and add $1/4$ teaspoon cayenne pepper. Makes 14 ounces. Consume once daily.

BENIGN PROSTATIC HYPERPLASIA/BPH (ENLARGED PROSTATE)

Benign prostatic hyperplasia, also known as benign prostatic hypertrophy, or BPH, is a common health condition among men who are in their mid-40s or older. The prostate gland is located below the bladder and surrounds the urethra. As the prostate enlarges, it applies pressure on the urethra, causing it to narrow. This can make normal urination difficult.

Common symptoms of benign prostatic hyperplasia include a more frequent than normal need to urinate, particularly during the night; incomplete or difficult urination; weak urine flow; dribbling; and burning sensations during urination. In some cases, BPH can also lead to infections of the prostate, as well as the kidneys. In can also be a precursor of prostate cancer, since both conditions are, at least in part, due to the buildup of toxins, which primarily store themselves in fatty tissue. (In men, the most concentrated area of fatty tissues is within the prostate gland, while in women it is within the breasts. This helps to explain why the incidence of both breast and prostate cancer continues to rise, and is also appearing at a higher rate in men and women under 40 years of age. The increase in both types of cancer corresponds with the continued rise in the amounts of man-made pollutants that are being emitted into the environment each and every day.)

Juicing can help prevent and slow the progression of BPH—and in many cases even reverse it—for a variety of reasons. These include the abundant supply of essential nutrients that juices contain, as well as their potent properties of detoxification. Since both poor nutrition and toxic buildup directly affect the health of the prostate gland, it makes good sense for all men over 40 years of age to consider making juicing a part of their overall daily health care routine.

JUICING RECIPES

• Juice 4 medium carrots, 1 medium cucumber, 2 garlic cloves, and 3 celery stalks.
Makes 16 ounces. Consume once daily.

• Juice 4 ounces watermelon (high in lycopene), 4 ounces black cherry, and 4 ounces black grapes.
Makes 8 ounces. Consume once to twice daily.

• Juice 3 medium carrots, 1 bunch parsley, 1 garlic clove, and 1 ounce turmeric.
Makes 8–10 ounces. Consume once to twice daily.

• Noni juice: 4–8 ounces, one to three times a day, can also be helpful.

• Juice 2 medium tomatoes, 3 celery stalks, $\frac{1}{2}$ medium beet, and $\frac{1}{2}$ bunch parsley.
Makes 16 ounces. Consume once daily.

BLADDER INFECTIONS (*See* CYSTITIS)

BLEEDING

The rich supply of nutrients that juices contain can help stimulate the body's repair mechanisms, which are called into play when bleeding occurs. The following juice recipes are among the most effective for this purpose. Ginger, cinnamon, and cayenne are also excellent at helping to stop bleeding. (Note: Bleeding that is continuous requires immediate medical attention.)

JUICING RECIPES

● Juice 4 medium carrots, 1 medium beet, and 1 ounce ginger root. Makes 12 ounces. Consume one to three times daily.

● Use 8 ounces apple juice with 1 teaspoon ginger, every two hours for acute heavy bleeding.

● Juice 1 medium apple, 2 medium pears, and add 1 teaspoon cinnamon. Makes 8 ounces. Consume one to three times daily.

● Juice 3 medium carrots, $1/2$ bunch spinach, $1/2$ medium beet, and 2 celery stalks. Can add $1/8$–$1/4$ teaspoon cayenne pepper. Makes 16 ounces. Consume once daily.

BLEEDING GUMS (*See* PERIODONTAL DISEASE)

BODY ODOR

Body odor refers to unpleasant smells emitted from the body. Although the most common cause of body odor is poor hygiene, which enables dried sweat and dirt to remain on skin for hours at a time, creating foul smells, body odor can also be due to a variety of other factors, including poor diet, nutrition deficiencies, constipation, and other gastrointestinal problems. The abundant supply of nutrients found in fresh-squeezed fruit and vegetable juices can help counteract each of these problems. When combined with good hygiene, juicing can help to quickly eliminate body odor.

JUICING RECIPES

● Juice 3 medium carrots, 3 celery stalks, and $1/2$ bunch parsley. Makes 12 ounces. Consume one to three times daily.

● Juice 1 medium apple, 2 medium lemons, 4 ounces cranberries, and add 1 tablespoon noni juice. Makes 8 ounces. Consume once daily.

● Juice 3 medium carrots, $1/2$ medium beet, 2 garlic cloves, and add 2 ounces wheatgrass juice. (See Wheatgrass Juice inset on page 146.) Makes 12 ounces. Consume once daily.

BOILS

Boils are slight red bumps on the skin that are pus-filled and inflamed. They can manifest anywhere on the body, but most commonly occur at or near the site of an infected hair follicle on the skin. In most cases, the infection is caused by the bacteria *Staphylococcus aureus*. Juicing is an appropriate self-care remedy for helping to prevent and resolve boils because the nutrients that juices contain help to enhance the body's immune system, which is necessary to fight infection.

JUICING RECIPES

• Juice 3 medium carrots, $1/4$ head lettuce, 2 ounces spinach, and 4–8 leaves of yellow dock. Makes 10 ounces. Consume twice daily.

• Juice 4 medium carrots, 1 medium beet, and 3–4 celery stalks. Makes 16 ounces. Consume once daily.

• Juice 4 medium carrots, $1/2$ medium beet, and 1 medium cucumber. Makes 16 ounces. Consume once to twice daily.

HEALTHY TWIST
🍎 Consider adding 1–2 ounces wheatgrass juice (see inset on page 146) and 2–3 garlic cloves in all of the above recipes.

BREAST DISORDERS (*See* FEMALE HEALTH PROBLEMS)

BRONCHITIS

Bronchitis is a respiratory condition that is characterized by inflammation of the bronchial airways. There are two types of bronchitis—acute and chronic. Acute bronchitis is characterized by deep, dry, or wet cough that tends to resolve within one to two weeks. Acute bronchitis usually results from a cold, flu, or, in some cases, sinusitis, although it can also develop due to exposure to bacterial or viral infection or from exposure to chemical irritants.

Chronic bronchitis typically occurs without exposure to infectious agents, and can often develop as a progression of acute bronchitis. It can linger for months or recur on a regular basis. In addition to coughing, chronic bronchitis can also be accompanied by wheezing and sensations of breathlessness.

Both acute and chronic bronchitis symptoms include deep, dry, or wet cough and inflammation of the bronchial airways. Other symptoms include chills, fever, excessive production of mucus, and the frequent need to expectorate phlegm and sputum. Both forms of bronchitis can also result in diminished immune function, leading to greater susceptibility to other conditions, including infections and pneumonia. Because of this, all cases of chronic bronchitis should be treated by a holistic health care professional.

JUICING RECIPES

• From Dr. Ralph Weiss: Use 1 teaspoon horseradish, 1 teaspoon fresh lemon juice, and 1 ½ teaspoons best virgin olive oil. Mix well. It's hot, so take small amounts slowly. Best taken after meals, when mucus develops.

• Juice 4 medium carrots, 4 celery stalks, 2 garlic cloves, and ⅛ ounce turmeric. Makes 16 ounces. Consume once to twice daily.

• Juice 2 medium lemons, 1 medium orange, 4 ounces pineapple, and consider 1 tablespoon noni juice.
Makes 8 ounces. Consume once to twice daily.

• Juice 3 medium carrots, 1 bunch parsley, 2 garlic cloves, and 1 medium cucumber. Makes 12 ounces. Consume once daily.

HEALTHY TWIST

❧ Consider adding rosemary leaves, basil, and teas of slippery elm or licorice to the above recipes for additional health benefits.

BRUISES

Bruises or contusions refer to marks on the skin. Typically, bruise marks are dark blue or black. Bruises form as a result of blood leaking out of small blood vessels known as capillaries. The blood then collects in small pools underneath the skin. Usually, this blood leakage is due to accidents or injury, but bruises can also be due to nutritional deficiencies, especially of vitamin C and bioflavonoids. In some cases, however, bruises can indicate a bleeding disorder, in which case prompt medical attention is required. The following juices are excellent remedies to help prevent bruising and to speed recovery time when bruising has already occurred.

JUICING RECIPES

• Juice 4 medium carrots with 1 medium beet.
Makes 12 ounces. Consume once daily.

• Juice 2 medium oranges, 2 medium lemons, and 1 teaspoon acerola cherry powder (or 2 ounces of frozen cherries). Makes 10 ounces. Consume once to twice daily. (An excellent source of frozen acerola is available through a company called Sambazon. For more information, visit www.sambazon.com.)

● Juice 3 medium carrots, 2 burdock roots, 2 garlic cloves, and 1 bunch spinach. Makes 12 ounces. Consume once daily.

● Juice 2 medium apples, 3 medium carrots, and add 2 ounces ginger root or 1 teaspoon cinnamon. Makes 14 ounces. Consume once to twice daily.

BURNS

Burns are caused by exposure to the skin to fire or hot or extreme cold temperatures. Burns are categorized according to their severity. The least severe category of burns is known as first-degree burns. Such burns only affect the top layer of the skin, known as the epidermis, and are characterized by reddened skin that peels away after several days, and which normally heals quickly. Second-degree burns are more severe and usually result in blistering of the skin due to damage below the epidermis. In most cases, however, second-degree burns heal without scarring.

The most severe category is third-degree burns, in which serious skin damage occurs. Often the skin appears charred, or the skin may be burned away to reveal muscle and bone tissue. Third-degree burns require the immediate attention of a burn specialist.

Proper nutrition is essential for full recovery from burns. Since fresh-squeezed juices supply a wide range of nutrients, including essential enzymes, juicing can often help to speed healing. The following juice recipes are particularly helpful for helping to treat burns.

JUICING RECIPES

● Juice 2 medium carrots, $\frac{1}{4}$ medium cantaloupe, and $\frac{1}{2}$ cup currants. Makes 10 ounces. Consume once to twice daily.

● Juice 4 medium carrots, 1 medium beet, and 1 medium cucumber. Makes 16 ounces. Consume once daily.

● Juice 3 medium carrots, 1 bunch cilantro, 1 medium cucumber, and $\frac{1}{2}$ cup peppermint leaves. Makes 12 ounces. Consume once daily.

HEALTHY TWIST

🐛 Consider adding aloe juice ($\frac{1}{4}$ cup) and 1–2 ounces wheatgrass juice to any of the above juices. (See Wheatgrass Juice inset on page 146.) Aloe vera gel can also be applied topically.

BURSITIS

Bursitis is a health condition that is caused when one or more bursa in the body develop inflammation. A bursa is a cavity that is shaped like a small sac. Bursae (the plural form of bursa) are part of the connective tissue surrounding the joints. They are responsible for secreting lubricating fluids in order to reduce friction between tendons and bone, and tendons and ligaments, as joints move. Bursitis can be acute or chronic. In addition to localized pain and tenderness in the area of the affected bursa, swelling and skin reddening can also occur. Normal range of motion within the joint can also be affected, resulting in limited or "frozen" movement. The joints that are most susceptible to bursitis are those of the elbows, hips, and shoulders. Although many cases of bursitis are due to misalignment of, or physical trauma to, the joints, nutritional deficiencies (especially magnesium) and chronic inflammation can also cause or contribute to the condition. When the latter factors are involved, juicing can be helpful in treating bursitis.

JUICING RECIPES

• Juice 2 medium carrots, 2 celery stalks, $1/2$ medium cucumber, $1/2$ medium beet, and add $1/4$ ounce turmeric and $1/8$–$1/4$ ounce ginger. Makes 12 ounces. Consume once daily.

• Juice 4 medium carrots, 3 celery stalks, 1 medium beet, and 2 garlic cloves. Makes 16 ounces. Consume once daily.

• Juice 8 ounces black cherries, 2 medium apples, and add 1 tablespoon noni juice. Makes 12 ounces. Consume once to twice daily.

CADMIUM POISONING (*See also* HEAVY METAL TOXICITY)

Cadmium is one of the few mineral elements that have no healthy purpose in the body. It is extremely toxic, even in low doses. Unfortunately, for more than half a century, cadmium use by various industries has led to high levels of cadmium residues in our air, water, and land. Cadmium is often found in the phosphate compounds that are part of commercial fertilizers. This has caused cadmium to increasingly been found in commercially grown food crops.

Although the amount of cadmium levels in food is relatively low, animals that are fed such crops have been found to have high concentrations of cadmium in their kidneys and livers. (This fact alone is a compelling reason to avoid eating non-organic foods, as well as meats and poultry that are derived from animals raised and slaughtered in commercial "factory" farms.) Cadmium is also a component of cigarettes, and is released in the smoke. This is another reason why secondhand exposure to cigarettes is unhealthy.

Because of these and other factors related to the release of cadmium into our environment, it is not surprising that the incidence of low-grade cadmium poisoning is on the rise in the populations of industrialized nations. Over time, the buildup of cadmium residues in the body can result in a variety of health symptoms. These include respiratory problems, muscle aches, chills, fever, dizziness, headache, coughs, chest pain, and an impaired sense of smell. Kidney and liver damage, as well as the complete failure of these organs, can also occur, as can a loss of bone mass, leading to osteoporosis and arthritic symptoms. Gout can also be related to cadmium poisoning. Juicing is recommended for cadmium poisoning, as well as for all other types of environmental poisoning, due to the detoxification properties juices possess. The following juices are particularly useful in this regard.

JUICING RECIPES

- Juice 3 medium carrots, 2 celery stalks, 1/4 bunch parsley, 1/4 bunch cilantro, and 1/2 medium cucumber. Makes 14 ounces. Consume once daily.

- Juice 3 medium carrots, 1 medium beet, 2 burdock roots, and 1/2 medium black radish. Makes 14 ounces. Consume once daily.

- Juice 2 medium apples, 8 ounces pineapple, 4 ounces cranberries, and 1 medium pear. Makes 16 ounces. Consume once to twice daily.

HEALTHY TWIST

❦ Consider supplementing with zinc (100–200 mg) and niacin (50–500 mg, until skin flushing occurs; start with a low dose) to further enhance detoxification.

CANCER

Cancer is the term given to a wide range of conditions that occur when normal, healthy cells in the body cease to function and mature properly. As cells stop functioning correctly and no longer progress to their natural cell death, they begin to mutate and multiply uncontrollably. In the process, cancer cells act as parasites within the body, diverting energy and sustenance (nutrients) from healthy cells, to the detriment of the body and its organ systems. If this process is not reversed, eventually cancer cells form into cancerous tumors. Ultimately, cancer cells metastasize, meaning that they break off from localized tumors to spread throughout other areas of the body to form other tumor masses.

Two of the most potent contributing factors to cancer are environmental toxins and poor diet. Poor diet alone is estimated to cause over one-third of all cancer cases in the United States each year, according to the National Cancer Institute (NCI). For this reason, the NCI now recommends that we eat at least five to nine servings of fruits and vegetables each day.

Juicing provides a variety of anti-cancer benefits. These include the ability of the various nutrients juices contain to neutralize toxic substances known as carcinogens, which act as triggers for cancer. A particular class of nutrients, known as *anutrients,* act as blocking agents that help to prevent carcinogens from reaching and interfering with healthy cells and tissues. Anutrients are found in high concentrations in a variety of vegetables, such as broccoli, cabbage, cauliflower, garlic, kale, leeks, and onions, as well as in certain fruits, such as grapefruit, lemons, and oranges. The juices from such fruits and vegetables provide excellent anti-cancer benefits.

Another reason why fresh-squeezed juices can be helpful for preventing and reversing cancer has to do with the detoxification properties they contain. This aspect of juicing helps the body to rid itself of toxins and other unhealthy substances that can cause and exacerbate cancer. In today's increasingly toxic world, the benefits of detoxification cannot be overemphasized.

Still another benefit that fresh-squeezed juices provide is immune enhancement. A healthy immune system is essential for both fighting cancer and for preventing the onset of cancer in the first place. Even in a healthy state, our bodies create hundreds of thousands of cancer cells each and every day. Under normal circumstances, a healthy immune system is able to target and eliminate these cells, ensuring that no harm is caused to the body. When immunity becomes impaired, however, increasing numbers of cancer cells are able to escape detection by natural killer (NK) cells and other cells of the immune system, making it easier for cancer to gain a foothold in the body.

One area of potential confusion regarding cancer and juicing has to do with the sugar content of juices. It is well known that cancer cells thrive on certain types of sugar. Therefore, while it is true that people with cancer should eliminate their consumption of white sugar, high sugar foods, and canned juices, we do not feel that this restriction applies to fresh-squeezed juices for the reasons discussed above, as well as the fact that the abundant supply of vitamins, minerals, and enzymes found in fresh juices act together as powerful anti-cancer agents.

JUICING RECIPES

- Juice 4 medium carrots, 1 medium beet (roots and tops), 2 garlic cloves, and 2 ounces wheatgrass. Makes 16–18 ounces. Consume once daily.

- Juice 1 cup fresh raw cabbage and 4 medium carrots. Especially for gastric and colon cancers. Makes 14 ounces. Consume once to twice daily.

- Juice ½ cup grapes, ¼ cup black cherries, and ¼ cup black currants. You can also add 1 medium apple. Makes 10 ounces. Consume once to twice daily.

- Drink wheatgrass juice. Consume 2-4 ounces daily. (See inset on page 146.)

- Juice 4 medium carrots and 4 sprigs of asparagus. Makes 10 ounces. Consume once daily.

- Juice 1 medium apple, 3–4 medium carrots, and 3 celery stalks. Makes 16 ounces. Consume once to twice daily.

- Juice 1 medium apple, ⅓ medium papaya, 4 ounces pineapple, and add 1 tablespoon noni juice. Makes 10 ounces. Consume once to twice daily.

CANDIDIASIS (SYSTEMIC YEAST OVERGROWTH)

Candidiasis, also known as systemic *Candida albicans* infection, is an increasingly common health condition characterized by unhealthy and systemic overgrowth in the body of a yeast called *Candida albicans*. *Candida albicans* is present in almost everyone to some extent in the lower gastrointestinal tract and, in women, the vagina. When the body is healthy, it is kept in check by the immune system and naturally occurring, healthy bacteria in the lower intestine, such as acidophilus and bifidobacteria. Disruptions in the population of healthy bacteria in the gut enable *Candida albicans* to pass beyond the lower intestine to travel through the intestinal walls, where it enters into the bloodstream. As this occurs, the yeast begins to mutate, transforming itself into a harmful fungus that infects body tissues and organs, creating a wide variety of health problems. This condition is known as candidiasis.

Symptoms of candidiasis can vary widely. They include allergies, anxiety and depression, chronic fatigue, cognition problems, earache, fungal infections, gastrointestinal problems, headache, accelerated heartbeat, hives and rashes, mood swings, respiratory problems, sexual dysfunctions (including loss of libido), skin problems, and vaginitis. Candidiasis can also impair the healthy functions of the body's organs, including the heart and liver, as well as interfere with the functioning of the central nervous system. It can also compromise immune function and exacerbate various autoimmune disorders and diseases, including AIDS and cancer.

Juicing—along with an anti-candidiasis diet that eliminates processed foods, as well as foods that are high in sugars and simple carbohydrates—can significant improve, and eventually eliminate, candidiasis. Juices deliver excellent nutritional benefits that can help to repair impaired digestion caused by candidiasis, while also improving immune function and helping the body to detoxify. The key is to always add 1–3 cloves of garlic to the vegetable juices that are used. Excellent fruit juice choices include blueberry, pineapple, papaya, and noni.

JUICING RECIPES

- Juice 3 medium carrots, 3 celery stalks, and 2 garlic cloves.
Makes 12 ounces. Consume once to twice daily.

- Juice 3 medium carrots, $1/2$ medium cucumber, $1/2$ bunch cilantro, and 1–2 garlic cloves.
Makes 10 ounces. Consume once to twice daily.

- Juice 3 celery stalks, $1/4$ head cabbage, $1/4$ medium onion, and 1 medium cucumber.
Makes 12 ounces. Consume once daily.

- Juice 8 ounces pineapple, $1/2$ medium papaya, and add 2 tablespoons noni juice.
Makes 8 ounces. Consume once to twice daily.

CANKER SORES

Canker sores are painful ulcers that can form on the surface of the mouth, inner cheek, or tongue. Typically, canker sores, which can be as large as a centimeter or more in diameter, have a red surface area with a white center. The following juice remedies can help relieve canker sore symptoms and speed healing.

JUICING RECIPES

- Juice 4 medium carrots, 2 celery stalks, and $1/4$ medium cantaloupe.
Makes 16 ounces. Consume once daily.

- Juice 1 medium apple, 1 medium pear, and 8 ounces blueberries.
Makes 8–10 ounces. Consume once to twice daily.

- Juice 3 medium carrots, ¹/₂ medium beet, and ¹/₂ medium cucumber. Makes 12 ounces. Consume once to twice daily.

CONSIDERATION

■ Avoid high-acid fruits (pineapple, citrus, tomato).

CARBUNCLES

Carbuncles are a class of boils that cause an infection that spreads underneath the skin. The infectious organism is usually *Staphyloccus aureus.* Carbuncles are similar to regular boils, except that they develop more slowly and tend to occur over a larger area. They are extremely painful, swollen, and red, and may be accompanied by general feelings of fatigue, debilitation, and fever. Generally, they also contain a copious amount of pus. The most common areas of the body where carbuncles can form are the nape of the neck, buttocks, or the thighs. Because of the various ways in which fresh-squeezed juices support the body's immune system, which is the first line of defense against infection, juicing can do much to relieve carbuncle symptoms. Excellent juice remedies include the following.

JUICING RECIPES

- Juice 4 medium carrots, ¹/₂ medium beet, 3 celery stalks, and 2 garlic cloves. Makes 16 ounces. Consume once daily.

- Juice 3 medium carrots, 1 bunch parsley, 1–2 ounces wheatgrass juice, 1 medium cucumber, and 6–8 leaves of yellow dock. (See Wheatgrass Juice inset on page 146.) Makes 16 ounces. Consume once daily.

- Juice 8 ounces pineapple, ¹/₂ medium papaya, 1 medium pear, and add 1 tablespoon noni juice. Makes 10 ounces. Consume once to twice daily.

CARDIOMYOPATHY

Cardiomyopathy, a weakness of the heart muscle, is the name given to describe disease in the primary muscles of the heart, especially the myocardium. Symptoms of cardiomyopathy can vary widely, ranging from chest pain, dizziness, and fatigue, to arrhythmia and congestive heart failure. Although many cases of cardiomyopathy prove to be benign, in other cases the disease can result in sudden death, especially during times of physical exertion or exercise. All people with cardiomyopathy should seek immediate medical attention. To help improve symptoms related to cardiomyopathy, the following juice recipes can be helpful.

JUICING RECIPES

• Juice 4 medium carrots, 1 medium cucumber, $^1/_2$ bunch spinach, $^1/_4$ head lettuce, $^1/_4$ pound alfalfa sprouts, and 2 garlic cloves.
Makes 20 ounces. Consume once daily.

• Juice 8 ounces blueberries, 4 ounces cranberries, 8 ounces pomegranate, and $^1/_2$–1 cup pitted hawthorn berries.
Makes 12 ounces. Consume once to twice daily.

• Juice 3 medium carrots, 1 bunch parsley, 2 garlic cloves, and add 2 ounces wheatgrass juice. (See Wheatgrass Juice inset on page 146.)
Makes 12 ounces. Consume once daily.

• Juice 4 medium carrots, $^1/_4$ medium onion, 3 celery stalks, and add $^1/_2$ tablespoon flax oil.
Makes 16 ounces. Consume once daily.

HEALTHY TWIST

🌿 Cayenne pepper can also be added to all of the above juice recipes, as well as used as a seasoning with meals, including soups.

CELLULITE

Although not a disease, cellulite is of concern for many people—especially women, who are more apt to develop cellulite than men are—because of the unsightly dimples that it causes to form on the body, most noticeably on the buttocks. Cellulite can also affect the arms, knees, stomach, and thighs. Such dimpling occurs due to a breakdown in the body's lymphatic system, which results in a buildup of waste by-products in the spaces between the cells, along with an increase in the body's overall percentage of body fat compared to lean muscle mass. Because juicing provides excellent benefits for the lymphatic system, and can also be useful for reducing overall body fat, it is an excellent self-care remedy for preventing and reversing cellulite buildup.

JUICING RECIPES

• Juice 1 medium beet, 3 medium carrots, 1 medium black radish, 2 burdock roots, and 1–2 garlic cloves. **Makes 14 ounces. Consume once daily.**

• Juice 3 medium carrots, 8 ounces Jerusalem artichoke, 2 garlic cloves, and $^1/_2$ bunch parsley. **Makes 12 ounces. Consume once to twice daily.**

• Juice 8 ounces cantaloupe, $^1/_2$ medium papaya, 3 medium lemons, and 4 ounces cranberries. **Makes 12 ounces. Consume once to twice daily.**

CELLULITIS

Cellulitis is a disease characterized by inflammation of the body's connective tissues due to bacterial infections. Typically, cellulitis results when inflammation that occurs as a natural response to a localized skin infection spreads beyond the infected area into other tissues. Areas of the skin affected by cellulitis appear red and swollen and usually feel hot and tender to touch. The most common areas of the body where cellulitis occur are on the lower legs and on the face, but it can potentially occur anywhere. Because cellulitis can spread rapidly, and also penetrate beneath the skin to affect underlying tissues and potentially spread into the bloodstream and the lymphatic system, it is a potentially serious, and in some cases, life-threatening condition, and therefore requires immediate medical attention.

While not a cure for cellulitis, juicing can help to relieve symptoms and boost the body's immune response as it deals with the associated bacterial infection. Useful juice remedies for cellulitis include the following.

JUICING RECIPES

• Juice 3 medium carrots, 1–2 garlic cloves, 1 ounce turmeric root, and 1 medium cucumber. Makes 12 ounces. Consume once to twice daily.

• Juice 4 medium carrots, ½ medium beet, 2 garlic cloves, and 6–8 leaves yellow dock. Makes 12 ounces. Consume once daily.

• Juice 3 medium carrots, 3 celery stalks, and 1 ounce turmeric root. Makes 12 ounces. Consume once daily.

CHICKENPOX (*See also* SHINGLES)

Chickenpox, also called varicella (after the varicella-zoster virus), is a highly contagious and common childhood health condition, but it can also affect adults who were spared chickenpox as children. In children, chickenpox is generally a mild condition characterized by a low-grade fever and rash of blisters. It is most contagious on the day before the rash breaks out. Once the rash breaks out, blisters appear over the course of four to five days that are extremely itchy. In most cases, chickenpox will run its course within a week of its onset, and younger children usually experience milder symptoms compared to older children. In adults, exposure to chickenpox can result in shingles, which can be more painful and more difficult to treat.

JUICING RECIPES

- Juice 3 medium oranges with 2 medium lemons.
Makes 12 ounces. Consume once daily.

- Juice 4 medium carrots and $1/2$ bunch watercress during acute stage.
Makes 12 ounces. Consume once daily.

- Juice 2 medium apples, 8 ounces blueberries, and add 1 tablespoon noni juice. Makes 10 ounces. Consume once daily.

CHRONIC FATIGUE SYNDROME (CFS)

CFS (also known as chronic fatigue immune dysfunction syndrome, or CFIDS) is a complex disease condition characterized by severe and often debilitating fatigue and muscle pain and/or muscle weakness. An overriding symptom of CFS is constant fatigue that does not improve with rest or sleep, and which is made worse even by minor activity. Other symptoms of CFS can include allergic reactions, anxiety attacks, breathing problems, depression, digestion problems, dizziness, headache, heightened sensitivity to cold and heat as well as light and sound, irregular heartbeat, low grade fever, memory problems, night sweats, rash, recurring infections, and swollen lymph glands.

One of the keys to successfully treating CFS is to rid the body of any infectious agents and toxins that may be sapping the body's energy and strength. To accomplish this, both the body's immune system and its systems of detoxification and elimination must be supported. In additional, in many cases, it is important to restore proper adrenal gland function. The thyroid gland may also need support. The following juice recipes work well in aiding in the achievement of all of these tasks, and therefore are excellent self-care remedies for coping with chronic fatigue syndrome.

JUICING RECIPES

- Juice 3 medium carrots, 2 celery stalks, and add 2 ounces wheatgrass juice. (See Wheatgrass Juice inset on page 146.)
Makes 12 ounces. Consume once daily.

- Juice 3 medium carrots, 4 celery stalks, 2 garlic cloves, and $1/2$ bunch parsley. Makes 12 ounces. Consume once to twice daily.

- Juice 3 medium carrots, $1/4$ head cabbage, 1 medium cucumber, and 1–2 garlic cloves. Makes 14–16 ounces. Consume once daily.

• Juice 8 ounces blueberries, 2 medium apples, and add 1 tablespoon noni juice. Makes 10 ounces. Consume once to twice daily.

CIRRHOSIS

Cirrhosis is a term commonly used to describe various chronic liver diseases that result in abnormal changes to liver cells. These changes, in turn, cause the liver to become hardened and inflamed, leading to liver damage. The liver is responsible for carrying out over 1,500 functions in the body each day, including storing and filtering blood, producing bile to help digest fats, and transforming sugars and carbohydrates into glycogen, which the body requires for energy.

Initial symptoms of cirrhosis of the liver include constipation or diarrhea, fatigue, fever, indigestion, itches and rashes, and variations in normal stool color. As the disease progresses, additional symptoms result, such as abdominal swelling and pain, jaundice (the skin taking on a yellowish tinge), internal bleeding, and overall swelling of the body. If allowed to progress, cirrhosis can result in complete liver failure, leading to coma and death.

Cirrhosis requires ongoing professional medical attention. Juicing can be helpful because juices can aid in digestion and detoxification, as well as support many of the functions the liver is responsible for because of the many nutrients that juices contain.

JUICING RECIPES

• Juice 1 medium beet, 1 medium black radish, 2 burdock roots, and 3–4 medium carrots.
Makes 16 ounces. Consume once daily.

• Drink wheatgrass juice. Consume 1-2 ounces daily. (See inset on page 146.)

• Juice 4 ounces black cherries, 1 medium pear, 4 ounces pineapple, and add 1 tablespoon noni juice.
Makes 6–8 ounces. Consume once to twice daily.

• Juice 2 medium pears, 8 ounces blueberries, and 1/2 medium papaya.
Makes 10 ounces. Consume once to twice daily.

HEALTHY TWIST

Add raw flaxseed oil and garlic to the above recipes as tolerated to provide further benefits.

COLD / FLU (*See also* VIRAL INFECTIONS)

Colds and flu are two of the most common disease conditions, with colds affecting an estimated 50 percent of all Americans each year, while flu affects 5-20 percent of the population with 200,000 people hospitalized and about 36,000 annual deaths, according to the CDC. Both conditions have similar symptoms, but typically symptoms of flu are more severe and last longer. In some cases, flu can even result in death, especially among young children and elderly people with weakened immune systems. Common symptoms of both cold and flu include aches, coughing, fatigue, headache, runny nose, sinus congestion, sneezing, and sore throat. In cases of the flu, fever can also occur, as can diarrhea and vomiting.

Unlike conventional physicians, naturopathic physicians and other holistic health care professionals do not seek to suppress common cold and flu symptoms because they recognize that symptoms such as coughing and sneezing are actually attempts by the body to eliminate the viruses that are responsible for both conditions. When such viruses attack the body, the body's immune system responds by trapping and engulfing viruses with mucus that it then expels in the form of phlegm. Fever is another immune response that the body uses to neutralize and eliminate infectious microorganisms. Therefore, naturopaths typically allow fevers to run their course, unless body temperature exceeds 104 degrees Fahrenheit.

All of the body's healing mechanisms that come into play during times of colds and flu can be greatly assisted by drinking two or more glasses of fresh-squeezed juices each day. Excellent juice choices include the following.

JUICING RECIPES

• Juice 3 medium lemons, 1 medium orange, 2 ounces pineapple, $\frac{1}{4}$ cup black currants. You can also add some elderberry juice.
Makes 8 ounces. Consume once to twice daily.

• Juice 3 medium carrots, $\frac{1}{2}$ medium beet, 1 medium tomato, and $\frac{1}{2}$ medium green pepper. You can also add $\frac{1}{4}$ bunch watercress.
Makes 8 ounces. Consume once daily.

• Juice 4 medium carrots and 2–3 celery stalks.
Makes 12 ounces. Consume once to twice daily.

• Juice 3 medium carrots, $\frac{1}{4}$ bunch spinach, 1 medium beet, and $\frac{1}{2}$ medium cucumber. Makes 14 ounces. Consume once daily.

HEALTHY TWIST

☙ Add small doses of onion ($\frac{1}{4}$ medium size) or 2–4 garlic cloves to the above juices for additional benefits.

COLD SORES (HERPES SIMPLEX)

Cold sores are small fever blisters that form in and around the mouth. They are caused by the virus herpes simplex 1 (HSV1). Nearly everyone develops cold sores at some point in their lives. In addition to the blisters themselves, cold sores can sometimes also be accompanied by other symptoms, such as fatigue, fever, neck pain, and swollen lymph glands. One of the primary factors that can enable cold sores to develop is nutritional deficiencies, making juicing an excellent self-care remedy for preventing and reversing cold sores. The following juices are particularly useful.

JUICING RECIPES

• Juice 4 medium carrots, 4 celery stalks, $\frac{1}{2}$ bunch parsley, and 1–2 garlic cloves. Makes 16 ounces. Consume once daily.

• Juice 3 medium carrots, 1 medium black radish, $\frac{1}{2}$ bunch cilantro, and 1 medium cucumber.
Makes 14 ounces. Consume once daily.

• Juice 3 medium carrots, 1 medium beet, and 1 medium cucumber.
Makes 14 ounces. Consume once daily.

HEALTHY TWIST

☙ Also consider adding 1 ounce of *ranunculus bulbosa* (mountain buttercup or St. Anthony's turnip—use the greens) to the above recipe. This is one of the under-appreciated eclectic herbal treatments both topically and internally for herpes 1 and 2.

CONSIDERATION

■ Avoid citrus, pineapple, and all nuts, and consider supplementing with 1,000 mg of the amino acid lysine one to two times daily.

COLIC

Colic is a common health condition among newborn babies. In most cases, newborns affected by colic will experience it sometime between the third week and the third month of their young lives. The primary symptom of colic is crying that lasts for two to three hours a day and which occurs for no apparent reason. The following juices can help soothe babies afflicted with colic, and can be administered via a bottle.

JUICING RECIPES

- Juice $\frac{1}{2}$ cup cherries, 1 medium apple, and $\frac{1}{2}$ ounce ginger root.
Makes 8 ounces. Consume once daily.

- Juice 1 medium apple, 1 medium pear, and add $\frac{1}{4}$ teaspoon cinnamon.
Makes 6 ounces. Consume once to twice daily.

- Juice 2 medium carrots, 1 medium apple, and $\frac{1}{2}$ ounce ginger root.
Makes 8 ounces. Consume once daily.

COLITIS

Colitis is a condition of the colon that is characterized by inflammation, as well as abdominal pain, diarrhea, flatulence and, in some cases, fever. It is primarily caused by lack of fiber in the diet, poor eating habits, poor diet, nutritional deficiencies, and food allergies. The following juices can be helpful for reversing and preventing colitis.

JUICING RECIPES

- Juice 3 medium carrots, $\frac{1}{4}$ head cabbage, 1–2 garlic cloves, and 2 celery stalks.
Makes 16 ounces. Consume once daily.

- Juice $\frac{1}{4}$ head cabbage, 1 medium papaya, 2–3 medium carrots, and add 2 ounces wheatgrass juice. (See Wheatgrass Juice inset on page 146.)
Makes 20 ounces. Consume once daily.

- Juice $\frac{1}{2}$ small head cabbage, 8 ounces broccoli, and $\frac{1}{2}$ medium beet.
Makes 8 ounces. Consume one to three times daily.

- Juice 8 ounces blueberries, $\frac{1}{2}$ medium papaya, and 1 medium apple.
Makes 10 ounces. Consume once to twice daily.

HEALTHY TWIST

🌱 Drink juice of $\frac{1}{2}$ medium lemon with warm water each morning, followed by: carrot and apple or carrot, beet, and cucumber juice (8 ounces).

🌱 Aloe vera added to the above juices, or to 8 ounces of filtered water, can also be helpful.

CONSIDERATION

■ Avoid citrus juices.

CONSTIPATION

Constipation is one of the most common gastrointestinal problems in the United States. In addition to sluggish bowels and infrequent elimination, other symptoms of constipation include fatigue, flatulence, hemorrhoids, and stomach upset. Headaches can also occur with constipation. In some cases, blood in the stool and rectal bleeding can also occur, both of which require immediate medical attention.

Like many other gastrointestinal conditions, constipation is largely due to poor eating habits, poor diet, nutritional deficiencies, and dehydration (lack of sufficient water intake throughout the day). Other potential causes include food allergies, environmental toxins, low thyroid function (see hypothyroidism, page 199), and the overuse of laxatives as well as pharmaceutical drugs.

The following juice combinations are all excellent for preventing and relieving constipation.

JUICING RECIPES

- Juice 3 medium carrots, 1/2 medium beet, and 3 celery stalks with 1 teaspoon garlic or yellow onion juice.

Makes 14 ounces. Consume once daily.

- Juice 3 medium carrots, 1 medium apple, and 1 medium lemon.

Makes 12 ounces. Consume once to twice daily.

- Juice 3 medium carrots, 2 celery stalks, and 1/4–1/2 bunch spinach.

Makes 12 ounces. Consume once daily.

HEALTHY TWIST

For cases of chronic constipation, add one or more of the following: 1–2 garlic cloves, 1/8–1/4 yellow onion, 1 black radish, 1/2 bunch spinach, 1/2–1 bunch watercress, or 2–4 ounces fresh dandelion root to carrot, beet, celery, cabbage, cucumber, and tomato juice (equal parts or as taste decides).

COUGHS

Coughs are usually caused by the need to expel something from the air passages. Productive coughing brings up mucus, while an unproductive, dry cough does not.

If coughing becomes persistent, seek prompt medical attention, as this may be a sign of a more serious underlying health problem. The following juices can help to relieve cough symptoms.

JUICING RECIPES

● Juice 4 medium carrots, $^{1}/_{4}$ bunch lettuce, 1 garlic clove, and 2 celery stalks. Makes 14 ounces. Consume once to twice daily.

● Juice 3 medium lemons with 1 medium orange.
Makes 6 ounces. Consume two to three times daily.

HEALTHY TWIST

🌢 Hot pear juice with cinnamon stick. You can also add cardamom and cumin to any of the above juices.

CONSIDERATION

▦ Avoid or limit wheat and dairy products.

CYST

A cyst is a growth below the surface of the skin. Typically, cysts are soft and filled with a whitish-brown material that can sometimes ooze onto the skin surface. Most types of cysts are harmless (benign) and do not require medical treatment. However, in cases of large cysts, surgery is sometimes recommended to remove them. Medical treatment may also be advised if cysts become infected (usually by bacteria). In women, cysts in the breasts and ovaries should be monitored by a health professional to rule out breast and ovarian cancer. The following juice remedies can help to prevent and reverse cysts that are noncancerous.

JUICING RECIPES

● Juice 3 medium carrots, 2 burdock roots, $^{1}/_{2}$ medium cucumber, and 2 garlic cloves. Makes 12 ounces. Consume once daily.

● Juice 4 medium carrots, 1 medium black radish, $^{1}/_{2}$ medium cucumber, and 1 ounce turmeric root. Makes 12 ounces. Consume once to twice daily.

● Juice 3 medium carrots, 1 medium beet, 1 bunch parsley, 2 celery stalks, and 1–2 garlic cloves. Makes 16 ounces. Consume once daily.

CYSTITIS

Cystitis, also known as bladder infection or urinary tract infection, is characterized by irritation anywhere within the urinary tract, from the urethra all the way to the end of the bladder lining. It most often occurs in women who are sexually active and women who have entered into menopause, and in many cases can be chronic and recurring. Symptoms of cystitis include pain or burning sensations during urination, more frequent than normal urination, and pain located in the lower back and/or over the pubic region. If left untreated, cystitis can affect the kidneys. When this happens, additional symptoms can include blood in the urine, chills, fever, nausea, vomiting, back pain, and pain in the loins. All cases of cystitis should be monitored by a physician in order to avoid the onset of more serious problems.

Because of their ability to improve the overall health of the urinary tract, including ridding it of potentially infectious microorganisms that can cause irritation, the following juices are recommended for cystitis.

JUICING RECIPES

- Juice 3 medium carrots, 1 medium cucumber, $1/2$ bunch parsley, and 1–2 garlic cloves. **Makes 12 ounces. Consume twice daily.**

- Juice 8 ounces cranberries, 2 medium pears, and add 1 tablespoon noni juice. **Makes 8 ounces. Consume once to twice daily.**

- Juice 12 ounces watermelon and 2 medium pears.
Makes 10 ounces. Consume once to twice daily.

CONSIDERATION

■ Drink 8–12 glasses of pure water daily.

DEMENTIA

Dementia is a disorder of the brain that has become increasingly common in the last half century among Americans as they age. Among the many reasons for the rise in cases of dementia is the lack of nutrition found in today's standard American diet. (In cultures around the world that eat plentiful supplies of fresh fruits and vegetables, along with whole-grain foods, wild-caught fish, and other healthy foods, dementia and other brain disorders are rare.)

Dementia is a serious condition, with symptoms that can be similar to Alzheimer's disease. Symptoms can range from depression, fatigue, forgetfulness, and memory loss to disorientation and aggressive or paranoid behavior. In some cases, people suffering from dementia also lose their ability to speak clearly and comprehend vocabulary and words, and experience problems understanding numbers. They can also feel disoriented in terms of time and space.

Because of the abundant supply of nutrients that fresh-squeezed juices can deliver to the brain, juicing can be of benefit to people with dementia. In addition, juices can improve the health of the arteries, thereby helping to ensure proper blood and oxygen supply to the brain. Juicing is by no means a cure for dementia, however, and people who suffer from it should seek prompt medical attention so that all of the causes of their condition are determined and properly dealt with.

JUICING RECIPES

• Juice 3 medium carrots, 1 medium beet, 3 celery stalks, 1/4 bunch cilantro, and 1–2 garlic cloves. Makes 16 ounces. Consume once daily.

• Juice 8 ounces blueberries, 8 ounces black grapes, and 2 pears. Makes 12 ounces. Consume once to twice daily.

• Juice 3 medium carrots, 1/2 bunch watercress, 3 celery stalks, and 1 garlic clove. Makes 12 ounces. Consume once daily.

HEALTHY TWIST

🌿 Dr. Bailey's Power Smoothie can also be helpful (See Chapter 6, page 96).

🌿 Also consider supplementing with 1/4 cup ginkgo berries or 1–2 capsules, 1–2 teaspoons DHLA and 50–100 mg zinc, lecithin, phosphatidyl choline, or phosphatidyl serine (2 caps).

DEPRESSION

Depression is an emotional disorder that is becoming increasingly common in the United States in recent years. Although all of us are susceptible to temporary feelings of depression from time to time, which usually quickly resolve themselves, chronic depression is far more serious, and in some cases even life-threatening. Symptoms of chronic depression vary, and can include ongoing feelings of despair, fear, grief, hopelessness, panic, and a lack of self-worth. Physical symptoms are also common, such as accelerated heartbeat, high blood pressure, and gastrointestinal problems. In some cases, chronic depression can lead to suicide.

Although depression is considered to be a condition related to emotions, nutritional deficiencies and an excess of internal toxins can also be a major contributing factor. For this reason, regularly drinking fresh-squeezed juices that are abundant in a wide range of nutrients can be helpful in relieving symptoms of depression.

JUICING RECIPES

• Juice 3–4 medium carrots, 3 celery stalks, 1/4 bunch lettuce, 1/4 bunch parsley, and 1/4 cup hypericum flowers (commonly referred to as St. John's Wort). Makes 16 ounces. Consume once daily.

- Juice 1 medium apple, 4 ounces pineapple, and add 1 tablespoon noni juice. Makes 6 ounces. Consume once to twice daily.

- Juice 3 medium carrots, 2 medium apples, and 1 medium pear. Makes 16 ounces. Consume once to twice daily.

DERMATITIS

Dermatitis is a general term that is used to describe several types of skin disorders that are characterized by inflammation of the skin's upper layer. The most common symptoms of dermatitis are flaking, itching, scaling, and thickening of the skin. Crusts can also form on the skin, further exacerbating symptoms.

One of the factors involved in dermatitis is over-acidity in the body. By restoring proper acid-alkaline balance, many cases of dermatitis will naturally resolve themselves. The following juices are all useful for helping to maintain proper acid-alkaline balance, and therefore are recommended for people who suffer from dermatitis.

JUICING RECIPES

- Juice 3 medium carrots, $\frac{1}{2}$ medium beet, $\frac{1}{2}$ medium cucumber, and 2 celery stalks.
Makes 14 ounces. Consume once to twice daily.

- Juice 2 medium carrots, 2 celery stalks, and 1 medium apple.
Makes 12 ounces. Consume once daily.

- Juice $\frac{1}{2}$ medium cantaloupe, and add 2 tablespoons of seabuckthorn (*hippophae rhamnoides*). (An excellent source of seabuckthorn is available at the following website: www.sibu.com.)
Makes 12 ounces. Consume once to twice daily.

DIABETES

Diabetes (diabetes mellitus) is a degenerative disease that is caused by the body's inability to produce an adequate supply of insulin or, in some cases, no insulin at all (Type I diabetes) or by insulin resistance, a condition in which the cells of the body resist insulin's attempts to regulate blood sugar levels (Type II diabetes). Insulin is a hormone manufactured by the pancreas. Among its functions in the body is the metabolism of glucose, a type of sugar that is one of the cells' main sources of energy. In both types of diabetes, proper regulation of blood sugar is disrupted, leading to chronic elevated blood sugar levels. Both types of diabetes can also result in disruptions in the body's ability to metabolize carbohydrates, fats, and proteins.

Type I diabetes is primarily a condition that occurs in childhood, which is why it is sometimes referred to as juvenile diabetes. It is primarily triggered by defective genes that cause pancreatic function to become impaired. It can also be caused by viral infections that damage the cells of the pancreas. Type II diabetes, on the other hand, is largely a consequence of the standard American diet, with its high sugar content and poor overall nutritional value, along with a sedentary lifestyle and the increasing tendency of Americans to be overweight or obese. Of the two types of diabetes, Type II is far more prevalent, accounting for over 90 percent of all cases of diabetes in the United States.

People with diabetes are advised not to eat foods that are high in sugar and simple carbohydrates. Such foods rank high on what is known as the glycemic index, a measurement of the sugar and simple carbohydrate content. Interestingly, many vegetables, such as carrots, have a higher glycemic index when they are cooked than do the fresh juices that can be prepared from them. Because of this fact, certain juices, such as the ones listed below, can be very helpful for managing diabetes symptoms, especially those related to Type II diabetes. For additional benefit, Dr. Bailey also recommends the Power Smoothie he developed (see Chapter 6, page 96). A number of his patients with Type II diabetes were able to totally reverse their condition within two months, by juicing, following a sensible diet, and making the Power Smoothie a part of their daily routine.

JUICING RECIPES

- Juice 1 cup string beans, $\frac{1}{4}$ cup parsley, $\frac{1}{2}$ medium cucumber, 2–3 celery stalks, and $\frac{1}{4}$ cup watercress.
Makes 10 ounces. Consume once daily.

- Juice 3 medium carrots, 2 celery stalks, $\frac{1}{4}$ bunch parsley, and $\frac{1}{4}$ bunch spinach.
Makes 12 ounces. Consume once daily.

- Juice $\frac{1}{4}$ head lettuce, $\frac{1}{4}$ bunch spinach, 2 medium carrots, 2 medium Jerusalem artichokes, and 1–2 garlic cloves.
Makes 10 ounces. Sip one glass three times daily.

DIARRHEA

Diarrhea is a common health problem that afflicts nearly everyone at some time in their lives. Typical diarrhea symptoms are loose, watery stools and a frequent need to go to the bathroom. Abdominal cramps and pain, as well as flatulence, can also occur. Although most cases of diarrhea are not serious, diarrhea that lasts for more than a few days may be an indication of a more serious health problem, and therefore should be attended to by a physician.

Juicing is an excellent remedy for diarrhea for a variety of reasons. In addition to the many nutrients that juices contain that help to improve overall gastrointestinal health, juices can also help to prevent and reverse the dehydration that can occur during bouts of diarrhea, as well as replacing salts in the body known as electrolytes that are often flushed from the body when diarrhea strikes.

JUICING RECIPES

- Juice 3 medium carrots with 1 medium apple.
Makes 12 ounces. Consume once to twice daily.

- Juice 2–3 medium carrots, 3 celery stalks, and 1 medium apple.
Makes 14 ounces. Consume once daily.

- Juice 2 medium carrots, 3 celery stalks, and 1/4 head cabbage.
Makes 12 ounces. Consume once to twice daily.

- Juice 1 medium papaya, 1 medium apple, 2 medium lemons, and 4 ounces pineapple.
Makes 16 ounces. Consume once daily.

DIVERTICULITIS

Diverticulitis is an intestinal disorder that is characterized by balloon-like sacs or pouches that extend out from the intestinal walls, which are affected by chronic inflammation. Symptoms of diverticulitis include abdominal pain (which can often be severe and be mistaken for appendicitis), constipation, and mucus in the stools. The primary cause of diverticulitis is a poor diet that lacks fresh fruits and vegetables and other foods rich in fibers. In cultures around the world where such foods make up the traditional diet, diverticulitis is extremely rare. Juicing is therefore an excellent self-care remedy for both preventing and reversing diverticulitis. Especially useful juices for this purpose include the following.

JUICING RECIPES

• Juice 3 medium carrots, $\frac{1}{4}$ head cabbage, 3 celery stalks, and 1–2 garlic cloves. Makes 16 ounces. Consume once daily.

• Juice 3 medium carrots, $\frac{1}{2}$ medium beet, and 3 celery stalks.
Makes 14 ounces. Consume once to twice daily.

• Juice 8 ounces blueberries, 2 medium pears, 1 ounce ginger, and add 1 tablespoon noni juice. Makes 8 ounces. Consume once to twice daily.

ECZEMA

Eczema is a skin disorder characterized by inflammation of the skin that is usually accompanied by blisters, reddish bumps, itching, scaling, and swelling of the affected skin area. In some cases, crusting and oozing can also occur.

As with dermatitis (see page 178), one of the factors involved in eczema is over-acidity in the body. By restoring proper acid-alkaline balance, many cases of eczema will naturally resolve on their own. The following juices are all useful for helping to maintain proper acid-alkaline balance, and therefore are recommended for people who suffer from eczema.

JUICING RECIPES

• Juice 1 cup black currants and 1 cup red grapes, and consider adding 2 tablespoons of seabuckthorn.
Makes 12-14 ounces. Consume once daily.

• Juice 3 medium carrots, $\frac{1}{2}$ medium beet, $\frac{1}{4}$ bunch spinach, $\frac{1}{2}$ cucumber, and $\frac{1}{4}$–$\frac{1}{2}$ bunch parsley.
Makes 14 ounces. Consume once daily.

HEALTHY TWIST

😺 Green juices made from any combination of green vegetables (8–16 ounces), and wheatgrass juice (1–2 ounces, one to two times a day) can also be helpful. (See Wheatgrass Juice inset on page 146.)

EDEMA

Edema refers to the abnormal buildup of fluids in the body. Typically, these fluids, which are composed primarily of salt and water, begin to pool in the spaces between the cells. Most commonly, this fluid buildup occurs in the extremities, but edema can occur anywhere in the body, including in the brain, as well as along the spine, knees, and in the lungs. Symptoms of edema include bloating and swelling of the affected area of the body, puffy and stretched skin, and, in some cases, unhealthy weight gain due to fluid retention.

Edema is caused by a variety of factors, including poor diet and nutritional imbalances, as well as impaired function of the lymphatic system. Fresh-squeezed juices can help correct such imbalances in the body due to the rich supply of nutrients they supply, making juicing a useful self-care approach for reversing and preventing edema.

JUICING RECIPES

• Juice equal parts pear, pineapple, watermelon, and cranberries
(6 ounces of each will typically make 16 ounces).
Consume 8 ounces twice daily.

• Green juices made from any combination of green vegetables,
plus parsley, watercress, lettuce, and dandelion leaf.
Consume 8 ounces twice daily.

• Juice 1 medium cucumber, 1/4 bunch parsley, 2 celery stalks, and
2 medium carrots.
Makes 12 ounces. Consume once to twice daily.

ENDOMETRIOSIS

Endometriosis is an increasingly common condition among women in the United States and other Western nations. It is caused by tissues that should normally only be found inside the uterus developing elsewhere in the body, such as the pelvic cavity (on the ovaries, fallopian tubes, and within the pelvic walls), the bladder, the intestines, and, in some cases, the appendix and the rectum. In rare cases, endometriosis can also develop inside the vagina, and even in the brain, lungs, and spine. It can also occur as a result of cesarean sections (C-sections) and on the sites of scars formed as a result of laparoscopic surgery.

The main symptom of endometriosis is pain in the pelvic area that usually corresponds to menstruation. At times, the pain can be so severe as to be debilitating. In many cases, endometriosis can also trigger the development of adhesions and scar tissue inside the pelvis that can eventually distort women's internal anatomy. As it progresses, it can also cause internal organs to fuse together, resulting in a condition known as "frozen pelvis."

In his practice, Dr. Bailey has found the following juice remedies to be helpful in relieving endometriosis symptoms. They can also help to prevent endometriosis from occurring in the first place.

JUICING RECIPES

• Juice 1 cup black currants and 1 cup red or purple grapes, and 2 tablespoons of noni juice.
Juice enough to make an 8-ounce serving and drink twice daily.

• Juice 3 medium carrots, 1 medium beet, 1 burdock root, 1–2 garlic cloves, and $1/4$ cup raspberry leaf.
Makes 12 ounces. Consume once to twice daily.

• Juice 3 medium carrots, 8 ounces broccoli, $1/2$ bunch parsley, 3 celery stalks, and 1 garlic clove. Makes 14 ounces. Consume once to twice daily.

EPILEPSY

Epilepsy is a condition that impairs the brain's normal electrical activity, resulting in convulsions, abnormal motor function suck as jerky and distorted movements, impaired functioning of the nervous system, and, in some cases, a temporary loss of consciousness. Epilepsy is a very serious health condition that must be treated by a physician or other health care professional.

While the exact cause of epilepsy is unknown, it is known that nutritional deficiencies, as well as a buildup of toxins in the body due to constipation and sluggish elimination, can worsen the condition. Since fresh-squeezed juices provide abundant nutrients and can also aid in improving elimination, as well as the body's overall detoxification mechanisms, juicing can provide some degree of benefit for people suffering from epilepsy.

JUICING RECIPES

• Juice 3 celery stalks, 2 medium carrots, and $1/2$ head lettuce.
Makes 12 ounces. Consume three glasses daily.

• Juice 1 cup black currants, 2 medium pears, and add 1 tablespoon noni juice. Makes 8 ounces. Consume once daily.

• Juice 8 ounces coconut, 1 medium mango, 1 medium pear, and add 2 capsules or 1 full dropper passion flower extract or tincture.
Makes 6–8 ounces. Consume once to twice daily.

EXHAUSTION

Exhaustion, which is characterized by an extreme feeling of fatigue that is often accompanied by feelings of listlessness, is often due to a combination of overwork, stress, and poor nutrition. Fresh juices can help to reverse nutritional deficiencies related to exhaustion, and can also help to relieve some forms of stress. As the digestion of solid foods requires energy, juices are one of the easiest, safest, and most beneficial foods for exhaustion. The following juice combinations can be especially helpful.

JUICING RECIPES

• Juice 3 medium carrots, 2 medium apples, and ¼ medium cantaloupe.
Makes 18 ounces. Consume once to twice daily.

• Juice 3 medium carrots, 3 celery stalks, and add 2 ounces wheatgrass juice. (See Wheatgrass Juice inset on page 146.)
Makes 12 ounces. Consume twice daily.

• Juice 4 medium carrots, 1 bunch spinach, 2 celery stalks, and ½ medium beet.
Makes 16 ounces. Consume once daily.

EYE DISORDERS / VISION PROBLEMS

Poor diet and nutritional deficiencies, especially a lack of antioxidant vitamins and minerals, have been linked to a variety of eye and vision problems, including cataracts, glaucoma, macular degeneration, and night blindness. Poor nutrition can also impair the proper function of eye muscles that control eye movement, further affecting visual performance. According to Glen Swartout, OD, a holistically oriented vision specialist, eye and vision problems can also be due to acid-alkaline imbalances in the blood. Blood that is overly acidic causes the muscle tone of eye muscles to increase, turning them inward and impairing their ability to function properly. Gastrointestinal problems can also contribute to vision problems.

Juices that are rich in antioxidants and enzymes can play a significant role in protecting overall eye health, and can also help to reverse, or at least slow the progression of, a number of eye and vision problems. If you suffer from eye problems, be sure to make one or more of the following juice combinations a part of your daily dietary intake.

JUICING RECIPES

● Juice 4 medium carrots, $1/4$ bunch spinach, and 1–2 garlic cloves. Makes 12 ounces. Consume once daily.

● Juice $1/2$ cup blueberries, $1/2$ cup goji berries, and $1/4$ cup cranberries. Makes 6 ounces. Consume once to twice daily.

● Juice 12 ounces cantaloupe, 2 medium apples, and 2 ounces of frozen acai berries. Makes 14–16 ounces. Consume once daily.

● Juice 4 medium carrots, 3 celery stalks, and $1/2$ medium cucumber. Makes 14 ounces. Consume once to twice daily.

FEMALE HEALTH PROBLEMS

Poor diet and nutritional deficiencies can cause or exacerbate a variety of common female health problems, including menstrual problems, premenstrual syndrome (PMS), bladder infections (cystitis—for more on this topic see page 167), vaginal infections, ovarian cysts, fibrocystic breast disease, and uterine fibroids. Poor diet and nutritional imbalances can also cause problems during menopause, such as hot flashes, and can play a significant role in the onset of certain types of cancers, including breast, cervical, endometrial, and ovarian cancer. (For more on cancer, see page 162.) Because of the many nutritional benefits juices provide, juicing can help to prevent female health conditions, as well as relieve their symptoms. However, women who suffer from any of the above conditions are advised to also work with a holistic health care professional with an expertise in women's health issues who can help them create a comprehensive treatment plan.

In his practice, Dr. Bailey has found the following juice combinations to be particularly useful for female health conditions.

JUICING RECIPES

● Equal parts carrot and apple juice. Consume 8–16 ounces daily.

● Juice 1 cup cranberries and $1/2$ cup red grapes. Makes 8 ounces. Consume once to twice daily.

● Juice 3 medium carrots, 2 celery stalks, $1/4$ bunch spinach, $1/4$ bunch parsley, and 1–2 garlic cloves. Makes 12 ounces. Consume once daily.

● Juice 1 medium apple, 4 ounces cranberries, 4 ounces blueberries, and 1 tablespoon noni juice. Makes 8 ounces. Consume once to twice daily.

- Juice 3 medium carrots, $1/2$ medium beet, $1/2$ medium cucumber, $1/4$ medium sweet onion, and $1/4$ bunch spinach.
Makes 14 ounces. Consume once daily.

- Watermelon juice. Consume 8 ounces daily.

FERTILITY / INFERTILITY

The following juice combinations can help to enhance fertility and reverse infertility associated with poor diet and poor nutrition. They can also improve the overall health of the endocrine system, helping to ensure a proper balance of hormone levels, which are necessary for conception and healthy pregnancy to occur.

JUICING RECIPES

- Juice 4 medium carrots, $1/2$ medium yam, 3 celery stalks, $1/2$ medium beet, and 2 garlic cloves.
Makes 18 ounces. Consume once daily.

- Juice 3 medium carrots, 8 ounces Jerusalem artichokes, $1/2$ bunch cilantro, and 2 celery stalks.
Makes 14 ounces. Consume once daily.

- Juice 4 ounces cranberries, 4 ounces pomegranate, 8 ounces raspberries, and add 1 tablespoon noni juice.
Makes 8–10 ounces. Consume once to twice daily.

HEALTHY TWIST

🐸 Consider Dr. Bailey's Power Smoothie (see Chapter 6, page 96).

🐸 Consider supplemental zinc (50–100 mg) and 1–2 tablespoons essential fatty acids.

FEVER

Fever refers to body temperature above the normal level of 98.6 degrees Fahrenheit. Nearly everyone experiences fever at some point in their lives. In most cases, fever is temporary and breaks within 24–48 hours. Symptoms of fever can be mild or severe, depending on how high body temperature becomes, as well as the overall health of persons with fever prior to developing it. In addition to feeling hot, fever symptoms can include excessive perspiration, increased thirst, dehydration, fatigue, headache, muscle aches, and dizziness.

It is important to recognize that fever is one of the body's defense mechanisms to protect itself from invading bacteria, viruses, and other harmful microorganisms. For this reason, holistic health practitioners prefer to allow fevers to run their course so long as body temperature remains below 104 degrees. In cases of fever above 104 degrees, as well as in cases that last longer than 48 hours, medical attention should be sought, however.

Juicing is an excellent way to assist immune function, which can include fever when the body is exposed to infectious microorganisms. The following juices provide a variety of immune benefits, and can also help alleviate symptoms of fatigue, thirst, and dehydration associated with fever.

JUICING RECIPES

- Juice 2 medium lemons with 1 medium grapefruit.
Makes 8 ounces. Consume once to twice daily.

- Juice 1 medium orange, 1 medium apple, and $\frac{1}{4}$ pound pineapple with $\frac{1}{4}$ pound grapes and as an option, consider 2 tablespoons noni juice.
Makes 10–12 ounces. Consume once to twice daily.

- Juice 3 medium carrots and 4 celery stalks.
Makes 12 ounces. Consume once daily.

FLATULENCE

Flatulence refers to the buildup and passing of intestinal gas, also known as flatus, formed by the fermentation of or incomplete digestion of foods. Common symptoms of flatulence include abdominal discomfort and distention, mild chest pains, and, in some cases, heartburn due to trapped gas. While most cases of flatulence are temporary, chronic cases can be an indication of a more serious gastrointestinal problem, or even cancer. If you suffer from chronic flatulence, seek immediate medical attention.

Two of the most common causes of flatulence are poor diet and a lack of essential nutrients, including digestive enzymes. Since fresh juices provide a rich supply of enzymes and other nutrients, juicing is an excellent self-care remedy for preventing and reversing flatulence.

JUICING RECIPES

- Juice $\frac{1}{2}$ medium papaya with 6 ounces grapes or 1 medium lemon and 1 medium orange.
Makes 8 ounces. Consume once to twice daily.

- Juice 3 medium carrots, 1 bunch parsley, and 1 ounce ginger.
Makes 8 ounces. Consume once to twice daily.

- Juice 3 medium carrots, ¼ bunch parsley, ¼ medium beet, 3 celery stalks, and add 1 tablespoon of garlic or yellow onion juice.
Makes 14 ounces. Consume once daily. Note: For the first few days, before flatulence is improved, the garlic may add to the external odor.

- Juice ½ medium papaya and 12 ounces blueberries.
Makes 8 ounces. Consume twice daily.

FLU (*See* COLD / FLU)

FOOD POISONING

Food poisoning is caused by eating food that has been contaminated by harmful bacteria or viruses, such as the *E. coli* virus. Foods that contain harmful chemical residues can also cause food poisoning. The onset of food poisoning symptoms can vary greatly, depending on the cause. In many cases, symptoms can occur within 1–12 hours, while in other cases symptoms may not become apparent for as long as 24–96 hours.

Symptoms of food poisoning can vary as well, ranging from abdominal pain, diarrhea, fever, nausea, excessive perspiration, vomiting, and a loss of energy and strength. Juicing can help to quickly resolve food poisoning, primarily by aiding the body to detoxify and eliminate harmful chemicals and microorganisms that trigger the above symptoms, as well as helping to improve the overall health and functioning of the gastrointestinal system. The following juice combinations are particularly recommended for food poisoning.

JUICING RECIPES

- Juice 4 medium carrots, 1 medium beet, ½ ounce turmeric root, ¼ ounce ginger root, and garlic—the more the better.
Makes 14 ounces. Consume once daily.

- Juice 2 medium lemons, 1 medium orange, 4 ounces pineapple, ⅓ medium papaya, and add 1 tablespoon noni juice.
Makes 14 ounces. Consume once daily.

- Juice 3 medium carrots, 2 burdock roots, 1 medium black radish, and 2 cloves of garlic.
Makes 10 ounces. Consume one to three times daily.

FRACTURES

Fractures are breaks within one of more of the body's bones. While juicing is by no means a cure for fractures, the many nutrients that fresh-squeezed juices provide can help speed the healing process.

JUICING RECIPES

• Juice 1 bunch watercress, $1/2$ medium beet, and 2 medium carrots. Makes 8 ounces. Consume twice daily.

• Juice 8 ounces coconut and 1 medium papaya. Makes 10 ounces. Consume twice daily.

• Consider 6–8 leaves comfrey, 2 tablespoons dried or fresh horsetail, and 2 tablespoons dried or fresh *eupatorium perfoliatum* (boneset) in any combination of green juices.

• Juice 4 medium carrots, 1 medium beet, and 1 bunch parsley. Makes 14–16 ounces. Consume once daily.

FUNGAL INFECTIONS

Fungal infections are caused by harmful fungi, as well as various types of molds, mildew, and yeast, such as *Candida albicans* (see Candidiasis on page 164). Many cases of fungal infection affect only the skin and nails, while in other cases fungal infections can target the body's internal organs. The following juices can help to relieve symptoms of fungal infection, as well as shorten recovery time.

JUICING RECIPES

• As a general guideline, it is important to dilute all fruit juices with equal amounts water; consider papaya and noni juice.

• Add 2–4 garlic cloves to all vegetable juices.

• Juice citron and apply topically.

• Juice 3 medium carrots, 8 ounces Jerusalem artichokes, 4 ounces green beans, and 4 ounces asparagus. Makes 14 ounces. Consume once daily.

• Juice 3 medium carrots, 3 celery stalks, 2 garlic cloves, and $1/4$–$1/2$ bunch cilantro. Makes 12 ounces. Consume once to twice daily.

• Juice 8 ounces pineapple, 2 medium lemons, $1/4$ medium papaya, and add 2 tablespoons noni juice. Makes 8 ounces. Consume once to twice daily.

GALLSTONES / GALLBLADDER PROBLEMS

The gallbladder is a small organ located beneath the liver. Its primary function is to store bile manufactured by the liver, and to then secrete it into the intestines after eating in order to help transport fats contained in foods. One of the most common gallbladder problems is the formation of gallstones which, if left unchecked, can block the cystic duct, a small tube through which the gallbladder receives bile from the liver. When gallstones become lodged within the gallbladder or the cystic duct, the gallbladder can become inflamed, creating pain in the right side of the abdomen, as well as, in some cases, in and around the right shoulder blade. Gallstones can also result in another problem known as cholecystitis, which is an infection of the cystic duct caused by gallstones that are trapped within it. Gallstones can also travel down the common hepatic duct and create blockages there with reflux back to the liver or even worse, they can become lodged where the pancreas and liver ducts join and cause acute pancreatitis, which is a life-threatening condition.

Not all cases of gallstones result in noticeable symptoms, and many people have gallstones but are unaware of it. Preventing and eliminating gallstones, even if they do not result in symptoms, is still advisable, however, due to the link between the gallbladder and proper digestion and healthy liver function. The following juice combinations are excellent for maintaining gallbladder health.

JUICING RECIPES

• Juice 3 medium carrots, $\frac{1}{2}$ medium beet, and $\frac{1}{2}$ medium cucumber (also add a little garlic, black radish, or fresh dandelion roots).
Makes 12 ounces. Consume once to twice daily.

• Juice $\frac{1}{2}$ cup grapes, 1 medium pear, $\frac{1}{2}$ medium grapefruit, and 1 medium lemon.
Makes 10 ounces. Consume once daily.

• Juice 3 medium carrots, 2 burdock roots, 1–2 ounces turmeric, and 1–2 garlic cloves.
Makes 10 ounces. Consume once to twice daily.

HEALTHY TWIST

❧ Consider adding 1–2 capsules of Chelidonium (Celandine) and 1–2 teaspoons milk thistle oil to the above juicing recipes. Avoid eggs and pasteurized milk.

GAS (*See* FLATULENCE)

GASTRITIS

Gastritis is a gastrointestinal disorder characterized by inflammation in the stomach. It can be caused by infectious viruses, fungi, parasites, as well as bacteria, such as *Heliobacter pylori,* which has also been linked to the majority of cases of stomach ulcer. The overuse of pharmaceutical drugs, including aspirin and other common pain medications, can also cause gastritis, as can impaired immune function.

The following juice combinations are recommended for gastritis because of their ability to reduce and reverse inflammation, as well as for their immune-boosting properties, which can enhance the body's ability to destroy unhealthy bacteria and viruses.

JUICING RECIPES

- Juice 3 medium carrots, $\frac{1}{2}$ medium cucumber, $\frac{1}{2}$ ounce ginger root, 1 garlic clove, and 1–2 tablespoons aloe juice.
Makes 10 ounces. Consume once to twice daily.

- Juice 3 medium carrots, 1 medium cucumber, and $\frac{1}{4}$ head cabbage.
Makes 16 ounces. Consume once daily.

- Juice 8 ounces blueberries, 2 medium pears, and $\frac{1}{4}$ medium papaya.
Makes 8 ounces. Consume twice daily.

HAIR LOSS

Although most cases of baldness have a hereditary cause or influence, especially male pattern baldness, hair loss can also occur as a result of poor diet, nutritional deficiencies, impaired digestion and gastrointestinal function, premature aging, parasites, hormonal imbalances, and hypothyroidism (low thyroid function). The many nutrients that fresh-squeezed juices contain can be beneficial for all of these contributing factors, and therefore can help to prevent, halt, and reverse certain types of hair loss. The following juice combinations are especially helpful.

JUICING RECIPES

- Juice 3 medium carrots, $\frac{1}{2}$ medium beet, $\frac{1}{2}$ bunch spinach, 2–4 ounces nettle leaf, and 4 ounces alfalfa sprouts.
Makes 12 ounces. Consume once to twice daily.

- Juice 4 medium carrots, 2 burdock roots, $^1/_2$ bunch cilantro, and 2 celery stalks. Makes 14 ounces. Consume once daily.

- Juice 3 medium carrots, 1 medium beet, and 1 medium apple. Makes 14 ounces. Consume once daily.

HEALTHY TWIST

🍎 Consider adding a little onion juice or garlic to the above juices for added benefit.

HALITOSIS (*See* BAD BREATH)

HEADACHES (*See also* MIGRAINE)

Headaches rank among the most common of all health conditions, affecting nearly everyone at least once in their lives. In most cases, headaches are temporary, but in others, they can prove debilitating, depending on their type. Migraine headache is an example of this latter type of headache, as are headaches that continually recur or persist for long periods of time. Such headaches should be attended to by a physician, as should all cases of headaches that are accompanied by blurring vision, convulsions, dizziness, fever, and head trauma.

There are many potential causes of headaches. These include physical factors, such as spinal misalignments, muscle spasms and muscle tension, and physical trauma or injury. Other potential causes of headache include allergies, constipation, poor diet, poor digestion, hormonal imbalances, infections, and nutritional deficiencies. Juicing can often prove beneficial for headaches caused by this second class of factors due to the abundant supply of nutrients juices contain.

JUICING RECIPES

- Juice 4 medium carrots and 4 celery stalks. Make 14 ounces. Consume once to twice daily.

- Juice 3 medium carrots, $^1/_2$ medium beet, 1 medium cucumber, and $^1/_4$ bunch parsley. Makes 14 ounces. Consume once to twice daily.

- Juice 3 medium carrots, 3 celery stalks, $^1/_4$ bunch spinach, $^1/_4$ bunch parsley, and $^1/_4$ head lettuce. Makes 16 ounces. Consume once daily.

- Juice $^1/_2$ medium papaya, 6 ounces cantaloupe, and add 1 tablespoon noni juice. Makes 8 ounces. Consume once to twice daily.

HEARING PROBLEMS / EAR DISORDERS

Like all other aspects of the body's health, good hearing and proper ear function is in large part dependent on a healthy diet and an optimum supply of nutrients. While there are many other factors that can contribute to ear and hearing disorders, diet and nutrition should never be overlooked. By providing your body with the nutrition it needs, you can help to ensure that certain other factors that can cause ear and hearing problems, such as allergies, infection, and the buildup of fluids in the ear canals, are prevented or minimized. The following juice remedies, all of which are rich in immune-boosting antioxidants, are especially useful for this purpose.

JUICING RECIPES

- Juice 4 medium carrots, 2 celery stalks, and 2 garlic cloves.
Makes 12 ounces. Consume once daily.

- Juice 3 medium carrots, $\frac{1}{2}$ bunch cilantro, $\frac{1}{2}$ bunch parsley, and dilute with 1 cup nettle tea.
Makes 16 ounces. Consume once daily for chronic complaints, three times daily for acute conditions.

- Juice 3 medium carrots, 1 bunch watercress, 1 ounce ginger root, and 1 ounce turmeric root.
Makes 8 ounces. Consume twice daily.

HEALTHY TWIST

🍂 Consider supplementing with 50–100 mg of zinc.

HEART DISEASE (*See* ARRHYTHMIA; CARDIOMYOPATHY)

HEAVY METAL TOXICITY (*See also* CADMIUM POISONING)

Heavy metal toxicity occurs when metals such as cadmium, lead, mercury, nickel, and other poisonous chemical compounds build up within the body. Typically, heavy metals and other chemical toxins gravitate to the fat cells in the body, as well as in the bones, brain, central nervous system, and various organs and glands. As they accumulate, these toxins can cause a variety of health problems.

A wide variety of health symptoms can be caused by heavy metal poisoning, depending on the toxin in question and the degree of its accumulation. Symptoms range from allergies, arthritis, digestive and gastrointestinal problems, and impaired immunity, to mental and cognition problems, including Alzheimer's and dementia, and an increased risk of chronic degenerative diseases, including heart disease and cancer.

Juicing is recommended for treating and preventing heavy metal poisoning, as well as for all other types of environmentally related illnesses, due to the detoxification and immune-enhancing properties that fresh-squeezed juices possess. The following juices are particularly useful.

JUICING RECIPES

- Juice 4 medium carrots, 1 bunch cilantro, 1 medium beet, and 1 ounce turmeric root.
Makes 14–16 ounces. Consume only once per day.

- To support liver, kidneys, and skin: Juice 4 medium carrots, 2 celery stalks, 2 burdock roots, $\frac{1}{2}$ medium beet, 2 garlic cloves, $\frac{1}{2}$ bunch cilantro, and 2 teaspoons flaxseed or currant oils.
Makes 16 ounces. Consume once daily.

- Juice 3 medium carrots, 3 celery stalks, 2 burdock roots, and add 2 ounces wheatgrass juice. (See Wheatgrass Juice inset on page 146.)
Consume once daily.

- Juice $\frac{1}{2}$ medium papaya, 8 ounces pitted black prunes or plums, and 2 medium lemons.
Makes 14 ounces. Consume once daily.

HEALTHY TWIST

🌿 Consider niacin (50–500 mg, or until skin flushing is achieved) and saunas for further benefits.

HEMORRHOIDS

Hemorrhoids are distended veins in the lining of the anus. They can occur internally inside the anus, or externally near the opening of the anus. Hemorrhoid symptoms include itching in and around the anus, pain and discomfort during bowel movements and when sitting, and, in some cases, minor bleeding. While quite common in the United States and other Western nations, hemorrhoids are virtually nonexistent among native societies that follow a diet rich in natural, unprocessed foods and plenty of fresh fruits and vegetables. Juicing is therefore an excellent self-care remedy for preventing and reversing hemorrhoids.

JUICING RECIPES

- Juice 3 medium carrots and $1/2$ bunch parsley.
Makes 8 ounces. Consume once to twice daily.

- Juice 3 medium carrots, $1/4$ bunch spinach, 3 celery stalks, and $1/4$ bunch parsley.
Makes 14 ounces. Consume once daily.

- Juice 4 medium carrots and 4 ounces watercress.
Makes 10 ounces. Consume once daily.

HEALTHY TWIST

🌶 Consider 1–3 capsules of horse chestnut extract as indicated and 1–3 tablespoons of ground supplemental fiber or 1–3 teaspoons of powdered fiber (8 ounces water for each tablespoon).

HEPATITIS

Hepatitis is a disease of the liver and is characterized by inflammation of the liver, as well as damage to, and premature death of, liver cells. The most common cause of hepatitis is infection by a virus that can occur in five strains: A, B, C, D, and E. Other common causes include overconsumption of alcohol; drug abuse; regular use of medications, including pain relievers such as acetaminophen; and exposure to toxic chemicals and other environmental pollutants. Hepatitis can either be short-term, or acute, or chronic, potentially leading to liver failure. Symptoms of hepatitis include pain in the right abdominal area over the liver, jaundice, extreme fatigue, loss of appetite, fever, nausea, vomiting, and unhealthy weight loss. All forms of hepatitis should be attended to by a physician or other health care specialist. To help ease symptoms, the following juice combinations are also recommended.

JUICING RECIPES

- Juice 1 medium beet, 3 medium carrots, 2 garlic cloves, and 2 ounces wheatgrass juices. (See Wheatgrass Juice inset on page 146.)
Makes 12 ounces. Consume once daily.

- Juice 3 medium carrots, 2 garlic cloves, 2 burdock roots, and 1 medium black radish, also consider adding flax oil.
Makes 10 ounces. Consume once daily.

- Juice 1 medium apple, 1 medium lemon, and 1 cup black currants.
Makes 8 ounces. Consume once to twice daily.

- Juice 1 medium apple, $1/3$ medium papaya, 2 medium lemons, and add 1 tablespoon noni juice. Makes 10 ounces. Consume once daily.

HERPES SIMPLEX (*See* COLD SORES)

HICCUPS

Hiccups are extremely common and are caused by constriction of the vocal chords as a result of a sudden contraction of the diaphragm. In the vast majority of cases, hiccups are not serious. In some cases, however, hiccups can become ongoing, to the point where they may require medical intervention and, in extreme cases, even surgery. To avoid hiccups when juicing, remember to drink slowly and "chew" your juices, swishing them around in your mouth before swallowing. Also try not to eat or drink when you are upset.

HYPERGLYCEMIA (HIGH BLOOD SUGAR)

Hyperglycemia is characterized by chronic elevations in the body's blood sugar levels. The primary contributing factors for hyperglycemia are poor diet and poor nutrition, and insulin resistance due to diabetes (for more on Diabetes, see page 178). Like diabetics, people with high blood sugar are advised not to eat foods that are high in sugar and simple carbohydrates. Such foods rank high on what is known as the glycemic index, a measurement of the sugar and simple carbohydrate content. Interestingly, many vegetables, such as carrots, have a higher glycemic index when they are cooked than do the fresh juices that can be prepared from them. Because of this fact, certain juices, such as the ones listed below, can be very helpful for managing blood sugar levels. Initially, there may be some elevation of serum glucose levels after juice consumption; this tends to reduce within a few weeks of regular intake of fresh vegetable juices. For additional benefit, Dr. Bailey also recommends the Power Smoothie he developed (see page 96), which has enabled many of his patients with hyperglycemia to completely reverse their condition within two months, by juicing, following a sensible diet, and making the Power Smoothie a part of their daily routine.

JUICING RECIPES

- Juice 2 medium carrots, 3 celery stalks, 1 garlic clove, and 3 medium Jerusalem artichokes. Makes 14 ounces. Consume once daily.

- Juice 1 medium grapefruit, 2 medium lemons, and $\frac{1}{2}$ medium papaya. Makes 14–16 ounces. Consume once to twice daily. Can substitute 6 ounces pineapple for papaya for individual taste.

- Juice 2 medium carrots, 1 bunch parsley, 1 garlic clove, and 1 cup green beans. Makes 10 ounces. Consume once to twice daily.

HYPERTENSION (HIGH BLOOD PRESSURE)

High blood pressure, also known as hypertension, is a common health condition in the United States, affecting an estimated 25 percent of all adults. It is characterized by above-normal blood pressure levels that force the heart to beat harder. Left unchecked, high blood pressure can cause damage to the walls of blood vessels, especially the arteries. This damage, in turn, can cause a buildup of cholesterol deposits in the arteries, since the release of cholesterol is one of the mechanisms the body uses to repair damaged areas in the arteries. If high blood pressure is allowed to progress, it can eventually lead to a variety of heart conditions, including heart attack and stroke. In some cases, it can also result in damage to other body organs, including the brain and kidneys. Therefore, high blood pressure should be carefully monitored by a health care practitioner.

Often times, high blood pressure can be present without any noticeable symptoms. When symptoms do occur, they include difficulty breathing, pressure on the chest, dizziness, fatigue, headaches, insomnia, and problems with digestion and gastrointestinal function. As with many other chronic health problems in the United States, high blood pressure is largely due to poor diet and a lack of proper nutrition, as well as hardening of the arteries caused by unhealthy eating habits and nutritional deficiencies, and unhealthy lifestyle habits, such as smoking and alcohol and drug abuse. The regular use of pharmaceutical drugs can also cause or make high blood pressure worse, as can stress.

By managing stress, eating healthy foods, and making juicing a part of your daily health routine, most cases of high blood pressure can be significantly improved. The following juice combinations can be especially helpful.

JUICING RECIPES

- Juice 3 medium carrots, 1 medium cucumber, $\frac{1}{4}$ bunch parsley, $\frac{1}{4}$ head lettuce, and 1–2 garlic cloves. Makes 14 ounces. Consume once to twice daily.

- Juice 3 medium carrots, 1 bunch parsley, $\frac{1}{2}$ medium cucumber, and 1 ounce ginger root. Makes 14 ounces. Consume once to twice daily.

- Juice 12 ounces watermelon and 4 ounces pitted hawthorn berries, or dilute with 1 cup hawthorn tea. Makes 10 ounces or diluted with tea it makes 16 ounces. Consume once daily.

HYPERTHYROIDISM

Hyperthyroidism is the name given to excessive production of thyroid hormones by the thyroid gland. An overabundance of thyroid hormones in the body can result in a variety of health complaints. These include accelerated heartbeat and erratic pulse, anxiety, bulging eyes, chest pains, diarrhea and other gastrointestinal problems, fatigue, goiter (abnormal enlargement of the thyroid gland), moist skin and excessive perspiration, tremors, and unhealthy weight loss. Hyperthyroidism should be monitored by a health care professional. The following juice combinations can also help.

JUICING RECIPES

- Juice 3 medium carrots, 2 celery stalks, $\frac{1}{4}$ bunch spinach, and parsley. Makes 12 ounces. Consume once daily.

- Juice $\frac{1}{4}$ head cabbage, 4 ounces watercress, and $\frac{1}{4}$ bunch spinach. Makes 6 ounces. Consume once to twice daily.

- Juice 3 medium carrots, 8 ounces broccoli, and $\frac{1}{2}$ head kale. Makes 12 ounces. Consume once to twice daily.

HYPOGLYCEMIA (LOW BLOOD SUGAR)

Hypoglycemia is a condition characterized by fluctuating or lower than normal blood sugar levels. It can be caused by a variety of factors, including poor diet (especially the consumption of too much sugar and simple carbohydrates), poor digestion, nutritional imbalances, lack of digestive enzymes, and a regular pattern of missed meals. In some cases, hypoglycemia can also be due to abnormal functioning of the pancreas, which can result in erratic production of insulin, which the body needs to regulate blood sugar levels.

Symptoms of hypoglycemia are usually most noticeable in the middle of the afternoon. They can include anxiety, digestion problems, dizziness, drowsiness, feelings of intense hunger, headache, loss of strength, rapid heartbeat, and difficulties related to cognition and memory.

A healthy diet of regular meals free of processed foods, sugar, and simple carbohydrates is essential for maintaining proper blood sugar levels. The following juice combinations are also recommended.

JUICING RECIPES

- Juice 2 medium carrots, $1/2$ medium beet, 2 burdock roots, 2 medium Jerusalem artichokes, and 1–2 garlic cloves.
Makes 12 ounces. Consume once daily.

- Juice 2 medium apples and 3 medium carrots.
Makes 16 ounces. Drink as two separate servings, 1–2 hours apart.

- Juice 3 medium carrots, 3 celery stalks, 2 burdock roots, and 2 garlic cloves. Makes 14 ounces. Drink once daily.

CONSIDERATION

■ If you find you cannot tolerate the above juice combinations, you can dilute them with pure, filtered water and still receive benefit.

HYPOTHYROIDISM

Hypothyroidism is the name given to below normal production of thyroid hormones by the thyroid gland. A deficiency of thyroid hormones in the body can result in a variety of health complaints. These include allergies, brittle hair and nails, constipation, depression, digestion and gastrointestinal problems, hair loss, headaches, impaired immune function, and slurred speech. In children, hypothyroidism can also stunt growth.

Hypothyroidism is far more common in the United States than hyperthyroidism (page 198), and often overlooked or misdiagnosed by many physicians. A simple way to test yourself for hypothyroidism is the Broda Barnes Test, named after Dr. Broda Barnes, one of the first physicians to recognize the prevalence of hypothyroidism. To perform the test, you will need a standard thermometer, which you will place beside your bed before you go to sleep. When you awake in the morning, before you get out of bed, place the thermometer under you right armpit for fifteen minutes without moving. Do this for three to five consecutive days. If your body temperature during that time is consistently below 97.5°F, more than likely you suffer from hypothyroidism. (Note: Women should avoid performing the Broda Barnes Test during the beginning and middle of their menstrual cycle, due to a normal decrease in body temperature that can occur during this time.)

Hypothyroidism is caused by a variety of factors, including poor diet, nutritional deficiencies, lack of digestive enzymes, and hormonal imbalances. In some cases, it can also be a sign of impaired liver function or liver disease. The following juice combinations are rich in nutrients that support the health of the thyroid gland. People with low thyroid function should make it a point to drink one or more of them each day, as well as eating a healthy diet. To improve results, also consider adding seaweeds such as kelp to your diet for their rich iodine content, a necessary mineral for proper thyroid function.

JUICING RECIPES

- Juice 3 medium carrots, 3 celery stalks, 2 burdock roots, and 1 medium beet. Makes 16 ounces. Consume once daily.

- Juice 1 medium papaya, 2 medium pears, 8 ounces blueberries, and 2 medium lemons. Makes 16 ounces. Consume once daily.

- Juice 3 medium carrots, $\frac{1}{2}$ head of spinach, 2 garlic cloves, and $\frac{1}{2}$ medium green pepper. Makes 10–12 ounces. Consume once daily.

HEALTHY TWIST

🐛 Limit the raw juice of cabbage, broccoli, kale, and cauliflower, as these foods can interfere with thyroid function. To enhance the benefits of the above recipes, add kelp to them.

IMPOTENCE

Impotence, which is also known as erectile dysfunction, affects men who are primarily in their late 40s or older. It is characterized by an inability to achieve or maintain an erection. Once commonly dismissed by conventional physicians as a natural consequence of aging, today most medical experts agree that impotence is in fact a potential sign of overall declining health, a view that has long been held by natural healing systems such as naturopathic medicine, traditional Chinese medicine (TCM), and Ayurveda, the system of traditional medicine that originated in ancient India. Moreover, physicians now recognize that erectile dysfunction can also be a sign of developing heart disease, especially among men in their 40s and 50s. Therefore, all men who experience impotence should see a physician to rule out more serious health problems.

Although some cases of impotence are psychological in nature, they are rare compared to cases due to physical causes. These include poor diet and nutritional deficiencies, along with hormonal imbalances, chronic stress, alcohol and drug abuse, cigarette smoking, and being unhealthily over-weight or obese. Since juicing can help to address these factors, drinking fresh juices on a regular basis can also be beneficial for men who suffer from impotence. In addition to the juice combinations recommended below, men should also consider supplementing with zinc. Certain herbs might also help, such as ginseng. (To most effectively use herbs for your health care needs, consult with a knowledgeable herbalist or a health care practitioner trained in herbal medicine.)

JUICING RECIPES

- Juice 3 medium carrots, 3 celery stalks, $1/2$ medium beet, and 1–2 garlic cloves.
Makes 12 ounces. Consume once daily.

- Juice $1/4$ medium cantaloupe and $1/4$ cup cranberries.
Makes 8 ounces. Consume once to twice daily.

- Juice 3 medium carrots, $1/2$ bunch watercress, 1 bunch parsley, and 2 celery stalks.
Makes 14–16 ounces. Consume once daily.

HEALTHY TWIST

❦ Consider supplementing with zinc (20–50 mg, once per day).

INFLAMMATION

As we discussed in Chapter 3, inflammation is a natural healing mechanism employed by the body to help heal wounds and to deal with invading harmful microorganisms. In such cases, inflammation is only temporary and subsides once the problems it is meant to address are dealt with. When inflammation becomes chronic, however, it can set the stage for a wide variety of health problems to occur, including serious illnesses such as heart disease and cancer. Poor diet, nutritional deficiencies, and lack of enzymes are some of the primary causes of chronic inflammation, as are diets that are rich in foods that create an overly acidic effect inside the body once they are digested. Juicing helps to address all of these factors, making it an excellent way to prevent and reverse chronic inflammation. The following juices are particularly useful because of their anti-inflammatory properties.

JUICING RECIPES

- Juice $1/2$ cup currants with 1 cup black or red grapes.
Makes 6 ounces. Consume three times daily.

- Juice 8 ounces pineapple with 1 medium papaya.
Makes 10 ounces. Consume once to twice daily.

- Juice 8 ounces blueberries, $\frac{1}{2}$ medium papaya, and add 1 tablespoon noni juice.
Makes 6 ounces. Consume once to twice daily.

- Juice 3 medium carrots, 1 medium cucumber, 3 celery stalks, and 2 garlic cloves.
Makes 14–16 ounces. Consume once to twice daily.

HEALTHY TWIST

Consider adding cold-pressed flaxseed and sunflower oils to your favorite vegetable juices.

INSOMNIA

Of all sleep disorders that affect Americans, the most common is insomnia. According to sleep experts, nearly 60 percent of all adults in the United States suffer from some form of insomnia at least once a week. There are three types of insomnia. The most common form is characterized by difficulty sleeping upon going to bed. This type is known as sleep-onset insomnia. Another type of insomnia, known as sleep-maintenance insomnia, is characterized by frequent awakenings during the night, with difficulty falling back to sleep each time. The third type of insomnia, known as early-wakening insomnia, occurs when people wake up after only a few hours of sleep and are unable to return to sleep. All three forms of insomnia leave people feeling tired and exhausted throughout the day.

There are many factors that can cause insomnia, including psychological conditions such as anxiety, depression, unresolved emotional upsets, and chronic stress. Other factors include poor sleeping habits, unhealthy diets, habitually eating late in the evening, poor nutrition, and hormonal imbalances, especially a lack of the hormone melatonin. Juicing can help to correct dietary and nutritional factors that contribute to insomnia. Because juicing can also enhance the overall health of the endocrine system, which is responsible for hormone production and regulation, regularly drinking juices can help alleviate hormonal imbalances, which may contribute to insomnia. Such juices include the following.

JUICING RECIPES

- Juice 3 medium carrots, 1–2 celery stalks, and $\frac{1}{2}$ head lettuce.
Makes 12 ounces. Consume one hour before bed.

- Coconut milk with passionflower fruit (equal parts).
Consume 8 ounces before bed.

- Juice 6 ounces cantaloupe, 4 ounces blueberries, and add 1 tablespoon noni juice.
Makes 4 ounces. Consume before bed.

IRREGULAR HEARTBEAT (See ARRHYTHMIA)

IRRITABLE BOWEL SYNDROME (IBS) (See also FOOD POISONING)

Irritable bowel syndrome, or IBS, is a gastrointestinal disorder that affects an estimated 40 million Americans, according to Dr. Mark Pimentel, Director of the Gastrointestinal Motility Program at Cedars-Sinai Medical Center, and author of *The New IBS Solution*. Unlike other gastrointestinal conditions, which are characterized by inflammation, ulceration, or damage to the lining of the intestinal walls, IBS typically does not cause alterations to intestinal tissues, making it difficult for physicians to accurately diagnose it.

An effective diagnosis is made even more difficult because of the variety of symptoms that can be caused by IBS, all of which can be mistaken for it. These include abdominal pain, bloating, constipation, diarrhea, flatulence, nausea, and unhealthy weight loss. Symptoms of IBS also tend to fluctuate, at times being noticeable and severe, and at other times seeming to have faded away, only to recur at a later date.

Because of how difficult IBS is to detect, until recently, most conventional physicians attributed it to psychological factors, such as anxiety and chronic stress. Today, however, IBS is recognized as a legitimate physical condition. According to Dr. Pimentel, who has conducted a number of published clinical studies on IBS, the primary cause of the disease is bacterial infection in the stomach and small intestine, which is often precipitated by a bout of food poisoning. Other contributing factors can include poor diet, nutritional deficiencies, impaired immunity, and a lack of fiber in the diet.

In Chapter 3, you learned how juicing can help improve immune function, as well as enhance overall digestion and gastrointestinal function. Because of these healing properties that juices contain, juicing can play a positive role in alleviating IBS symptoms, and in many cases reversing it. Moreover, regularly drinking fresh-squeezed juices can help to ensure that you are receiving an abundance of essential nutrients. Recommended juices for IBS include the following.

JUICING RECIPES

- Juice $1/4$ head cabbage, 4 ounces broccoli, 3–4 medium carrots, 2 celery stalks, and $1/4$ bunch parsley. Makes 16 ounces. Consume once daily.

- Juice 12 ounces blueberries, 2 medium pears, 2 medium apples, and add 1–2 teaspoons slippery elm powder. Makes 16 ounces. Consume once daily.

- Juice 3 medium carrots, $1/2$ medium beet, 1 medium cucumber, and 1 garlic clove. Makes 10 ounces. Consume once daily.

JAUNDICE (*See also* CIRRHOSIS; GALLSTONES / GALLBLADDER PROBLEMS; HEPATITIS; LIVER SUPPORT)

Jaundice is a symptom of gallbladder or liver disease. It is characterized by a yellowing of the skin and the whites of the eyes and can be accompanied by a variety of other symptoms. Such symptoms include abdominal pain and swelling, dark urine, fatigue that can often be severe, fluid retention within the abdomen, gastrointestinal problems, nausea, and vomiting.

As we mentioned, jaundice is typically an indication of a more serious underlying condition, such as cirrhosis, gallbladder problems, hepatitis and other types of liver disease (including liver cancer), and liver toxicity. It can also be caused by pernicious anemia. If you are experiencing any of the symptoms of jaundice, seek immediate medical attention and ask your physician to run appropriate blood tests.

As you've already learned, juicing provides many benefits for the liver, as well as for the gallbladder. Therefore, juicing should always be considered as a self-care treatment for jaundice. The best juices for jaundice and overall gallbladder and liver support include the following.

JUICING RECIPES

- Juice 3–4 medium carrots, 1 medium beet, 2 garlic cloves, 2–3 celery stalks, 1 medium black radish, and fresh dandelion root, if available. Makes 16 ounces. Consume two to three times daily.

- Juice 1 cup red grapes, 1 medium pear, and 1 medium lemon. Consider adding 1 tablespoon noni juice. Makes 8 ounces. Consume once to twice daily.

- Juice 3 medium carrots, 2 celery stalks, and $1/4$ bunch parsley. Makes 10 ounces. Consume once to twice daily.

- Juice 3 medium carrots, 1 medium beet, and $1/2$ medium cucumber. Makes 12 ounces. Consume once daily.

JOINT PAIN (*See also* ARTHRITIS; INFLAMMATION)

Joint pain ranks among the most common of health complaints in the United States, especially among people who are middle-aged and older. One of the primary causes of joint pain that is not due to injury of the joints is chronic inflammation in the tissues that surround the joints. Because of the many anti-inflammatory benefits that fresh-squeezed juices provide, juicing on a daily basis is highly recommended for such cases of joint pain, along with a healthy diet that is free of processed foods, sugars, unhealthy fats and oils, and simple carbohydrates. Beneficial juices for alleviating joint pain include the following.

JUICING RECIPES

● Juice 3 medium carrots, $1/2$ medium cucumber, and 4 ounces watercress.
Makes 10 ounces. Consume once to twice daily.

● Juice 4 ounces pineapple, 1 medium papaya, 1 medium pear, and 1 tablespoon noni juice.
Makes 12 ounces. Consume once daily.

● Juice 3 medium carrots, 3 celery stalks, 1–2 garlic cloves, and 4–6 leaves of mustard greens.
Makes 14 ounces. Consume once daily.

KIDNEY STONES

Kidney stones are a fairly common health condition in the United States, and are primarily caused by poor diet and nutritional deficiencies. Kidney stones can occur within the kidneys themselves, or along the rest of the urinary tract, including the bladder and urethra. Although many cases of kidney stones do not cause symptoms and therefore escape detection, if kidney stones are not treated, they can eventually create blockages in the urinary tract, creating serious problems.

Symptoms of kidney stones include abrupt and severe, stabbing pains in the back and down into the genital region. They can also cause abdominal swelling, blood in the urine, chills, fever, nausea, and vomiting. When kidney stones pass from the kidneys, the pain can be excruciating, and is often likened to the pain women experience during childbirth.

In addition to following a healthy diet, it is important to consume adequate amounts of healthy fluids throughout the day in order to prevent kidney stones and relieve their symptoms. Pure, filtered water is especially recommended, as are at least two 8-ounce glasses of fresh-squeezed juices each day. The following juices can be especially helpful.

JUICING RECIPES

• Juice 2 medium lemons and add to 16 ounces water.
Consume 8 ounces three times daily.

• Juice 3 medium carrots, $1/2$ medium beet, 1 medium cucumber, and $1/4$ bunch parsley; consider adding some garlic and/or horseradish root.
Makes 14 ounces. Consume once to twice daily.

• Juice 1 pound cranberry and 1 pound watermelon.
Consume 8 ounces three times daily.

LARYNGITIS

Laryngitis is characterized by hoarseness when speaking or a partial loss of the voice itself. It is caused by the voice box (larynx) of the throat becoming inflamed. It can also be due to irritations of the trachea (windpipe) or the pharynx, the part of the throat that is located behind and below the root of the tongue. In many cases, laryngitis is due to overexertion of the throat, such as what happens during bouts of screaming or lengthy periods of speaking or singing. It can also be caused by allergies, bacterial infection, and exposure to chemical irritants and pollutants. In some cases, it can also be an accompanying symptom of colds, flu, and other respiratory conditions, such as bronchitis.

The following juice combinations can help to soothe inflammation and irritation of the throat, thereby relieving laryngitis symptoms.

JUICING RECIPES

• Juice 3 medium carrots and 4 ounces pineapple.
Makes 8 ounces. Consume two to three times daily.

• Juice 3 medium carrots and 1 medium apple.
Makes 12 ounces. Consume twice daily.

• Juice 3–4 medium carrots with 2–3 celery stalks.
Makes 12 ounces. Consume once to twice daily.

• Juice 3 medium carrots, $1/2$ medium beet, $1/2$ medium cucumber, and $1/2$ ounce ginger root.
Makes 10 ounces. Consume once to twice daily.

HEALTHY TWIST

🐝 Consider 2–4 capsules hyssop or 8 ounces strong tea (infusion) in tonic drink (see Chapter 6 for more on tonics).

LIVER SUPPORT (*See also* CIRRHOSIS; HEPATITIS)

As we've previously mentioned, your liver is responsible for carrying out over 1,500 functions in the body each day, including storing and filtering blood; producing bile to help digest fats; transforming sugars and carbohydrates into glycogen, which the body requires for energy; and detoxifying the body of various toxins and pollutants. Because of the many important roles that the liver performs in the body, optimum liver function is essential for overall good health. The following juices can help to support the health of the liver and its many functions due to the abundance of nutrients they provide, and because of their detoxification properties.

JUICING RECIPES

• Juice 4 medium carrots, 1 medium beet, 1 medium black radish, 2 burdock roots, 2 celery stalks, and 1–2 garlic cloves.
Makes 18 ounces. Consume once daily.

• Juice 3 medium carrots, $^1/_2$ medium beet, 3 celery stalks, and 1–2 garlic cloves.
Makes 14 ounces. Drink once to twice daily.

• Juice $^1/_2$ medium papaya, 4 ounces pineapple, 2 medium lemons, and 1 medium mango.
Makes 12 ounces. Consume once daily.

LONGEVITY (*See* ANTI-AGING / LONGEVITY)

LUPUS

Lupus is an autoimmune disease that affects the health of the blood and causes the body's connective tissues and joints to become inflamed. There are two types of lupus. The first, known as discoid lupus erythematosus (DLE) primarily affects areas of the skin and, in some cases, the joints. Systemic lupus erythematosus (SLE) is more serious, since it can cause dysfunctions in the body's organs due to how it negatively affects the blood. In some cases, SLE can even prove fatal, due to its ability to cause organ failure.

In cases of DLE, common health symptoms include red, circular rashes on the face, neck, chest, scalp, or elbows, which can often result in scarring. DLE can also cause permanent hair loss. Rashes can also occur in cases of SLE, although typically they are located on the cheeks and the nose and do not leave scars. Other symptoms of SLE include anemia, fatigue, fever, high blood pressure, muscle pain and muscle contractions, inflammation of the lungs (pleurisy) and heart membrane (pericarditis), joint swelling (especially of the hands and fingers), kidney problems, and swollen lymph nodes.

Both cases of lupus should be overseen by a health care practitioner. The following juice combinations can also be used to alleviate lupus symptoms.

JUICING RECIPES

• Juice 4 medium carrots, 3 celery stalks, 2 garlic cloves, and add 1/2–1 tablespoon flaxseed oil or black currant oil.
Makes 14 ounces. Consume once daily.

• Juice 2 medium apples, 2 medium pears, 1 ounce ginger, and add 1 tablespoon noni juice. Makes 12 ounces. Consume once to twice daily.

• Juice 3 medium carrots, 1/4 head cabbage, 1–2 garlic cloves, and 1/2 cucumber. Makes 12 ounces. Consume once to twice daily.

CONSIDERATION

■ Avoid or observe response to tomatoes, peppers, and potatoes.

MALNUTRITION (*See* NUTRITIONAL DEFICIENCY)

MEASLES

Measles, which is caused by viral infections, is a very common health condition among children and pre-teens. (Adults can develop measles as well, if they did not do so as children, but such cases are rare.) While not serious, measles can be very uncomfortable. And, in the case of children who suffer from serious immune disorders, it can cause significant health risks. Therefore, the parents of such children need to seek immediate medical attention.

There are two types of measles, each caused by and named after a different strain of virus. The most common form is rubeola, or hard measles, which is characterized by fever and coughing in its initial stage, and then followed by a rash that usually first breaks out on the face, and then quickly (within 24 hours) spreads to the rest of the body. Typically, the rash fades once the fever breaks, which usually occurs within five days.

Rubella, or German measles, is less common than hard measles. It, too, initially manifests with a fever, followed by reddened cheeks and an accompanying rash. Unlike rubeola, the rash associated with German measles is finer and can also be accompanied by swollen lymph glands in the neck and behind the ears. In most cases, German measles only lasts for three days and does not pose a serious health threat. However, it can be life-threatening to unborn babies whose mothers contract it during pregnancy, and can also result in serious birth defects once the babies are born.

The following juice combinations can help soothe symptoms of both types of measles, as well as boost immunity so that the body is able to more quickly heal itself.

JUICING RECIPES

- Juice $1/4$ pound pineapple and 1–2 medium pears.
Makes 6 ounces. Consume three times daily.

- Acute stage: Juice 1 medium orange, 1 medium lemon, 2 medium carrots, and $1/4$ bunch watercress. Makes 10 ounces. Consume once daily.

- Juice 2 medium carrots, 1 burdock root, 1–2 garlic cloves, and 3 celery stalks. Makes 10 ounces. Consume once daily.

MENOPAUSE

Menopause is a natural stage in every woman's life that occurs once the menstrual cycle ends (usually by the time women are in their late 40s or early 50s). At this time, the ovaries stop producing as much estrogen, a hormone that triggers menstruation. As with many health conditions, menopause that causes uncomfortable symptoms is virtually nonexistent in cultures around the world where a healthy, natural diet is followed and where women are respected and honored for this significant passage into another stage of their lives. By contrast, here in the United States, many women experience a variety of symptoms as they enter into menopause. These include hot flashes and vaginal dryness that can be accompanied by anxiety, depression, mood swings, and stress, as well as edema (water retention) and unhealthy weight gain. Many women also become more susceptible to bacterial infections during menopause, as well as candidiasis (systemic yeast overgrowth). They also have a higher risk of developing heart disease, osteoporosis, and fibroids, as well as breast and other types of cancer. To a large degree, all of these problems are due to imbalanced ratios of estrogen to progesterone (another hormone) which, ironically, can be further aggravated by the use of synthetic hormones that are so often prescribed for menopausal women by physicians.

While juicing itself is not a complete solution for preventing symptoms of menopause, the following juices can help to minimize such symptoms. For best results, seek the assistance of a holistically oriented health practitioner who specializes in women's health issues, and be sure to eliminate all unhealthy foods and beverages from your diet.

JUICING RECIPES

• Juice $\frac{1}{2}$ cup black currants, 1 cup black or purple grapes, and 1 medium apple.
Makes 10 ounces. Consume once to twice daily.

• Juice 3 medium carrots, $\frac{1}{2}$ medium beet, $\frac{1}{2}$ medium cucumber, and 1 garlic clove. Consider adding a small amount of raspberry leaf.
Makes 10 ounces. Consume once to twice daily.

• Juice 3 medium carrots, 2 burdock roots, 1 bunch watercress, and $\frac{1}{2}$ bunch parsley.
Makes 12–14 ounces. Consume once daily.

• Juice 12 ounces cantaloupe, 2 medium apples, and add 1 tablespoon noni juice.
Makes 16 ounces. Consume once daily.

MIGRAINE (*See also* HEADACHES)

Migraine is a specific type of headache that afflicts more than 12 million people in the United States. Unlike other types of headaches, migraine headaches usually strike one side of the face, particularly the eye and surrounding temple, causing throbbing pain that is often accompanied by other symptoms. These include blurred vision, dizziness, nausea, sensitivities to light, and vomiting. Many migraine sufferers are temporarily debilitated by their symptoms until they pass.

To most appropriately treat migraine headaches, it is necessary to first determine all of the potential factors that can trigger their onset. These include allergies (both food and environmental), musculo-skeletal imbalances and related problems, digestive and gastrointestinal problems, poor diet, and nutritional deficiencies. It is also necessary for migraine sufferers to learn how to effectively manage stress, which is another primary trigger of migraines.

The following juice combinations can help to relieve migraine symptoms, especially those that are caused by poor diet, nutritional imbalances, and gastrointestinal problems.

JUICING RECIPES

- Juice 4 medium carrots and 4 celery stalks.
Makes 14 ounces. Consume once to twice daily.

- Juice 3 medium carrots, $\frac{1}{2}$ medium beet, 1 medium cucumber, and $\frac{1}{4}$ bunch parsley.
Makes 14 ounces. Consume once to twice daily.

- Juice 3 medium carrots, 3 celery stalks, $\frac{1}{4}$ bunch spinach, $\frac{1}{4}$ bunch parsley, and $\frac{1}{4}$ head lettuce. Makes 16 ounces. Consume once daily.

- Juice $\frac{1}{2}$ medium papaya, 6 ounces cantaloupe, and add 1 tablespoon noni juice.
Makes 8 ounces. Consume once to twice daily.

HEALTHY TWIST

🍒 Consider adding Boswellia (1–3 capsules), 1–2 ounces turmeric, $\frac{1}{2}$ cup black cherry juice or 2 tablespoons black cherry concentrate, and/or 3 capsules nettles to the above recipes.

MONONUCLEOSIS

Mononucleosis, also known as "mono," is an acute disease caused by a viral infection that in most cases affects teenagers between the ages of 14 to 18. It can also affect adults, however. Mono primarily affects the lymph glands and respiratory system. But, if it is allowed to progress, it can also affect various organs in the body, including the liver and spleen, and, in rare cases, the heart and kidneys. The primary viruses associated with mononucleosis are the cytomegalovirus and the Epstein-Barr virus, both of which are members of the herpes group of viruses. Due to how infectious mononucleosis is, it is sometimes called the "kissing disease" because it can be transmitted by a kiss from persons affected with it. People with mononucleosis are advised to avoid contact with others until they recover.

People with mononucleosis typically experience an increase in abnormal white blood cells, which is a sign physicians use to diagnose the disease, since, in many ways, it can resemble the flu. The primary symptom of mononucleosis is extreme fatigue. Other symptoms include chills that alternate with fever, depression, swollen lymph glands, headache, and sore throat. Some people also develop bruises or rashes inside the mouth.

Conventional physicians often recommend antibiotic treatment for mononucleosis. This is usually unnecessary (except for cases where bacterial infection is also present), because antibiotics provide no benefit for viral infections. In some cases, they can even cause symptoms to worsen.

To properly treat mononucleosis, bed rest is advised, along with plenty of healthy fluids and light meals consisting primarily of soups and raw or slightly steamed vegetables. The following juice combinations are also recommended because of the variety of immune-boosting nutrients they provide. Please note, too, that in most cases, people with mono may require four to six weeks of proper rest before they fully recover from their symptoms. Aerobic exercise should be limited until four to six weeks past the symptom stage (sore throat, exhaustion), as mono is notorious for recurrence.

JUICING RECIPES

• Juice 3 medium carrots, $\frac{1}{2}$ medium beet, 1 medium tomato, and $\frac{1}{2}$ medium green pepper (also add a little garlic and onion).
Makes 16 ounces. Consume once daily.

• Juice 1 medium lemon, 1 medium orange, and 4 ounces pineapple.
Makes 6 ounces. Consume once to twice daily.

• Consume wheatgrass juice (1–2 ounces) daily, or add to other fresh juices. (See inset on page 146.)

• Juice 3 medium carrots, 2 burdock roots, 1 garlic clove, and 2 celery stalks. Consider Osha root (*lomatium,* best as an isolate) and/or Larix powder (1 teaspoon).
Makes 12 ounces. Consume once to twice daily.

MOTION SICKNESS

Motion sickness, as its name implies, is a condition caused by a reaction to motion, primarily during travel in cars, trains, boats, airplanes, and other vehicles. Symptoms of motion sickness vary and can include dizziness, fatigue, headache, nausea, panic attacks, and vomiting.

The following juice recipes can be helpful for both preventing and relieving symptoms associated with motion sickness.

JUICING RECIPES

• Juice 2 medium apples with 1 ounce ginger root.
Makes 8 ounces. Consume once to twice as needed.

• Juice 2 medium pears, 1 medium apple, and 1 teaspoon cinnamon.
Makes 8 ounces. Consume one to three times as needed.

• Juice 3 medium carrots, 3 celery stalks, and 2 ounces ginger.
Consume once.

MUMPS

Mumps is another fairly common childhood disease (although it can afflict adults as well), and one that can easily be spread to others through coughs and sneezes, due to how highly infectious it is. Although usually not serious, in some cases mumps can provoke other disease conditions, including convulsions, brain inflammation (encephalitis) and meningitis (inflammation of the brain and spinal cord). For this reason, children with mumps should be monitored by a health care practitioner.

Mumps are caused by viral infections. The primary symptoms of mumps are swollen lymph glands along the neck, and swollen salivary glands beneath the tongue, along with difficulty swallowing and speaking clearly. Other potential symptoms include fatigue, headache, muscle stiffness (especially in the neck), nausea, and vomiting.

As with mononucleosis (page 211), to properly treat mumps, bed rest is advised, along with plenty of healthy fluids and light meals consisting primarily of soups and raw or slightly steamed vegetables. The following juice combinations are also recommended because of the variety of immune-boosting nutrients they provide.

JUICING RECIPES

- Juice 2 medium oranges and 2 medium lemons.
Makes 10 ounces. Consume twice daily.
- Juice 3 medium carrots and $1/2$ bunch watercress.
Makes 8 ounces. Consume once to twice daily.
- Juice 2 medium apples, $1/2$ medium papaya, and 1 ounce ginger.
Makes 12 ounces. Consume once to twice daily.

MUSCLE CRAMPS

Muscle cramps are a condition in the body caused by the abnormal contraction of various muscles. They are not serious, but can be quite painful. Symptoms of muscle cramps include muscle tightness, as well as pain and sometimes burning sensations in the affected muscle. The primary causes of muscle cramps are a lack of exercise, poor diet, and nutritional deficiencies, especially those nutrients that are found in carrots and green vegetables, as well as certain fruits. Musculo-skeletal imbalances and other physical problems can also play a role. Useful juice combinations for preventing and reversing muscle cramps include the following.

JUICING RECIPES

- Juice 3 medium carrots, $\frac{1}{2}$ medium beet, 3 celery stalks, $\frac{1}{2}$ cucumber, and $\frac{1}{4}$ bunch watercress; consider also mustard greens.
Makes 16 ounces. Consume once daily as needed.

- Juice 3 medium carrots, 3 celery stalks, and 6–8 leaves of mustard greens. Makes 12–14 ounces. Consume once to twice as needed.

- Sweet fruit juices, such as papaya, pineapple, and noni.
Consume 16 ounces daily.

NAIL PROBLEMS

Nail problems are characterized by abnormal changes in the appearance of the finger or toenails. These include abnormally brittle, curving or thickening of nails, as well as bacterial or fungal overgrowth in and around the nails. Other nail problems include nails that easily chip or crack, darkened nails, white spots within the nails, and redness in the skin that surrounds nails. Though not serious, nail problems are often a sign of an underlying imbalance in the body, and in some cases can be due to disease conditions, such as allergies, arthritis, or metabolism problems. Other causes of nail problems include anemia, poor diet, poor circulation, nutritional imbalances (especially a lack of minerals and digestive enzymes), and dysfunctions in various organs of the body, such as the kidneys.

Nail problems related to poor diet and nutritional deficiencies can often be resolved by drinking the following juice combinations on a regular basis.

JUICING RECIPES

- Juice 3 medium carrots, $\frac{1}{2}$ medium beet, 3 celery stalks, and 1 ounce wheatgrass juice. (See Wheatgrass Juice inset on page 146.)
Makes 14 ounces. Consume once daily.

- Juice 3 medium carrots, $\frac{1}{4}$ head cabbage, and 1 bunch watercress.
Makes 12 ounces. Consume once to twice daily.

- Juice 1 medium papaya, 8 ounces coconut, 2 ounces peppermint leaves, and 1 medium lemon. Makes 12 ounces. Consume once to twice daily.

NAUSEA (*See also* MOTION SICKNESS; VOMITING)

Nausea is a health condition that typically occurs in the stomach or small intestine. It can lead to feelings of dizziness, gagging, and vomiting. In some cases, nausea can be due to psychological problems, such as anxiety, stress, and panic attacks. In most cases, however, it is due to such factors as poor diet, overeating, food poisoning, parasites, or the excessive consumption of alcohol. Cigarettes (including secondhand smoke) and drug use can also cause nausea, as can exposure to toxic chemicals and other pollutants. Nausea can also be due to ear problems, particularly within the inner ear and ear canal. Nutritional deficiencies and liver toxicity can also cause nausea.

The following juice combinations can quickly relieve nausea symptoms.

JUICING RECIPES

- Juice 2 medium apples with 1 ounce ginger root.
Makes 8 ounces. Consume every 2 hours as needed.

- Juice 2 medium pears, 8 ounces blueberries, and 1 teaspoon cinnamon.
Makes 6 ounces. Consume every 2 hours as needed.

- Juice 3 medium carrots, 3 celery stalks, and 2 ounces ginger root.
Makes 12 ounces. Consume once daily.

NEURALGIA / NEUROPATHY / NEURITIS

Neuralgia, neuropathy, and neuritis are related conditions of the nerves or the overall nervous system. Neuralgia is characterized by spasms that run along a specific nerve, causing intermittent pain. Neuropathy occurs when nerves outside of the spine, which comprise the peripheral nervous system, become disturbed or entrapped, due to diseases such as diabetes, structural problems such as carpal tunnel syndrome or degenerative disks and disk lesions, and poor diet and nutritional deficiencies. Neuritis is characterized by inflammation in specific nerve groups. All three conditions are similar in terms of their symptoms, which include constant or fluctuating pain, burning sensations, and uncomfortable tingling in the affected nerves and the areas of the body that surround them. Because all three conditions can also be indications of underlying disease, medical attention is advised in order to rule out more serious health problems.

To help relieve symptoms of these conditions, consider drinking one or more of the following juice combinations at least once a day.

JUICING RECIPES

- Juice 4 medium carrots, 8 ounces Jerusalem artichokes, $1/4$ medium onion, 1 garlic clove, and 2 celery stalks. Consider $1/4$ cup of hypericum flowers (commonly referred to as St. John's Wort).
Makes 16–18 ounces. Consume once daily.

- Juice 3 medium carrots, $1/2$ bunch parsley, 2 celery stalks, and $1/2$ head lettuce. Makes 14 ounces. Consume once to twice daily.

- Juice 8 ounces blueberries, 2 medium pears, 2 medium lemons, and either 1 tablespoon noni juice or 2 capsules ($1/2$ dropper) of passion flower. Makes 16–18 ounces. Consume once daily.

NOSEBLEEDS

Nosebleeds are caused by irritations in the mucous membrane inside the nose. They most commonly occur in childhood and in most cases are not serious. However, nosebleeds following physical trauma, such as accidents or injury, as well as nosebleeds that are recurring or do not cease, require immediate medical attention.

In addition to physical trauma, nosebleeds can be caused by nutritional deficiencies (especially vitamin C and vitamin K, as well as flavonoids), dry weather, forceful blowing of the nose, fingernail scratches, and environmental irritants, such as dust. Aspirin and drugs such as coumadin can also cause nosebleeds because of their blood-thinning properties.

To stop nosebleeds that are not due to trauma, sit or lie down and tip your head up and backward. As you do so, pinch your nostril for a few minutes while breathing through your mouth. If bleeding continues beyond five to ten minutes, apply crushed ice against your nose and cheek, and pack your nostril with cotton or gauze. Once bleeding stops, moisten the inside of your nostrils with soothing ointments such as aloe vera gel or liquid vitamin E.

To prevent nosebleeds from recurring, include plenty of dark, leafy green vegetables in your diet and regularly drink one or more of the following juices. By doing so, you will be providing your body with many of the nutrients it needs to ensure the overall health of the inner lining of your nose.

JUICING RECIPES

- Juice 3 medium carrots, $1/2$ medium beet, $1/4$ bunch spinach, and $1/2$ ounce ginger root or $1/4$ teaspoon cayenne.
Makes 10 ounces. Consume once at time of bleeding.

- Juice 2 medium apples and add $1/4$–$1/2$ teaspoon cinnamon.
Makes 8 ounces. Can consume once every hour as needed.

- Juice 1 medium grapefruit (scrape inner rind skin into juicer), 2 medium oranges, and 1 ounce citron. Makes 14–16 ounces. Consume once daily.

NUTRITIONAL DEFICIENCY

Nutritional deficiencies are a very common and often undiagnosed health risk in many Americans due to poor diet. Lack of all of the nutrients that your body requires each day to maintain optimal health sets the stage for a wide range of disease conditions to take root. Because of how quickly and completely the abundant supply of nutrients that juices contain is absorbed by the body, juicing is one of the best ways of ensuring that your body's nutritional needs are met. Almost all nutritional deficiencies can be addressed by daily drinking of fresh juices. Taste is important, so find the most pleasurable combinations. Spinach should be considered for its iron content, watercress for its high calcium content, and garlic to help address nutritional deficiencies due to yeast-related conditions.

JUICING RECIPES

• Juice 3 medium carrots and 2 medium apples.
Makes 16 ounces. Consume once to twice daily.

• Juice 3 medium carrots, 3 celery stalks, and $1/2$ medium beet. Add 1–2 garlic cloves. Makes 12–14 ounces. Consume once daily.

• Juice 3 medium carrots, $1/2$ bunch spinach, 2 celery stalks, and $1/2$ medium cucumber. Makes 16 ounces. Consume once daily.

• Juice $1/4$ medium cantaloupe, 1 medium apple, and 8 ounces blueberries. Add 1 tablespoon noni juice, 2 ounces frozen Acai berries (palm berry), or 2 ounces frozen acerola (available from www.sambazon.com). Makes 10 ounces. Consume once to twice daily.

OBESITY

Obesity is a condition of being extremely overweight (more than 20 percent of normal, healthy body weight). The United Sates is currently in the midst of an obesity epidemic, especially among children and teenagers, primarily due to poor eating habits, unhealthy diets, and nutritional deficiencies. Other causes of obesity include food allergies, insulin imbalance, and impaired ability in the body to properly burn calories (thermogenesis).

Left unchecked, obesity can cause premature death, as well as many serious health conditions. These include diabetes, gallstones and gallbladder disease, heart disease, high blood pressure, kidney and liver disease, respiratory problems, and stroke. Obesity also significantly increases the risk of certain types of cancers, including breast cancer, colon cancer, cancer of the rectum, and uterine cancer.

The following juice remedies can help to support healthy weight loss and improve nutritional deficiencies that are associated with obesity.

JUICING RECIPES

- Juice 2 medium carrots, 3 celery stalks, 1/2 bunch parsley, and 1/2 medium cucumber. Makes 12 ounces. Consume one to three times daily.

- Juice 2 medium carrots, 4 ounces green beans, 2 medium Jerusalem artichokes, and 1 garlic clove.
Makes 10 ounces. Consume one to three times daily.

- Juice 1 medium grapefruit, 2 medium lemons, and 2 medium green apples. Makes 18 ounces. Consume once to twice daily.

OSTEOPOROSIS

Osteoporosis is a degenerative bone condition that is characterized by bone loss that exceeds the body's ability to produce new bone tissue. All of us lose bone tissue, but when we are healthy, it is replaced by an equal amount of new bone tissue. For people with osteoporosis, the body is unable to create bone tissue equal to the amount that is lost. As a result, bones become brittle and porous and become more likely to fracture. In many cases, the skeleton may also shrink. Other symptoms of osteoporosis are bent posture and rounding of the upper back and shoulders, brittle fingernails, gum disease, leg cramps, joint pain, and loss of strength.

Both men and women, as they grow older, can develop osteoporosis, but it is more common among women, affecting approximately one-third of all women in the United States who are past menopause. By contrast, in other cultures around the world, where the diet is natural and rich in fresh fruits, vegetables, and whole grains, the incidence of osteoporosis is extremely rare.

Though it is often mistakenly considered to be a natural consequence of aging, in actuality osteoporosis is another chronic condition that is closely related to the standard American diet, which is both lacking in vital nutrients and overly acidic, meaning that it creates acid-alkaline imbalances in the body. Both of these factors, along with the hormonal imbalances that can occur during and after menopause (see page 209), are what set the stage for osteoporosis. Other contributing factors for osteoporosis include cigarette smoking and secondhand exposure to cigarettes, environmental pollution, hyper- and hypothyroidism (see pages 198 and 199), menstrual irregularities, early menopause, gastrointestinal problems, kidney and liver problems, lack of exercise, lack of regular exposure to sunlight, and over-reliance on pharmaceutical drugs, such as antibiotics and steroids, which can interfere with the healthy production of new bone tissues and the body's ability to absorb calcium and other minerals that are essential for healthy bones. Excessive consumption of carbonated beverages is known to promote calcium loss due to the phosphorus excess and its shared elimination with calcium through the parathyroid function. Women who have had hysterectomies (removal of the uterus), or who have below-normal body fat content, also have a higher risk for developing osteoporosis.

A regular juicing routine, along with a healthy diet, proper exercise, and daily exposure to sunlight, can help men and women avoid developing osteoporosis. Fresh juices provide an abundance of nutrients, including minerals, which are essential for healthy bones. Juices can also help the body to eliminate environmental toxins that can also be involved, as well as improve the overall health of the kidneys, liver, and gastrointestinal tract. The following juices are especially helpful in this regard.

JUICING RECIPES

- Juice 3 medium carrots, $\frac{1}{4}$ bunch parsley, 2 celery stalks, and $\frac{1}{2}$–1 cup watercress.
Makes 12 ounces. Consume once daily.

- Juice 8 ounces coconut, $\frac{1}{2}$ medium papaya, and blend with 1 medium banana.
Makes 14 ounces. Consume once to twice daily.

- Juice 4 medium carrots, $\frac{1}{2}$ head cabbage, and 3 celery stalks.
Makes 16–18 ounces. Consume once daily.

OTITIS MEDIA

Otitis media is a common ear problem among children that affects the middle ear. It is caused by infection and is the leading cause of hearing loss in children. Other contributing factors that can cause or exacerbate otitis media include allergies, the overuse of antibiotics, poor diet, nutritional deficiencies, inflammation, and the excessive buildup of earwax in the ear canal.

Besides hearing problems, symptoms of otitis media include earache and ear pain, alternating chills and fever, upper respiratory tract infection, and swelling of the eardrum and middle ear. If allowed to progress, the infections related to otitis media can result in meningitis (inflammation of the brain and spinal cord). Therefore, resistant cases of otitis media need to be overseen by a holistic health care practitioner.

The juices that follow can be helpful, used both preventively and therapeutically.

JUICING RECIPES

● Juice 3 medium carrots, 1–2 garlic cloves, ½ head lettuce, and 2 celery stalks. Consider nettles and hypericum flowers.
Makes 14 ounces. Consume once daily.

● Juice 3 medium carrots, 2 celery stalks, and 1 ounce turmeric or ginger root. Makes 10 ounces. Consume once to twice daily.

● Juice 4 medium lemons, 1 medium orange, 1 ounce citron, and add 1 tablespoon noni juice. Makes 8 ounces. Consume once to twice daily.

PANCREATITIS

Pancreatitis is a condition that affects the pancreas and is characterized by inflammation of that organ. Pancreatitis can be temporary (acute) or ongoing (chronic). Cases of acute pancreatitis usually eventually heal, while cases of chronic pancreatitis often prove resistant to healing, and can lead to irreversible damage to pancreas cells if not properly treated. Symptoms of pancreatitis are often not apparent. When they are, they most commonly include sharp, stabbing abdominal pain that can also radiate outwardly along the back. Other symptoms of pancreatitis include accelerated heart rate, digestive problems, dizziness, excessive perspiration, nausea, and vomiting.

One of the most common causes of acute pancreatitis is overconsumption of alcohol, which must be avoided in order for the condition to heal. Regular heavy or excessive consumption of alcohol can cause chronic pancreatitis, as can gallbladder and liver dysfunctions, poor diet, nutritional deficiencies, and the overuse of pharmaceutical drugs. In cases of chronic pancreatitis, medical attention is advised. For both forms of pancreatitis, the following juices can help to relieve symptoms.

JUICING RECIPES

● Juice 3 medium carrots, 2 medium Jerusalem artichokes, ½–1 medium beet, and 2 garlic cloves. Juice may be diluted 50/50 with water.
Makes 14 ounces. Consume once to twice daily.

● Juice 3 medium carrots, ¼ head cabbage, 2 celery stalks, and add 2 ounces wheatgrass juice. (See Wheatgrass Juice inset on page 146.)
Makes 14 ounces. Consume once daily.

● Juice ½ medium papaya with 2 medium apples.
Makes 12 ounces. Consume once to twice daily.

PARKINSON'S DISEASE

Parkinson's disease is a condition that slowly but progressively affects the central nervous system, causing degeneration of the various body functions that the central nervous system initiates and regulates. There is no known cure for Parkinson's disease, and no known definitive cause, although it is known that the disease involves imbalances in the supply of dopamine and acetylcholine, both of which are essential chemicals of the brain. Many health professionals also consider the buildup of heavy metals, as well as other environmental toxins, to be a factor in the onset and progression of the disease.

Initial symptoms of the disease often escape notice at first, but usually begin as slight tremors of the hands, arms, feet, or legs. In most cases, in the early stages of the disease, the tremor only affects one side of the body and is only apparent during times of rest, except for sleep, when it is completely absent. During movement, it also tends to disappear, but it can be aggravated by stress and lack of sleep. Other areas of the body that can be affected by tremor at the onset of Parkinson's disease are eyelids, forehead, jaw, and tongue. Another early warning sign of Parkinson's is a decrease in the amount of times the eyelids blink.

As the disease progresses, symptoms become increasingly noticeable and start to change. They include abnormally slow and distorted, shuffling movements, unbalanced gait, muscle stiffness, postural problems, and a shift of the tremor to both sides of the body. Some people with Parkinson's also develop what is known as Parkinson's mask, which is characterized by a frozen expression. Slurred speech and other difficulties of speech can also develop, as can depression, dementia, and fatigue. Eventually, people who suffer from Parkinson's disease can become completely incapacitated, requiring ongoing assistance in order to function. In all cases of Parkinson's, regular professional medical care is necessary.

Helping the body to detoxify and eliminate toxins can often help to slow the progression of Parkinson's disease. Juicing is an excellent way to help accomplish this. The following juice combinations can be especially useful.

JUICING RECIPES

- Juice 3–4 medium carrots, $1/4$ bunch spinach, and 1 garlic clove. Makes 10 ounces. Consume once daily.

- Juice 3 medium carrots, $1/2$ medium beet, 4 ounces radishes, 1 garlic clove, and $1/2$ medium cucumber. Makes 12 ounces. Consume once daily.

- Juice 3 medium carrots, $1/2$ bunch cilantro, 2 celery stalks, and 1 garlic clove. Makes 12 ounces. Consume once daily.

HEALTHY TWIST

👻 Consider 100 mg zinc, 2 tablespoons essential fats, and the following B vitamins: 100 mg each of B_1, B_2, and B_3.

PERIODONTAL DISEASE / BLEEDING GUMS

Periodontal disease is a disease of the gums, as well as the bones of the jaw in which teeth are set. It is characterized by inflammation and degeneration of the gums and jawbones. The most common type of periodontal disease is gingivitis, which primarily affects the gums, and results in inflamed and bleeding gums (particularly as a result of flossing and brushing the teeth). Left untreated, gingivitis can eventually spread into the base of the teeth and their underlying bones, causing a more serious form of periodontal disease known as periodontitis, which is one of the most common causes of bone loss among adults.

The primary causes of periodontal disease are poor dental habits, such as neglecting to floss and brush your teeth. This results in the buildup of bacteria and plaque in the surrounding gums and bone tissue. Other potential causes include poor diet, nutritional deficiencies (especially of vitamin C, as well as of calcium and various B vitamins), impacted food in the gums, smoking, and malocclusion (imbalanced bite).

Periodontal disease is extremely preventable if proper dental care is followed, including regular visits to your dentist. In most cases, it can also be reversed and eliminated so long as it has not progressed too far. Some cases that are resistant to proper treatment may be indications of more serious health problems, including diabetes and leukemia. Therefore, people who are unable to control periodontal disease despite proper treatment with a dentist are advised to see a physician to rule out more serious health conditions. To help prevent and reverse periodontal disease, be sure to brush your teeth after every meal and to floss your teeth at least twice a day. Also get regular dental checkups (every six months). Regularly drinking any of the following juice combinations can also be helpful. For added benefits, before swallowing, swish each sip of juice in your mouth.

JUICING RECIPES

• Juice 3 medium carrots, ½ bunch spinach, and 3 celery stalks.
Makes 14 ounces. Consume once to twice daily.

• Juice 3 medium carrots, 1 bunch watercress, and 1 ounce ginger.
Makes 10 ounces. Consume once to twice daily.

- Juice $1/2$ medium cantaloupe, 8 ounces blueberries, and 1 tablespoon noni juice. Makes 10 ounces. Consume once to twice daily.

HEALTHY TWIST

Consider cordyceps extract, hawthorn berries, and Sanguinaria (homeopathically) as supplements.

PLEURISY

Pleurisy is a lung condition caused by inflammation in the mucous membranes of the lungs and the thoracic cavity of the chest. These membranes are known as *pleura,* hence the condition's name. The primary cause of pleurisy is lung infection. Symptoms usually strike suddenly. The primary symptom is pain during inhalation. Coughing can also occur, which can trigger stabbing pains in the chest and within the area of the shoulder over the affected lung. As the condition takes hold, breathing usually becomes more shallow and rapid, as well.

The following juices can help conditions of pleurisy for a number of reasons. Rich with essential nutrients, they can help boost immune function, thereby helping the body to fight off the lung infection. And they can also assist in supporting detoxification and liver function, both of which are important when the body is seeking to rid itself of harmful microorganisms.

JUICING RECIPES

- Juice 3 medium carrots, 3 celery stalks, and $1/4$ bunch parsley. Makes 12 ounces. Consume two to three times daily.

- Juice 3 medium carrots, $1/2$ medium beet, $1/2$ medium cucumber, and 1–2 garlic cloves. Makes 10 ounces. Consume once to twice daily.

- Juice 8 ounces blueberries, 2 medium kiwis, 2 ounces pitted hawthorn berries (can add tincture or dilute with tea), and add 1 tablespoon noni juice. Makes 8 ounces. Consume once to twice daily.

PREGNANCY

Proper diet and nutrition are vitally important for healthy pregnancies that are successfully carried to term, as well as for the overall health of the mother and the newborn child. Making sure that the body's immune system and detoxification system are functioning properly is also important. Juicing is a self-care method that helps to accomplish these and many other tasks, thereby increasing the likelihood of a healthy pregnancy and delivery. Regularly drinking fresh juices can also help to prevent and relieve symptoms of morning sickness during the first trimester, and minimize unhealthy food cravings that many pregnant women experience prior to childbirth. The following juice combinations provide a rich source of essential nutrients to support the health of both the mother and her developing child throughout the course of pregnancy, and after the baby is born.

JUICING RECIPES

- Juice 3 medium carrots and 1 medium apple.
Makes 12 ounces. Consume once daily.

- Juice 3 medium carrots, 1–2 celery stalks, and 1/4 bunch parsley.
Makes 10 ounces. Consume once daily.

- Juice 3 medium carrots, 1 medium cucumber, and 1 bunch watercress.
Makes 12–14 ounces. Consume once daily.

PROSTATE PROBLEMS (*See* BENIGN PROSTATIC HYPERPLASIA)

PSORIASIS (*See also* DERMATITIS; ECZEMA)

Psoriasis is a chronic skin condition characterized by thick, reddened, scaly patches of skin. The most common areas of the body where psoriasis can occur are the arms, scalp, back, elbows, legs, and knees. In some cases, it also occurs behind the ears. Although psoriasis typically does not cause itching, it can be unsightly, leading to emotional discomfort and embarrassment.

A variety of factors can trigger or exacerbate psoriasis. These include allergies (both food and environmental), poor diet, nutritional deficiencies (including a lack of digestive enzymes), infections, and stress. The following juice recipes can help to address most of these factors and are very useful for relieving psoriasis symptoms and speeding healing.

JUICING RECIPES

- Juice 1 medium apple and 3 medium carrots.
Makes 12 ounces. Consume once to twice daily.

- Juice 3 medium carrots, 1 medium beet, 1/2 medium cucumber, and 2 garlic cloves. Makes 12 ounces. Consume once daily.

- Juice 1 cup blueberries and 1/2 cup black grapes.
Makes 6 ounces. Consume once to twice daily.

- Juice 3 medium carrots, 1/2 medium beet, 2 burdock roots, 1–2 garlic cloves, and consider yellow dock (5 percent, i.e. 1–3 leaves per quart). Makes 10 ounces. Consume once daily.

CONSIDERATION

■ Avoid juicing with citrus fruits until symptoms have significantly improved.

RASHES

Rashes are eruptions of the skin that cause redness, inflammation, and itching in the affected area. In the majority of cases, rashes are temporary and harmless. In some instances, however, rashes can be a sign of other health problems, such as allergies, a buildup of toxins and waste products in the body, exposure to environmental pollutants, gallbladder and liver problems, infections, poor diet, and nutritional deficiencies. Persistent rashes, as well as rashes that are accompanied by fever or joint pains, should be brought to the attention of a medical professional. The following juices are all helpful for soothing rash symptoms and speeding healing.

JUICING RECIPES

- Juice 3 medium carrots, 1/2 medium beet, 1 medium black radish, and 1 garlic clove. Makes 10 ounces. Consume once daily.

- Drink wheatgrass juice. Consume 2–4 ounces daily. (See inset on page 146.)

- Juice equal parts black currants and blueberries.
Consume 8 ounces twice daily.

- Juice 3 medium carrots, 1/2 head cabbage, and 2 celery stalks.
Makes 14 ounces. Consume once daily. Consider adding 1 cup nettle tea.

RINGWORM

Ringworm is a fungal infection of the skin. In most cases, ringworm appears as a red, ring-shaped blemish. It can also form blisters or be scaly in appearance. The most common areas of the body where ringworm occurs are the groin, inner thighs, feet, and toes, although it can be present anywhere on the body.

The fungal infections that cause ringworm are often preceded by poor hygiene and the buildup of sweat around the area of the groin, thighs, or feet due to wearing clothes or socks that are too tight. Candidiasis (systemic yeast overgrowth—see page 164) can also increase the risk of ringworm. To prevent and treat ringworm, be sure to bathe or shower at least once a day, and also wear clean underwear and socks. Drinking the following juices can also be helpful.

JUICING RECIPES

- Juice equal parts strawberries and fresh dates.
Consume 6 ounces twice daily.

- Juice 2 medium carrots, 2 celery stalks, and 2 garlic cloves.
Makes 8 ounces. Consume twice daily.

CONSIDERATION

■ Most vegetables juices, with as much garlic as desired, will be helpful.

■ Apply citron juice topically to relieve symptoms and speed healing.

SENILE DEMENTIA (*See* ALZHEIMER'S DISEASE)

SHINGLES (HERPES ZOSTER)

Shingles is a skin condition caused by the varicella-zoster virus. It also affects the central nervous system, causing symptoms of fatigue, fever, and gastrointestinal problems, followed (usually three to four days later) by the eruption of small, crust-like blisters on the skin, along various nerve lines. The eruptions can be extremely painful and sensitive to the touch. The most common sites on the body where shingles occur are on the side of the face, the chest, and ribcage. In most cases, shingles will heal within a week after the eruptions occur, but in some cases, the condition can recur, with the pain lasting for months at a time. Shingles that last beyond a two-week period could indicate more serious immune conditions, and should be treated by a health care professional. Shingles outbreaks near the eyes also require special attention because they can lead to blindness.

To relieve shingles' pain and speed healing, drink one or more of the following juice combinations at least twice a day.

JUICING RECIPES

- Juice 3 medium carrots, 3 celery stalks, 1/4 bunch parsley, 1–2 garlic cloves, and 1/4 head lettuce. Makes 14 ounces. Consume twice daily.

- Juice 4 medium carrots, 1/2 bunch spinach, and 1/2 medium beet.
Makes 12 ounces. Consume twice daily.

• Juice 8 ounces blueberries, 2 ounces citron, 1 medium apple, and add 1 tablespoon noni juice. Makes 8 ounces. Consume one to three times daily.

CONSIDERATION

■ Consider lysine supplementation (1,000–2,000 mg daily) and avoid foods that are high in the amino acid L-arginine, such as nuts, coffee, and chocolate.

SINUSITIS

Sinusitis is one of the most commonly occurring respiratory diseases in the United States. It occurs in two forms—acute and chronic. In both forms, inflammation strikes the mucous membranes of one or more of the sinus cavities. Acute sinusitis is usually temporary and due to a sinus infection, while chronic sinusitis tends to recur frequently. Left unchecked, chronic sinusitis can lead to additional sinus and breathing problems due to the degeneration of the mucous membranes of the sinuses as a result of ongoing inflammation. In addition to bacterial, fungal, and viral infections, sinusitis can also be caused by food allergies, candidiasis (page 164), nasal cysts and polyps, and structural problems in the sinus cavities, such as a deviated septum.

Symptoms of both acute and chronic sinusitis include congestion, chronic fatigue, fever, headache and facial pain, laryngitis, and postnasal drip. It can also be caused or exacerbated by environmental toxins, air that is too cold or dry, and smoking. Poor diet and nutritional deficiencies can also play a role.

To help relieve sinusitis symptoms, drink one or more of the following juices at least twice a day, however, since 1/4 onion is so potent, this drink should be limited to one time daily.

JUICING RECIPES

• Juice 3 medium carrots, 1/2 medium cucumber, 1/4 bunch parsley, 2 celery stalks, and 3–4 garlic cloves; also add nettle (as two opened capsules of powder). Makes 12 ounces. Consume once to twice daily.

• Juice 1 medium orange, 2 medium lemons, 1 ounce citron, and 2 ounces fresh peppermint leaves.
Makes 6–8 ounces. Consume once to twice daily.

• Juice 3 medium carrots, 1/2 bunch cilantro, 1/4 medium onion, and 3 celery stalks. Makes 14–16 ounces. Consume once daily.

SKIN PROBLEMS (*See also* ACNE; DERMATITIS; ECZEMA; PSORIASIS; RASHES; SHINGLES; SUNBURN)

Your skin is your body's largest organ of elimination. When your body becomes overburdened with toxins or succumbs to infections, skin problems can often result. Poor dietary habits and nutritional deficiencies can also lead to skin problems, as can liver problems, environmental pollutants, and sensitivities to synthetic fragrances and perfumes. Persistent skin problems can also be an indication of more serious, underlying health problems, in which case you should seek professional medical advice.

To help maintain the health of your skin, follow a high-fiber diet rich in unprocessed foods, healthy essential fatty acids, and plenty of fresh vegetables. Also be sure to drink plenty of pure, filtered water throughout the day and get regular exercise. The juices below are also recommended.

JUICING RECIPES

- Juice 3 medium carrots, $\frac{1}{2}$ medium cucumber, $\frac{1}{2}$ bunch parsley, and 2 tablespoons seabuckthorn. **Makes 12 ounces. Consume once to twice daily.**

- Juice $\frac{1}{2}$ medium papaya, 4 ounces currants, 4 ounces black grapes, and add 1 tablespoon noni juice. **Makes 8 ounces. Consume once to twice daily.**

- Juice 3 medium carrots, $\frac{1}{2}$ medium beet, $\frac{1}{2}$ medium cucumber, 1 burdock root, and add 1–2 tablespoons seabuckthorn.
Makes 14–16 ounces. Consume once daily.

- Juice 8 ounces watermelon, 8 ounces grapes, and add 2 ounces frozen acai berries. **Makes 10 ounces. Consume once to twice daily.**

- Juice 4 medium carrots and 2 medium apples.
Makes 16 ounces. Consume once daily.

CONSIDERATION

■ Emphasize essential fats, water, and high fiber in your diet.

SMOKING CESSATION

Smoking, especially smoking cigarettes, is one of the single most harmful lifestyle choices anyone can make. Unfortunately, once people start smoking, they very often quickly find themselves suffering from addiction to nicotine and various other of the more than 200 chemical ingredients that cigarettes contain. Researchers now understand that a large part of this addiction process is biochemical in nature.

Specifically, once addiction occurs, receptor sites in the brain are formed, which literally cause a physical and biochemical craving for the addictive substance. It is for this reason that people who suffer from addictions, including cigarettes, often are unable to quit their self-destructive habits. It's not a lack of will power that is involved but the powerful pull from the brain's receptor sites. Compounding this problem is the fact that the more times a person succumbs to his or her addiction, the more additional receptor sites specific to the addictive chemical are formed in the brains, further strengthening the biochemical cravings and, therefore, the addiction.

One of the keys to long-term successful recovery from addictions, including smoking, lies in shutting down the receptor sites that cause such craving. There are a number of ways that this can be achieved, including safe and natural methods such as detoxification therapies (including juice fasts; see Chapter 7), acupuncture, and dietary intervention. The following juice recipe, developed by Vaidya Priyanka, can also help to restore proper brain chemistry among smokers, making it easier to give up the smoking habit. (Vaidya Priyanka is one of the foremost Ayurvedic doctors in the world, coming from a 712-year lineage of women Ayurvedic healers from Kerala, India. Vaidyaji—as she is often called—is internationally respected and renowned.)

JUICING RECIPES

• Juice 1 medium apple, 1 celery stalk, 1 ½ teaspoons highest lignan flax oil, and ½ teaspoon turmeric. For other drug addictions, add 1 pinch clove powder to this recipe. Consume four to six times throughout the day as a 1-ounce serving, or with cravings. This drink will make smoking repugnant and significantly reduces cravings.

• For other juice recipes that can also be helpful, see Addictions on page 138.

SORE THROAT

Sore throats are a very common health condition and are rarely of serious concern. Sore throats can manifest in a variety of ways. They are characterized by inflammation of the throat, pain upon swallowing, and sensations of rawness. In some cases, symptoms can also include fever, laryngitis, postnasal drip, and swollen lymph nodes in the neck.

Most cases of sore throats are caused by bacterial or viral infection. But sore throats can also be due a number of other factors, including allergies, cigarettes and exposure to secondhand smoke, colds and flu, sinusitis, and enlarged tonsils (tonsillitis, see page 233). In some cases, sore throats can also be due to *Streptococcal* infection, which causes a specific type of sore throat known as strep throat. In people who suffer from immune deficiencies, strep throat should be carefully monitored by a health care practitioner, in order to avoid it causing rheumatic fever and other, more serious health conditions. Sore throats that last for more than ten days, or which are accompanied by a rash, should also be treated by a doctor.

To relieve symptoms of sore throat and to speed healing, the following juice combinations are recommended.

JUICING RECIPES

- Juice of red potato with equal parts carrot.
Consume 8 ounces once to twice daily.

- Juice 4 ounces pineapple, 1 medium apple, and $\frac{1}{2}$–1 ounce ginger root.
Makes 6 ounces. Consume two to three times daily.

- Add juice of 2 medium lemons and 1 teaspoon raw honey to 8 ounces hot water. Consume as much as desired.

- Juice 1 medium orange, 1 medium lemon, 1 tablespoon acerola powder or 2 ounces frozen acerola, and 1 ounce ginger root.
Makes 6–8 ounces. Consume one to three times daily.

SPORTS INJURIES / SPRAINS / STRAINS (*See also* FRACTURES)

Sports injuries, sprains, and strains are caused by accidents or other types of injuries, as well as overexertion of muscles due to exercise and stretching. Most cases of such conditions involve the soft tissues of the muscles or the joints themselves, which can sometimes become dislocated as a result of injury. Bone fractures also fall into this category, as do head injuries. In all cases, prompt medical attention should be sought.

Juicing is by no means a cure for sprains, strain, and other types of injury, but adding fresh juices to your daily diet can provide your body with an abundance of nutrients that can help to quicken your recovery time. The following juices can be particularly useful.

JUICING RECIPES

- Juice 3 medium carrots, 1 medium beet, 1 medium black radish, and 2 garlic cloves (can dilute with comfrey tea).
Makes 12 ounces. Consume once to twice daily.

- Juice 4 ounces pineapple, 1 medium papaya, 1 medium lemon, and 1 medium grapefruit. Consider adding 1 tablespoon noni juice and ginger. Makes 16 ounces. Consume once to twice daily.

- Juice 3 medium carrots, 2 burdock roots, 1 bunch watercress, $\frac{1}{2}$ medium beet, and 3 celery stalks. Makes 18 ounces. Consume once daily.

STOMACH ULCERS

Stomach ulcers are characterized by inflammation in the stomach, which can cause stomach pain (especially after eating and when lying down) and burning sensations in the stomach. In some cases, stomach ulcers can also result in stomach bleeding. Once thought to be primarily due to stress, since the 1990s it has been recognized that over 90 percent of all cases of stomach ulcer are caused by an overabundance of a type of bacteria known as *Helicobacter pylori* (*H. pylori*), which some researchers now speculate can also cause stomach cancer. (However, recent research indicates that *H. pylori* can be a normal flora without causing ulceration. Some researchers are now suggesting that *H. pylori* appears to thrive on ulcerated tissues and may not be causative.) Food allergies and the overuse of pharmaceutical drugs, especially aspirin and non-steroidal anti-inflammatory drugs (NSAIDs), as well as steroids and other types of pain relievers, can also cause stomach ulcers.

A related type of ulcer is duodenal ulcer, which affects the duodenum, the upper region of the small intestine, which is connected to the stomach by an organ known as the pylorus. Duodenal ulcers are caused by the same factors that cause stomach ulcers, including *H. pylori* infection.

The following juices can both relieve ulcer symptoms and help the body eliminate *H. pylori* infection.

JUICING RECIPES

- Combine 1–2 ounces wheatgrass juice in 8–16 ounces green juices (any combination of green vegetables). (See inset on page 146.)

- Juice 3 medium carrots, $\frac{1}{4}$ head cabbage, $\frac{1}{2}$ medium cucumber, and 1 garlic clove. Makes 14 ounces. Consume once daily.

- Raw potato juice can be added to carrot and celery. Consume 6 ounces twice daily.

- For duodenal ulcers: Drink raw cabbage juice throughout the day (can be mixed with carrot or celery). Consume 6 ounces three times daily.

SUNBURN (*See also* SKIN PROBLEMS)

Sunburn is a type of skin condition caused by overexposure to sunlight (more specifically, the ultraviolet radiation that sunlight emits). It primarily affects people who are fair-skinned, and symptoms typically appear within 12–24 hours after exposure. When sunburn occurs, the affected area of the skin turns some degree of red and painful to the touch. In some cases, sunburn can also result in skin blisters. Repeated incidences of sunburn can be dangerous because of how sunburn causes skin to prematurely age, making it more susceptible to skin cancer.

The following juices are recommended for sunburn, as well as for overall skin health, because they are rich sources of vitamin A and the carotene group of nutrients, which are necessary for the proper repair of damaged skin tissue.

JUICING RECIPES

• Juice 4 medium carrots. Makes 9 ounces. Consume once to twice daily.

• Juice 3 medium carrots and 1 medium cucumber.
Makes 12 ounces. Consume once to twice daily.

• Juice 8 ounces black grapes, 4 ounces currants, and 4 ounces blueberries. Makes 8 ounces. Consume once to twice daily.

• Juice 3 medium carrots and 2 medium green apples.
Makes 16 ounces. Consume once to twice daily.

• Carrot juice or combination of carrot and apple.
Consume 16–32 ounces daily.

CONSIDERATION

■ Aloe juice topically.

SWELLING

Swelling refers to any type of enlargement within the body. It can be caused by a number of factors, including allergies, infections, injuries, and water retention. Swelling that is persistent can be a sign of a more serious health condition, including cancer. For such cases, seek immediate medical attention.

To help reduce swelling, the following juices are recommended because of their rich nutrient content, including enzymes, which play an essential role in preventing and reducing swelling.

JUICING RECIPES

- Fresh pineapple juice (can add papaya). **Consume 8–16 ounces daily.**

- Juice 3 medium carrots, 3 celery stalks, 1 medium cucumber, and 1/4 bunch parsley. **Makes 16 ounces. Consume once daily.**

- Juice 3 medium carrots, 1 medium cucumber, 1 bunch parsley, and 2 garlic cloves. **Makes 14 ounces. Consume once daily.**

TONSILLITIS

Tonsillitis is caused by infection of the tonsils, which are organs located at the back of the mouth. Tonsils are part of your body's lymphatic system and play an important role in the functioning of your adrenal glands, which help to produce and regulate your body's energy.

The main causes of tonsillitis are bacterial and viral infections. Food allergies can also play a role, especially milk and dairy products. In addition to the tonsils becoming enlarged, symptoms of tonsillitis include neck and throat pain, difficulty swallowing, and fever. Other symptoms can include coughing, fatigue, headache, hearing problems (including temporary hearing loss), hoarseness, laryngitis, sore throat, and vomiting. In some cases, abscesses can also form on the tonsils themselves.

In the United States, tonsillitis, which primarily affects children, although it can also strike adults, is often treated by the surgical removal of the tonsils. Because of the tonsils' important roles as part of the lymphatic system and the adrenal system, such measures should be avoided if possible. The vast majority of tonsillitis cases do not require surgery. Instead, they can be treated by proper diet, proper nutrition, and natural healing therapies that boost immune function. The following juices can help to relieve symptoms and quicken recovery time. Patients are also advised to be tested for food allergies, which often go undetected.

JUICING RECIPES

- Juice 2 medium carrots, 1 medium beet, and 1 medium tomato.
Makes 12 ounces. Consume once daily.

- Juice 3 medium carrots with equal parts pineapple, orange, or apple and 1/2 ounce ginger or turmeric root.
Makes 16 ounces. Consume once daily.

- Juice 4 medium carrots, 3 celery stalks, and add 2–3 garlic cloves.
Makes 14 ounces. Consume once daily.

TUBERCULOSIS (TB)

Tuberculosis, often referred to as TB, is a specific type of lung infection that can be either short-lived or chronic. TB, in its early stages, can escape detection because it initially does not cause any health symptoms. Depending on the individual, TB can escape detection for as long as two years, before its symptoms become obvious. Meanwhile, lung lesions continue to grow until they become large enough to cause concern. Initial symptoms of TB are an unexplainable cough and flu-like symptoms. As TB progresses, additional symptoms, such as breathing difficulties, chest pain, fever, excessive perspiration, and unhealthy weight loss can occur. In many cases, blood can be coughed up, as well. Fluid buildup between the lungs and the wall of the chest can also occur. Left unchecked, TB can cause death. In addition to TB that affects the lungs, which is known as pulmonary tuberculosis, another form of TB, known as extra-pulmonary tuberculosis, can affect other parts of the body. Both types of TB require ongoing professional medical care.

A type of bacteria known as *Mycobacterium tuberculosis* is the cause of pulmonary tuberculosis. People who are most susceptible to TB are those who suffer from impaired immune function, alcoholics and drug abusers, diabetics, and people with AIDS. Poor diet and nutritional deficiencies also increase the risk of developing TB.

The following juices can help to relieve symptoms of tuberculosis and improve immune function.

JUICING RECIPES

• Raw potato juice. After juicing, allow the starch to settle and pour it off the juice. Combine with an equal amount of carrot juice. Add 1 teaspoon of olive or almond oil, 1 teaspoon of honey, and beat until it foams. Drink three glasses a day.

• Juice 4 medium carrots, 3 celery stalks, and add 2 ounces wheatgrass juice. (See Wheatgrass Juice inset on page 146.) Makes 16 ounces. Consume once daily.

• Juice 4 medium carrots, 2–4 garlic cloves, 1 medium beet, and 2 ounces turmeric root. Makes 14 ounces. Consume once daily.

URINARY PROBLEMS

Urinary problems refer to all health conditions that affect the urinary tract, which includes the kidneys, bladder, ureter (the tube that transports urine from the kidneys to the bladder), and urethra (the tube that carries urine from the bladder). Health conditions that fall under this category include dysuria, which is characterized by pain or burning sensations during urination; incontinence, a condition in which urination occurs without warning such as when coughing or sneezing; nocturia, which is characterized by an excessive need to urinate during the night; painful urination; and urination that requires straining, which is common among men who are middle-aged or older and is usually due to an enlarged prostate gland. In addition to painful or difficult urination, other symptoms of urinary problems include pus or blood in the urine.

Various factors can cause urinary problems. These include bacterial infections within the urinary tract, food allergies, cysts or uterine fibroids, bladder obstructions, and, in men, prostate infections, enlargement of the prostate gland (BPH), and prostate cancer. Various other disease conditions can also cause urinary problems, including diabetes and kidney disease. In order to effectively treat urinary problems, all of these factors must be screened for by a medical professional and, if present, addressed as well.

The following juices can help relieve symptoms associated with urinary problems, as well as help maintain the overall health of the urinary tract.

JUICING RECIPES

- Juice 3 medium carrots, $1/4$ bunch parsley, 3 celery stalks, and $1/2$ medium cucumber. Makes 14 ounces. Consume twice daily.

- Juice 1 cup cranberries and 1 cup red or purple grapes. Makes 6 ounces. Consume three times daily.

- Juice 4 medium carrots, 2 garlic cloves, $1/2$ bunch parsley, and 1 medium cucumber. Makes 16 ounces. Consume once to twice daily.

UTERINE FIBROIDS

Uterine fibroids are groups of firm, round tumors that develop within the uterus or on its surface. In most cases, the tumors are benign (noncancerous). They most commonly affect women who are in their 30s through their 50s. Women who suspect they have uterine fibroids should consult with their physicians to rule out the possibility of cancer.

Uterine fibroids can often occur without symptoms. When symptoms do occur, they include pain or a sensation of pressure in the pelvis and lower abdominal area, a frequent need to urinate, bleeding between menstruation cycles, and changes in menstrual flow (usually heavier than normal bleeding). A variety of factors can cause uterine fibroids, including poor diet, nutritional deficiencies, hormonal imbalances, and chronic emotional stress. To help prevent uterine fibroids, and to relieve their symptoms, the following juices are recommended.

JUICING RECIPES

- Juice 3–4 medium carrots, $\frac{1}{2}$ medium cucumber, $\frac{1}{2}$ bunch parsley, 4 ounces watercress, and 1–2 garlic cloves.
Makes 12 ounces. Consume once to twice daily.

- Juice 3 medium carrots, $\frac{1}{2}$ medium beet, 1 medium black radish, and add 1–2 teaspoons black currant oil.
Makes 10 ounces. Consume once to twice daily.

- Juice 1 medium pear, 8 ounces blueberries, 4 ounces cranberries, and 1 tablespoon noni juice.
Makes 6 ounces. Consume once to twice daily.

- For excessive or chronic bleeding: Juice 1 medium apple, 4 ounces black currants, and add 1 ounce ginger root or $\frac{1}{4}$ teaspoon cinnamon powder.
Makes 6 ounces. Consume three times daily.

CONSIDERATION

■ Avoid consuming coffee and other coffee-related products.

VAGINAL INFECTIONS (*See* FEMALE HEALTH PROBLEMS)

VARICOSE VEINS

Varicose veins are characterized by swollen, enlarged, and in some cases, twisted veins that most commonly occur on the lower legs and calves, as well as the inside of the legs. As varicose veins progress, they typically become blue or black. In addition to being unsightly, varicose veins can cause itching and burning sensations along the affected area. They are primarily caused by unhealthy diet, nutritional deficiencies, and a sedentary lifestyle. Obesity, pregnancy, and smoking are other contributing factors. The following juices can help prevent and reverse varicose veins because of the abundant supply of nutrients that they supply.

JUICING RECIPES

- Juice 3–4 medium carrots, $\frac{1}{2}$ bunch parsley, and 2–3 celery stalks.
Makes 12 ounces. Consume twice daily.

- Juice 3 medium carrots, $\frac{1}{2}$ medium beet, $\frac{1}{2}$ medium cucumber, $\frac{1}{4}$ bunch spinach, and 4 ounces watercress.
Makes 12 ounces. Consume once daily.

- Juice 8 ounces blueberries, 8 ounces black grapes, 2 medium lemons, 1 medium green apple, and 2 ounces frozen acerola cherries.
Makes 14 ounces. Consume once to twice daily.

VIRAL INFECTIONS (*See also* COLD / FLU)

Viral infections are any type of infection that is caused by a virus. There are literally hundreds of different types of viral infections, ranging from those that cause colds and flu, the herpes family of viruses, and the human immuno-deficiency virus (HIV). As a result, symptoms of viral infections can vary greatly, ranging from cold and flu symptoms, fatigue, fever, gastrointestinal problems, muscle aches, to AIDS, mononucleosis, and polio. Many cancer specialists now believe that viruses may also contribute to certain types of cancer. Heart disease can also be worsened by viral infections. Depending on the nature of the infecting virus, medical attention may be necessary and need to be ongoing. The following juices, all of which can help boost your body's immune and detoxification systems, can also be helpful, both for preventing and reversing the effects of viral infections.

JUICING RECIPES

- Juice 3–4 medium carrots, 3 celery stalks, $\frac{1}{2}$ medium beet, 1–2 garlic cloves, and $\frac{1}{2}$ ounce fresh turmeric root.
Makes 14 ounces. Consume once to twice daily.

- Juice $\frac{1}{2}$ medium papaya, 4 ounces pineapple, 4 ounces cranberries, and 1 tablespoon noni juice; consider adding cinnamon and ginger.
Makes 6–8 ounces. Consume once to twice daily.

- Juice 4 medium carrots, 3 celery stalks, $\frac{1}{2}$ medium beet, and 1–2 garlic cloves. Makes 16 ounces. Consume once daily.

- Juice 1 medium pear, 8 ounces blueberries, and add 1 tablespoon noni juice.
Makes 4 ounces. Consume twice daily.

- Juice 2 medium oranges and 2 medium lemons.

Makes 8 ounces. Consume two to three times daily.

HEALTHY TWIST

🍎 You can also add to the recipes above 1 ounce of citron, a citrus fruit that resembles lemons and limes, but which is larger and less acidic.

VISION PROBLEMS (*See* EYE DISORDERS / VISION PROBLEMS)

VOMITING

Vomiting is a fairly common health condition that can be accompanied by symptoms of fatigue, fever, nausea, stomach upset, and excessive perspiration. Vomiting can be caused by a variety of factors. These include food allergies, food poisoning, and infection by bacteria, fungi, parasites, and viruses. Overeating and excessive consumption of alcohol can also cause vomiting, as can motion sickness, pharmaceutical drugs, and gastrointestinal problems. Vomiting can also be due to other disease conditions, including diabetes and liver disease. Vomiting that does not cease, as well as vomiting that produces blood, require immediate medical attention. The following can help, as well.

JUICING RECIPES

- Any vegetable or fruit juice with 1 ounce fresh ginger root.

Consume 8 ounces every 30–90 minutes until nausea subsides.

HEALTHY TWIST

🍎 Probably the most common version of this uses 8 ounces of apple juice, but ginger goes well with most fruit selections.

WHOOPING COUGH

Whooping cough is a highly contagious respiratory condition that is caused by bacterial infection. It is characterized by coughing spasms that produce "whooping" sounds, which is why it is so named. Other symptoms of whooping cough include mucus buildup in the lungs, fatigue, loss of appetite, tearing eyes, and vomiting. Because of its infectious nature, it should be monitored by a physician. The following juices can also be helpful, in terms of relieving symptoms and speeding recovery.

JUICING RECIPES

• Juice 2 medium oranges and 2 medium lemons.
Makes 10 ounces. Consume three times daily.

• Juice 4 medium carrots with 4 ounces watercress.
Makes 10 ounces. Consume three times daily.

• Juice 3 medium carrots, 1 bunch parsley, and 2 garlic cloves.
Make 10 ounces. Consume twice daily.

WOUNDS (*See also* SKIN PROBLEMS)

Wounds refer to any type of damage to the skin and its underlying tissues, and range from minor cuts and scrapes to tears in the skin that require surgery to close. Juices that are rich in vitamin A, vitamin C, and the carotene family of nutrients are beneficial for all cases of wounds because of the skin-healing properties of such nutrients. Useful juices in this category include the following.

JUICING RECIPES

• Carrot juice plus any combination of beet, celery, and garlic juices.
Consume 8–24 ounces daily.

• Juice 12 ounces cantaloupe and 2 medium apples.
Makes 16 ounces. Consume twice daily.

• Juice 4 medium lemons, 1 medium orange, and 1 ounce of citron.
Makes 8 ounces. Consume once daily.

YEAST INFECTIONS (*See* CANDIDIASIS)

CONCLUSION

The juice combinations provided above are by no means the only juices that can be used to help relieve symptoms of illness. We encourage you to experiment with other combinations, as well, based on your juice preferences. As you do so, keep in mind that, overall, vegetable juices tend to provide more therapeutic benefits than fruit juices, although this is not a hard and fast rule. (Noni juice, for example, is a fruit juice that offers many therapeutic benefits.)

One other thing to remember is that the relief that fresh fruit and vegetables juices can provide are not always obvious initially. Like many other natural remedies, juices act on the body "from the inside, out," meaning that the bountiful nutrients that they contain first start to work on a cellular level. As the health of the body's cells improves, healthy improvements then start to spread outward to the tissues and organs, becoming increasingly obvious as they do so. Many times, however, especially in cases of long-standing health ailments, these benefits may require weeks or months before they truly become noticeable.

We encourage you to give your juicing regimen enough time to properly work. As you do so, you may find it helpful to remember an adage from traditional Chinese medicine (TCM), which states that for every year that an illness has been present, at least one month is required to heal it. The need for patience that is implied by this saying is, of course, in stark contrast to our societal desire for immediate results that can often send patients running from one "magic bullet" cure to another, only to ultimately be disappointed in their quest for a "quick fix" remedy.

On the other hand, some people who use juices as part of their overall self-care approach for dealing with illnesses, including many of Dr. Bailey's own patients, find that their health conditions begin to significantly improve within a few days or weeks after they begin juicing. The time involved is not important. What matters is that you provide your body with all that it needs to trigger its innate healing mechanisms. By making juicing a daily part of your health regimen, that is precisely what you will be doing, due to the abundance of vitamins, minerals, enzymes, and other nutritional co-factors you will be imbibing with every glass of juice you drink.

Conclusion

A t a time of an ever-increasing health care crisis in the United States and in many other nations around the world, it behooves all of us to take absolute responsibility for our health. This means doing all that we can on our own to become and stay healthy. Given the enormous health problems which we face today, both in terms of the rising spread of chronic, degenerative diseases and the various infectious and environmental factors that cause them, and the growing incapacity of our medical system to cope with them, self-care has never been as important as it is now. It's so important, in fact, that a number of medical experts have termed self-care the "medicine of the future." The challenges we face with regard to our health can only truly be addressed by conscious, ongoing self-care practices undertaken by each of us.

In this book, we have shared with you one of the simplest, yet most powerful, self-care methods for improving your health—juicing. You should now be aware of the many health benefits that juicing provides. Based on what you have learned, it is our hope that you will avail yourself of those benefits by purchasing your own personal juicer so that you can prepare a wide variety of fresh, health-promoting juices on a daily basis. By doing so, you will be literally drinking your way to good health while simultaneously protecting yourself from the all-too-numerous amounts of harmful toxins and synthetic chemicals in our environment. The more that you experiment with the juices you prepare, the more you will actively be participating in your personal health care, while at the same time having fun and regularly enjoying delicious, refreshing, and energizing drinks.

Another thing that we hope you have realized as a result of reading this book is the fact that good health is not and can never be the result of drugs, supplements, medical procedures, or money. Nor is it dependent on visits to your doctor. As the famed French philosopher Voltaire wrote, "The art of medicine consists of amusing the patient while Nature cures the disease."

Two centuries later, no less a medical authority than Dr. Albert Schweitzer echoed Voltaire's sentiments when he wrote, "It's supposed to be a professional secret, but I'll tell you anyway. We doctors do nothing. We only help and encourage the doctor within." Juicing is a potent means of encouraging the inner physician that Dr. Schweitzer wrote about, as well as a completely natural health option.

Of course, juicing in and of itself is not a magic bullet or wand when it comes to your health. That's why we've also provided you with guidelines for combining juicing with healthy eating and for fasting. By making use of these guidelines, as well as getting regular nonstrenuous exercise, you have at your disposal some of the most powerfully effective tools for creating health and preventing illness. We encourage you to actively make use of them.

With that said, let us raise a figurative glass to you (filled with delicious, fresh juice, of course). May your life journey be a healthy one, filled with self-discovery and adventure. And may every sip of juice you drink fill you with energy and enhance your well-being.

Juice Conversion Tables

Conversion of solid fruits and vegetables into juice is an inexact science, as these foods vary in moisture content and extraction by season, ripeness, and individual qualities. The type of juicer and the speed of the juicer also influence all fruit and vegetable conversions, especially papaya. (At low speed there was no juice from the papaya; at high speed there was a very nice and flavorful juice extracted.) The conversion tables that follow are based on the results Dr. Bailey achieved using the Breville juicer (see Resource List, page 249) at speeds recommended by the manufacturer's manual. Use these tables as a guide.

VEGETABLES			
FOOD	SOLID WEIGHT	JUICE WEIGHT	JUICE VOLUME
Asparagus	8 ounces	4 ounces	1/2 cup
Beans	5 ounces	2 ounces	1/4 cup
Beets	24 ounces	8 ounces	1 cup
Root (3 medium)	16 ounces	10 ounces	1 1/4 cup
Greens	8 ounces	3–6 ounces	7/8 cup
Black Radish (2 medium)	9 ounces	2–3 ounces	1/3 cup
Broccoli	13 ounces	3 ounces	3/8 cup
Cabbage (small head)	23 ounces	8 ounces	1 cup
Carrots (6 medium)	32 ounces	14 ounces	1 3/4 cup
Celery (medium head)	30 ounces	16 ounces	2 cups
Cilantro	(1 bunch)	2 ounces	1/4 cup

Food	Solid Weight	Juice Weight	Juice Volume
Cucumbers (2 medium)	16 ounces	8 ounces	1 cup
Ginger	2 ounces	2 tablespoons	
Onions	16 ounces	10 ounces	1¼ cup
Parsley (1 bunch)	2–3 ounces	⅓ cup	
Pepper	5 ounces	2 ounces	¼ cup
Spinach (2 bunches)	12 ounces	1 ½ cup	
Tomato (2 medium)	16 ounces	10 ounces	1⅛ cup
Turmeric	2 ounces	2 ½ tablespoons	

FRUITS			
Food	Solid Weight	Juice Weight	Juice Volume
Apples	42 ounces	20 ounces	2½ cups
Blueberries	8 ounces	2 ounces	¼ cup
Lemons	16 ounces	2 ounces	¼ cup
Melon	22 ounces	10 ounces	1¼ cup
Oranges	24 ounces	10 ounces	1¼ cup
Papaya (Low speed)	16 ounces	0	0
Papaya (High speed)	8 ounces	1 cup	
Pears	19 ounces	6 ounces	¾ cup
Pineapple	40 ounces	16 ounces	2 cups

Note: Weight of lemons, melon, oranges, and pineapple includes skin or peel and the pineapple top, all of which are not juiced.

References

Chapter 1

Davis, DR, Epp, MD, and Riordan, H. "Changes in USDA Food Composition Data for 43 Garden Crops, 1950 to 1999," *Journal for the American College of Nutrition* Dec. 2004, 23: 669–682.

Hall, Manly P. *The Secret Teachings of All Ages.* New York: Penguin Group, 2003. (pp. 346, 347, 351)

Koop, C. Everett. *Surgeon General's Report on Nutrition and Health.* U.S. Department of Health and Human Services, Washington, DC, 1988.

Pauling, Linus. *How to Live Longer and Feel Better.* New York: W. H. Freeman, 1986. (p. 57)

Powell, Owen. *Galen, On the Properties of Foodstuffs.* Cambridge, MA: Cambridge University Press, 2003. (p. 102)

U.S. Senate Document No. 264. United States Senate. Washington, DC, 1936.

Webster's New Universal Unabridged Dictionary. New York: Simon & Schuster, 1979. (p. 990)

Williams, Roger J. *Nutrition Against Disease.* New York: Pitman Publishing Corp, 1971. (p. 206)

Chapter 2

Adams, Francis, LLD. *The Genuine Works of Hippocrates.* Baltimore, MD: Williams and Wilkins Company, 1939. (p. 65)

Ehret, Arnold (Translated by Benedict Lust). *Rational Fasting* 1910, 3rd Ed. New York: Benedict Lust Publications, 1971. (pp. 75–76)

Gunther, Robert. *Greek Herbal Dioscorides.* Oxford, England: Oxford University Press, 1934. (pp. 46–47, 55, 81, 83–84)

Guthrie, Kenneth Sylvan. *The Pythagorean Sourcebook and Library.* Grand Rapids, MI: Phanes Press, 1988. (p. 179)

Hartmann, Franz, M.D. *Paracelsus, the Greatest of the Alchemists*. New York: The Theosophical Publishing Company, 1910. (pp. 3, 238)

Just, Adolf. *Return to Nature*. New York: Volunteer Press, 1903. (pp.134–135)

Lloyd, G.E.R. *Hippocratic Writings*. New York: Penguin Books, 1987. (pp. 24, 53, 170–185, 191–192, 201–203, 208–209, 230, 262)

Macfadden, Bernarr. *Encyclopedia of Physical Culture*, vol. VII. New York: Book Company, Inc., 1931. (p. 512)

Osol, A, and Ferrar, G. *The Dispensatory of the United States of America*, 25th Edition. Philadelphia: J.B. Lippincott Company, 1955. (pp. 823, 827, 1234, 1849)

Powell, Owen. *Galen, On the Properties of Foodstuffs*. Cambridge, MA: Cambridge University Press, 2003. (pp. 90, 97, 101–102, 105)

Robinson, James, M. *The Nag Hammadi Library*. New York: Harper Collins, 1990. (p. 128)

The Book of Jasher. Grantsville, UT: Archive Publishers, 1887, reprinted 2000. (p. 9)

Vaidya Bhagwan Dash, Junius. *A Handbook of Ayurveda*, New Delhi, India: Concept Publishing Company of New Delhi, India, 1983. (p. 76)

Walker, N.W. *Raw Vegetable Juices*. Norwalk Press Publishers, 1936. (pp.14–15)

Webster's New Universal Unabridged Dictionary. New York: Simon & Schuster, 1979. (p. 990)

Chapter 3

Appleton, Nancy. *Stopping Inflammation*. Garden City Park, NY: Square One Publishers, 2005. (pp. 5–7, 39–44)

Blauer, Stephen. *The Juicing Book*. Garden City Park, NY: Avery Publishing Group, 1989. (pp. 2–3)

Brown, Susan E, and Trivieri, Larry Jr. *The Acid-Alkaline Food Guide*. Garden City Park, NY: Square One Publishers, 2006. (pp. 9–41)

Davis, DR, Epp, MD, and Riordan, H. "Changes in USDA Food Composition Data for 43 Garden Crops, 1950 to 1999." *Journal for the American College of Nutrition* (Dec. 2004), 23: pp. 669–682.

"Juices may cut Alzheimer's risk" *British Broadcasting Company* (*BBC News*), August 31, 2006. Available at http://news.bbc.co.uk/go/pr/fr/-/2/hi/health/5298404.stm

Guyton, Arthur C. and Hall, John E. *Textbook of Medical Physiology*, Ninth Edition, Philadephia: W. B. Sanders Company, 1996.

Ivker, Robert; Anderson, Robert; and Trivieri, Larry Jr. *The Complete Self-Care Guide to Holistic Medicine.* New York: Tarcher/Putnam, 1999. (pp. 15–28)

Trivieri, Larry Jr. *The American Holistic Medical Association Guide to Holistic Health.* New York: John Wiley & Sons, 2001. (pp. 41–76)

Trivieri, Larry Jr. editor. *Alternative Medicine: The Definitive Guide,* Second Edition, Berkeley, CA: Celestial Arts/Ten Speed Press, 2002. (pp. 187–188)

U.S. Senate Document No. 264. United States Senate. Washington, DC, 1936.

Chapter 5

Bailey, Steven, ND. *The Fasting Diet.* Chicago: Contemporary Books, 2002. (pp. 139–143)

Batmanghelidj, F. *Your Body's Many Cries for Water.* Falls Church, VA: Global Health Solutions, Inc, 1992.

D'Adamo, Peter. *Eat Right 4 Your Type.* New York: G. P. Putnam's Sons, 1996.

Erasmus, Udo. *Fats and Oils.* Burnaby, Canada: Alive Pr, Ltd, 1989.

Erasmus, Udo. *Fats That Heal, Fats That Kill.* Burnaby, Canada: Alive Books, 1993.

Guyton, Arthur C, and Hall, John E. *Textbook of Medical Physiology,* Ninth Edition, Philadephia: W. B. Sanders Company, 1996.

Walcott, William, and Fahey, Trish. *The Metabolic Typing Diet.* New York: Broadway Books, 2000.

Chapter 7

Bailey, Steven, ND. *The Fasting Diet.* Chicago: Contemporary Books, 2002. (pp. 100–109, 114–118, 126–129)

Resource List

Acme Juicers (manufactured by Waring Products)

Waring Products
314 Ella T. Grasso Avenue
Torrington, CT 06790
Phone: 800-4WARING
  (800-492-7464)
Website: www.waringproducts.com

Braun Juicers

1 Gillette Park
Boston, MA 02127-1096
Phone: 800-BRAUN-11
  (800-272-8611)
Website: www.braun.com

Breville Juicers

Australia:
Website: www.breville.com.au

USA:
2851 East Las Hermanas Street
Rancho Dominguez, CA 90221
Phone: 866-BREVILLE
  (866-273-8455)
Website: www.brevilleusa.com
Canada:
2555 Aviation, Pointe Claire
Montreal, Quebec
H9P 2Z2

Phone: 866-273-8455
Website: www.breville.ca

England:
Pulse Home Products Limited
Vine Mill
Middleton Road
Royton
Oldham
Lancashire
OL2 5LN
Phone: 0161-652-1211
Website: www.breville.co.uk

Champion Juicers

Plastaket Manufacturing Co., Inc
6220 E. Highway 12
Lodi, CA 95240
Phone: 866-935-8423
Website: www.championjuicer.com

Green Power Gold, Green Star, and SoloStar Juicers

14109 Pontlavoy Avenue
Santa Fe Springs, CA 90670
Phone: 888-254-7336
Websites: www.greenstar.com;
  www.tribest.com

Juiceman Juicers

Salton, Inc.
1955 West Field Court
Lake Forest, IL 60045
Phone: 847-803-4600
Website: www.saltoninc.com

Jack LaLanne's Power Juicer

Tristar Products, Inc.
Phone: 800-532-0597
Website: www.powerjuicer.com

L'Equip Juicers

L'Equip, Inc.
101-B South 38th Street
Harrisburg, PA 17111
Phone: 800-816-6811 (USA);
    877-453-7847 (Canada)
Website: www.lequip.com

Miracle Pro Juicers

Miracle Exclusive, Inc.
Phone: 800-645-6360
Website:
    www.miracleexclusives.com

Moline Juicers

Moline Manufacturing Company
1531 Mansfield Court
Upland, CA 91784
Phone: 909-981-1420

Norwalk Juicers

Norwalk Sales & Service
808 South Bloomington
Lowell, AR 72745
Phone: 800-643-8645
Website: www.norwalkjuicers.com

Nutrifaster Juicers

Nutrifaster, Inc.
209 S. Bennett Street
Seattle, WA 98108
Phone: 800-800-2641
Website: www.nutrifaster.com

NutriSource Juicers

Back To Basics Products
675 West 14600 South
Bluffdale, UT 84065
Phone: 800-688-1989
Website:
    www.backtobasicsproducts.com

Omega Juicers

Omega Products, Inc
Harrisburg, PA 17111-4523
Phone: 717-561-1105
Website: www.omegajuicers.com

Panasonic Juicers

**Panasonic Corporation of North
    America**
Consumer Affairs Division,
    Panazip 2F-3
One Panasonic Way
Secaucus, NJ 07094
Phone: 800-405-0652 or
    800-211-7262
Website: www.panasonic.com

Wheateena Juicers

Sundance Industries
119 Broadway, # 1446
Newburgh, NY 12550
Phone: 845-565-6065
Website: www.sundanceind.com

WEBSITES FOR PURCHASING JUICERS

www.800wheatgrass.com/index.html

www.albionjuicer.com

www.amazon.com

www.bizrate.com

www.costplusjuicers.com

www.discountjuicers.com

www.ezjuicers.com

www.fernsnutrition.com/wheat-grass.html

www.gourmetgreens.com/about.html

www.harvestessential.com

www.healthnutalternatives.com

www.juicersforless.com

www.kitchenresource.com

www.livingright.com

www.mercantila.com

www.overstock.com

www.pleasanthillgrain.com/juicers.asp

www.productsforhealth.com

BOOKS

Fasting

Bailey, Steven. *The Fasting Diet.* Chicago: Contemporary Books, 2002.

This book provides comprehensive information about the health benefits of water and juice fasts, as well as detailed instructions for fasting.

Acid-Alkaline Balance

Brown, Susan E. and Trivieri, Larry. *The Acid-Alkaline Food Guide.* Garden City Park: Square One Publishers, 2006.

This book is the only book of its kind, providing quick reference charts for hundreds of commonly eaten foods based on their effects on the human body's internal pH.

Guerrero, Alex. *In Balance For Life.* Garden City Park, NY: Square One Publishers, 2005.

This book explores the importance of acid-alkaline balance for overall health.

RAW FOOD AND VEGETARIAN ORGANIZATIONS

Ann Wigmore Natural Health Institute
PO Box 429
Rincón, Puerto Rico 00677
Phone: 787-868-6307
Website: www.annwigmore.org

The Ann Wigmore Natural Health Institute carries on the work of the late Dr. Ann Wigmore, a pioneer in the use of wheatgrass juice and living foods for detoxifying and healing the body, mind, and spirit.

Center for Informed Food Choices
PO Box 16053
Oakland, CA 94610
Phone: 510-465-0322
Website: www.informedeating.org

The Center for Informed Food Choices (CIFC) promotes a diet based on whole, unprocessed, local, organically grown plant foods. CIFC educates the public about how our industrial food system, along with corporate-influenced government policies, is the root cause of a host of preventable public health, environmental, and social justice problems.

EarthSave International
PO Box 96
New York, NY 10108
Phone: 800-362-3648
Website: www.earthsave.org

EarthSave International is a global organization that promotes a sustainable, plant-based diet and supports people from all walks of life who are taking steps to promote healthy and life-sustaining food choices.

Green People
425 South 3rd Avenue, Suite #1
Highland Park, NJ 08904
Phone: 732-514-1066
Website: www.greenpeople.org

Green People is the world's largest online directory of holistic and environmentally friendly health products, including organic foods. They also provide a directory of groups and organizations devoted to organic farming, community supported agriculture, food co-ops, and health foods stores, listed by state (U.S.) and province (Canada).

Healthful Living International
PO Box 371053
Las Vegas, NV 89137-1053
Phone: 866-454-3454
Website:
  www.healthfullivingintl.org

Healthful Living International is a nonprofit group of doctors and educators dedicated to promoting self-healing methods based on the principles of Natural Hygiene, including a live raw foods and vegetarian diet.

Nature's First Law
PO Box 900202
San Diego, CA 92190
Phone: 800-205-2350 or
  888-RAW-FOOD
Website: www.rawfood.com

Nature's First Law provides an extensive listing of resources related to raw foods, including a nationwide directory of events and retreats related to raw foods, as well as an online raw foods community forum and an extensive supply of all-vegetarian health products.

The North American Vegetarian Society

PO Box 72
Dolgeville, NY 13329
Phone: 518-568-7970
Website: www.navs-online.org

Founded in 1974, The North American Vegetarian Society (NAV) is a non-profit educational organization dedicated to promoting the vegetarian way of life. Among the services offered by NAV is a directory of local vegetarian groups across the U.S. and Canada.

Organic Consumers Association (OCA)

6771 South Silver Hill Drive
Finland, MN 55603
Phone: 218-226-4164
Website:
www.organicconsumers.org

The Organic Consumers Association (OCA) is an online and grassroots non-profit public interest organization campaigning for health, justice, and sustainability. The OCA deals with crucial issues of food safety, industrial agriculture, genetic engineering, children's health, corporate accountability, Fair Trade, environmental sustainability, and other key topics. OCA is the only organization in the U.S. focused exclusively on promoting the views and interests of the nation's estimated 50 million organic and socially responsible consumers.

Vegetarian Resource Group (VRG)

PO Box 1463
Baltimore, MD 21203
Phone: 410-366-VEGE (8343)
Website: www.vrg.org

The Vegetarian Resource Group (VRG) is a non-profit organization dedicated to educating the public on vegetarianism and the interrelated issues of health, nutrition, ecology, ethics, and world hunger. In addition to publishing the Vegetarian Journal, VRG produces and sells cookbooks, other books, pamphlets, and article reprints.

Vegetarian Union of North America (VUNA)

PO Box 9710
Washington, DC 20016
Email: vuna@ivu.org
Website: www.ivu.org/vuna/english.html

The Vegetarian Union of North America (VUNA) is a network of vegetarian groups throughout the U.S. and Canada that promotes strong, effective, cooperative vegetarian movement throughout North America.

RAW FOOD AND VEGETARIAN PUBLICATIONS

Living Nutrition Magazine
PO Box 256
Sebastopol, CA 95473
Phone: 707-566-0404
Website: www.livingnutrition.com

Vegetarian Journal
The Vegetarian Resource Group (VRG)
PO Box 1463
Baltimore, MD 21203

Phone: 410-366-VEGE (8343)
Website: www.vrg.org

Vegetarian Times
PO Box 420235
Palm Coast, FL 32142-0235
Phone: 800-793-9161
Website:
    www.vegetariantimes.com

RESOURCES FOR NUTRITIONAL PRODUCTS

Acerola and Acai
Sambazon
Website: www.sambazon.com

NutriVitamin Enzyme Complex (Tyler)
Integrative Therapeutics, Inc.
Customer Service Department
9 Monroe Parkway, Suite 250
Lake Oswego, OR 97035
Phone: 800-931-1709
Website: www.integrativeinc.com

Living Water
Eclectic Institute
36350 S.E. Industrial Way
Sandy, OR 97055
Phone: 800-332-4372
Website: www.eclecticwater.com

Noni Juice
Tahiti Trader Company
7111-F Arlington Avenue
Riverside, CA 90503
Phone: 800-842-5309
Website: www.tahititrader.com

Seabuckthorn
The Seabuckthorn Company
Sibu Inc.
10421 South Jordan Gateway,
    Suite 500
South Jordan, UT 84095
Phone: 801-542-7500
Website: www.sibu.com

ONLINE RESOURCE FOR ORGANIC FARMS AND COMMUNITY SUPPORTED AGRICULTURE (CSA)

www.biodynamics.com/csa.html

www.buylocalfood.com/

www.eatlocal.net/

www.eatwellguide.org/

www.ecotrust.org/foodfarms/

www.foodroutes.org/

www.localharvest.org/farms/M9006

www.localharvest.org/csa/

http://newfarm.org/farmlocator/index.php

www.newfarm.org/features/0803/localfoodchall.shtml

www.organicconsumers.org/

www.wilson.edu/wilson/asp/content.asp?id=804

Raw Food and Vegetarian Online Resources

www.davidwolfe.com—The website of David Wolfe, a leading proponent of a raw foods diet.

www.envirolink.org—The online site of The EnviroLink Network, a non-profit organization founded in 1991. EnviroLink maintains a database of thousands of environmental resources, including vegetarianism.

www.forvegetarian.com—An online resource for a wide range of vegetarian topics.

www.fredericpatenaude.com—The website of raw foods expert Frederic Patenaude, publisher of the free online newsletter *Pure Health* & *Nutrition.*

www.fresh-network.com—An extensive online raw food resource for people in the United Kingdom.

www.happycow.net—This website provides an international listing of vegetarian and raw food groups and restaurants in six continents.

www.highvibe.com—An online raw food resource created by nutritionist Robert A. Dagger.

www.ivu.org—This website of the International Vegetarian Union, which was founded in 1908, provides a directory of vegetarian organizations around the world.

www.living-foods.com—The largest online community dedicated to promoting vegetarian and raw food diets. (Also located at www.rawfoods.com.)

www.organicexpress.com—An online shopping site that delivers organic foods directly to your door.

www.organicpages.com—An online resource for information about organic foods.

www.radicalhealth.com—An online information source about raw foods.

www.rawfamily.com—An online information site about raw foods maintained by the Boutenko family, all of whom cured themselves of chronic illnesses after adopting a raw foods diet.

www.rawfoods.com—See www.living-foods.com above.

www.rawfoodsnewsmagazine.com—An online news magazine devoted to covering a wide range of raw food topics.

www.rawganique.com—An online shopping site for organic produce; organic cotton, linen, and hemp clothing; organic bed and bath products; organic groceries; and other organic products, as well as health books.

www.rawtimes.com—An online raw foods information site.

www.thegardendiet.com—An online resource for information about raw foods and vegan diets.

www.vegan.com—An online resource providing a wide range of information related to a vegan diet.

www.vegdining.com—An online directory of vegetarian restaurants around the world.

About the Authors

Steven A. Bailey, ND, is a naturopathic physician and has been in private practice for twenty-four years, in Portland, Oregon. He has specialized in fasting and detoxification programs for these many years and has done personal fasts for the past forty years. He is the author of *The Fasting Diet* and a major contributor to *Alternative Medicine: The Definitive Guide.* He has also contributed to more than a dozen published books and has written hundreds of articles. He has hosted public radio shows for twenty years and has a cable access show, "The Doctor's Corner," that airs in the Portland area. He has taught, and lectures, at the National College of Naturopathic Medicine in addition to lecturing nationally at professional conferences.

After graduating college with dual degrees, Dr. Bailey became a counselor and program director at a federally accredited program for the adult disabled. Here, he started the nation's first union-waged program for the adult disabled. A vegetarian for over thirty years, Dr. Bailey enjoys a balanced family and professional life with his wife Susan and daughter Shayla. His passions include playing the flute, studying philosophy, fasting, meditation, and being a student of life. His life goals are to honor all life, live simply, and be the best person he can be.

Larry Trivieri, Jr., has been exploring natural and holistic healing methods for more than thirty years, and is a nationally recognized writer and journalist in the field of holistic and alternative medicine. In addition to writing numerous articles in many leading popular magazines, Trivieri is the author of *Health on the Edge: Visionary Views of Healing in the New Millennium* and *The American Holistic Medical Association Guide to Holistic Health;* and co-author of *The Acid-Alkaline Food Guide; Chronic Fatigue, Fibromyalgia & Lyme Disease;* and *The Complete Self-Care Guide to Holistic Medicine.* He is also the editor and co-author of both editions of the landmark health encyclopedia *Alternative Medicine: The Definitive Guide.*

In 2002, Trivieri founded the online health resource www.1healthy-world.com and is the author and publisher of its free online newsletter *The Health Plus Letter,* which is read by subscribers in more than thirty countries. A popular guest on radio and TV shows, Trivieri also lectures nationwide on a variety of health topics, with an emphasis on empowering self-care approaches that can be used to improve well-being. He resides in his home-town of Utica, New York.

Index

A

Abscess, 137
Acai berry, 83, 84
Acerola cherry, 84, 99
Acid-alkaline balance, 45–46, 70–75, 79, 111, 122
Acidic, 73
Acidosis, 73
Acne, 137–138. *See also* Skin problems.
Addictions, 138–139
Advanced glycation end products (AGEs), 49
AGEs. *See* Advanced glycation end products.
Aging, 139
AIDS, 140
Alcoholism, 140–141. *See also* Addictions.
Ali, Khalifah, 20
Ali, Muhammad, 20
Alkaline, 72, 73, 79, 122
Alkalizing. *See* Alkaline.
Allergies, 40, 141–142. *See also* Food allergies.
Allopath, 25
Allopathic medicine, 25
Almonds, 90
Alstat, Ed, 80
Alzheimer's disease, 47, 75, 142–143
Amebiasis, 143
American Journal of Medicine, 47
Amino acids, 35–36, 42
Amla, 23

Anemia, 22, 143–144
Ankylosing spondylitis, 144–145
Ann Wigmore Foundation, 146
Anoxia, 145
Anti-aging, 145–147
Antioxidants, 46–47
Anutrients, 163
Anxiety, 147–148
Archaeus, 17
Arrhythmia, 148–149
Arteritis, 149–150
Arthritis, 40, 150–152
Asafetida, 24
Asian pearl barley. *See* Job's tears.
Asthma, 152–153
Ayurveda, 16, 21–23, 29, 61–62, 89, 117, 119, 120, 200

B

Back pain, 153–154
Bad breath, 154
Banana, 98
Barnes, Broda, 199
Batmanghelidj, F., 79, 130
Bed sores, 155
Bee pollen, 84
Benign prostatic hyperplasia (BPH), 155–156
Benign prostatic hypertrophy. *See* Benign prostatic hyperplasia.
Bioavailability, 14
Biochemical individuality, 62
Bioflavonoids, 37
Black cherry, 84

OTHER SQUAREONE TITLES OF INTEREST

GOING WILD IN THE KITCHEN
The Fresh & Sassy Tastes of Vegetarian Cooking
Leslie Cerier

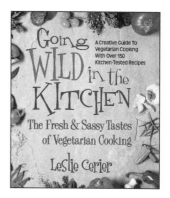

Going Wild in the Kitchen is the first comprehensive global vegetarian cookbook to go beyond the standard organic beans, grains, and vegetables. In addition to providing helpful cooking tips and techniques, the book contains over 150 kitchen-tested recipes for healthful, taste-tempting dishes—creative masterpieces that contain such unique ingredients as edible flowers; sea vegetables; and wild mushrooms, berries, and herbs. It encourages the creative side of novice and seasoned cooks alike, prompting them to follow their instincts and "go wild" in the kitchen by adding, changing, or substituting ingredients in existing recipes. To help, a wealth of suggestions is found throughout. A list of organic food sources completes this user-friendly cookbook.

$16.95 US • 240 pages • 7.5 x 9-inch quality paperback • ISBN 978-0-7570-0091-1

EAT SMART EAT RAW
Creative Vegetarian Recipes for a Healthier Life
Kate Wood

From healing diseases to detoxifying your body, from lowering cholesterol to eliminating excess weight, the many important health benefits derived from a raw vegetarian diet are too important to ignore. However, now there is another compelling reason to go raw—taste! In her new book *Eat Smart, Eat Raw,* cook and health writer Kate Wood not only explains how to get started, but also provides delicious kitchen-tested recipes guaranteed to surprise and delight even the fussiest of eaters.

Eat Smart, Eat Raw begins by explaining the basics of cooking without heat, from choosing the best equipment to stocking your pantry. What follows are twelve recipe chapters filled with truly exceptional dishes, including hearty breakfasts, savory soups, satisfying entrées, and luscious desserts.

$15.95 US • 184 pages • 7.5 x 9-inch quality paperback • ISBN 978-0-7570-0261-8

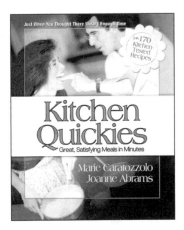

KITCHEN QUICKIES
Great, Satisfying Meals in Minutes
Marie Caratozzolo and Joanne Abrams

Ever feel that there aren't enough hours in the day to enjoy life's pleasures—simple or otherwise? Whether you're dealing with problems on the job, chasing after kids on the home front, or simply running from errand to errand, the evening probably finds you longing for a great meal, but with neither the time nor the desire to prepare one.

Kitchen Quickies offers a solution. Virtually all of its over 170 kitchen-tested recipes—yes, really kitchen tested—call for a maximum of only five main ingredients other than kitchen staples, and each dish takes just minutes to prepare! Imagine being able to whip up dishes like Southwestern Tortilla Pizzas, Super Salmon Burgers, and Tuscan-Style Fusilli—in no time flat! As a bonus, these delicious dishes are actually good for you—low in fat and high in nutrients!

$14.95 US • 240 pages • 7.5 x 9-inch quality paperback • ISBN 978-0-7570-0085-0

AS YOU LIKE IT COOKBOOK
Imaginative Gourmet Dishes with Exciting Vegetarian Options
Ron Pickarski

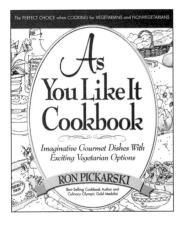

When it comes to food, we certainly like to have it our way. However, catering to individual tastes can pose quite a challenge for the cook. The *As You Like It Cookbook* is designed to help you meet the challenge of cooking for both vegetarians and nonvegetarians alike. It offers over 170 great-tasting dishes that cater to a broad range of tastes. Many of the easy-to-follow recipes are vegetarian—and offer ingredient alternatives for meat eaters. Conversely, recipes that include meat, poultry, or fish offer nonmeat ingredient options. Furthermore, if the recipe includes eggs or dairy products, a vegan alternative is provided. This book has it all—delicious breakfast favorites, satisfying soups and sandwiches, mouth-watering entrées, and delectable desserts.

$16.95 US • 216 pages • 7.5 x 9-inch quality paperback • ISBN 978-0-7570-0013-3

THE ACID-ALKALINE FOOD GUIDE

A Quick Reference to Foods & Their Effect on pH Levels

Dr. Susan E. Brown and Larry Trivieri, Jr.

In the last few years, researchers around the world have reported the importance of acid-alkaline balance to good health. While thousands of people are trying to balance their body's pH level, until now, they have had to rely on guides containing only a small number of foods. *The Acid-Alkaline Food Guide* is a complete resource for people who want to widen their food choices.

The book begins by explaining how the acid-alkaline environment of the body is influenced by foods. It then presents a list of thousands of foods—single foods, combination foods, and even fast foods—and their acid-alkaline effects. *The Acid-Alkaline Food Guide* will quickly become the resource you turn to at home, in restaurants, and whenever you want to select a food that can help you reach your health and dietary goals.

$7.95 US • 208 pages • 4 x 7-inch mass paperback • ISBN 978-0-7570-0280-9

GLYCEMIC INDEX FOOD GUIDE

For Weight Loss, Cardiovascular Health, Diabetic Management, and Maximum Energy

Dr. Shari Lieberman

The glycemic index (GI) is an important nutritional tool. By indicating how quickly a given food triggers a rise in blood sugar, the GI enables you to choose foods that can help you manage a variety of conditions and improve your overall health.

Written by leading nutritionist Dr. Shari Lieberman, this book was designed as an easy-to-use guide to the glycemic index. The book first answers commonly asked questions, ensuring that you truly understand the GI and know how to use it. It then provides both the glycemic index and the glycemic load of hundreds of foods and beverages, including raw foods, cooked foods, and many combination and prepared foods. Whether you are interested in controlling your glucose levels to manage your diabetes, lose weight, increase your heart health, or simply enhance your well-being, *The Glycemic Index Food Guide* is the best place to start.

$7.95 US • 160 pages • 4 x 7-inch mass paperback • ISBN 978-0-7570-0245-8

VICKI'S VEGAN KITCHEN
Eating with Sanity, Compassion & Taste
Vicki Chelf

Vegan dishes are healthy, delicious, and surprisingly easy to make. Yet many people are daunted by the idea of preparing meals that contain no animal products. For them, and for everyone who loves great food, vegetarian chef Vicki Chelf presents *Vicki's Vegan Kitchen,* a comprehensive cookbook designed to take the mystery out of meatless meals.

The book begins by offering tips for making nutritious food choices, as well as an extensive glossary of ingredients. Vicki then discusses the simple kitchen equipment you need to have on hand and explains basic cooking techniques. Following this are twelve chapters packed with over 350 recipes for delicious dips, scrumptious soups, pleasing pastas, decadent desserts, and much, much more. Whether you're interested in compassionate cooking, you value the benefits of a meat-free diet, or you just want to treat your family to a wonderful meal, *Vicki's Vegan Kitchen* will bring delectable vegan fare to your kitchen table.

$17.95 US • 368 pages • 7.5 x 9-inch quality paperback • ISBN 978-0-7570-0251-9

THE WORLD GOES RAW COOKBOOK
An International Collection of Raw Vegetarian Recipes
Lisa Mann

People everywhere know that meals prepared without heat can taste great and improve their overall health. Yet raw cuisine cookbooks have always offered little variety—until now. In *The World Goes Raw Cookbook,* raw food chef Lisa Mann provides a fresh approach to (un)cooking with recipes that have an international twist.

After discussing the healthfulness of a raw food diet, *The World Goes Raw Cookbook* tells you how to stock your kitchen with the tools and ingredients that make it easy to prepare raw meals. What follows are six recipe chapters, each focused on a different ethnic cuisine, including Italian, Mexican, Middle Eastern, Asian, Caribbean, and South American dishes. And from soups and starters to desserts, every one's a winner. There are even easy-to-follow instructions for growing fresh ingredients in your own kitchen garden.

Whether you are already interested in raw food or are exploring it for the first time, the taste-tempting recipes in *The World Goes Raw* can add delicious variety to your life.

$16.95 US • 194 pages • 7.5 x 9-inch quality paperback • ISBN 978-0-7570-0320-2

WHAT YOU MUST KNOW ABOUT VITAMINS, MINERALS, HERBS & MORE

Choosing the Nutrients That Are Right for You

Pamela Wartian Smith, MD, MPH

Almost 75 percent of your health and life expectancy is based on lifestyle, environment, and nutrition. Yet even if you follow a healthful diet, you are probably not getting all the nutrients you need to prevent disease. In *What You Must Know About Vitamins, Minerals, Herbs & More,* Dr. Pamela Smith explains how you can restore and maintain health through the wise use of nutrients.

Part One of this easy-to-use guide discusses the individual nutrients necessary for good health. Part Two offers personalized nutritional programs for people with a wide variety of health concerns. People without prior medical problems can look to Part Three for their supplementation plans. If you want to maintain good health or you are trying to overcome a medical condition, *What You Must Know About Vitamins, Minerals, Herbs & More* can help you make the best choices.

$15.95 US • 448 pages • 6 x 9-inch quality paperback • ISBN 978-0-7570-0233-5

WHAT YOU MUST KNOW ABOUT WOMEN'S HORMONES

Your Guide to Natural Hormone Treatments for PMS, Menopause, Osteoporosis, PCOS, and More

Pamela Wartian Smith, MD, MPH

Hormonal imbalances can occur at any age and for a variety of reasons. While most hormone-related problems are associated with menopause, fluctuating hormonal levels can also cause a variety of other conditions. *What You Must Know About Women's Hormones* is a clear guide to the treatment of hormonal irregularities without the health risks associated with standard hormone replacement therapy.

This book is divided into three parts. Part I describes the body's own hormones, looking at their functions and the problems that can occur if these hormones are not at optimal levels. Part II focuses on the most common problems that arise from hormonal imbalances, such as PMS, hot flashes, and endometriosis. Lastly, Part III details hormone replacement therapy, focusing on the difference between natural and synthetic hormone treatments.

Whether you are looking for help with menopausal symptoms or you simply want to enjoy vibrant health, this book can make a profound difference in your life.

$17.95 US • 256 pages • 6 x 9-inch quality paperback • ISBN 978-0-7570-0307-3

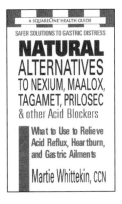

A SQUAREONE°HEALTH GUIDE

SAFER SOLUTIONS TO GASTRIC DISTRESS

NATURAL
ALTERNATIVES
TO NEXIUM, MAALOX,
TAGAMET, PRILOSEC
& other Acid Blockers

What to Use to Relieve
Acid Reflux, Heartburn,
and Gastric Ailments

Martie Whittekin, CCN

NATURAL ALTERNATIVES TO NEXIUM, MAALOX, TAGAMET, PRILOSEC & OTHER ACID BLOCKERS

What to Use to Help Relieve Acid Reflux, Heartburn, and Gastric Ailments

Martie Whittekin, CCN

With millions of Americans suffering from heartburn, acid reflux, and other gastric ailments, it's no wonder that stomach medications are the best-selling drugstore remedies. Ads claim that these meds can relieve pain quickly, but don't tell you that they fail to treat the cause of the problem. This book offers safer, more effective alternatives to popular heartburn and acid reflux medications.

Written by Martie Whittekin, an experienced clinical nutritionist, *Natural Alternatives to Nexium* examines the underlying causes of acid-related gastric ailments. Most important, it highlights effective natural alternatives—both those that provide immediate relief and those that offer long-term relief. If you suffer from the pain of recurrent gastric upset, this book can make a profound difference in the quality of your life.

$7.95 US • 272 pages • 4 x 7-inch mass paperback • ISBN 978-0-7570-0210-6

NATURAL ALTERNATIVES TO VIOXX, CELEBREX & OTHER ANTI-INFLAMMATORY PRESCRIPTION DRUGS

What to Use to Help Relieve Arthritis Pain and Inflammation

Carol Simontacchi, CCN, MS

A SQUAREONE°HEALTH GUIDE

SAFER SOLUTIONS TO COX-2 INHIBITORS

NATURAL
ALTERNATIVES
TO VIOXX, CELEBREX
& other Anti-Inflammatory
Prescription Drugs

SECOND EDITION

What to Use to Help
Relieve Arthritis Pain
and Inflammation

Carol Simontacchi

Beyond today's headlines is an underlying truth—COX-2 inhibitors can be dangerous to your health. For those looking for other options, health expert Carol Simontacchi has created a guide to using safer natural alternatives.

Natural Alternatives to Vioxx first examines the causes of arthritis pain and inflammation, and then looks at both pharmaceutical and holistic approaches to this condition. The book then discusses the most effective supplements available, including bromelain, curcumin, cat's claw, fish oil, ginger, glucosamine, chondroitin, and SierraSil. Each supplement is examined for its action, scientific documentation, and dosage, and a special section supplies anti-inflammatory recipes. Here is a vital resource for those looking for a safer solution.

$5.95 US • 128 pages • 4 x 7-inch quality paperback • ISBN 978-0-7570-0278-6

What You Must Know About Statin Drugs & Their Natural Alternatives

A Consumer's Guide to Safely Using Lipitor, Zocor, Mevacor, Crestor, Pravachol, or Natural Alternatives

Jay S. Cohen, MD

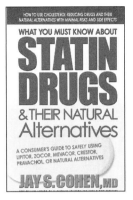

The statins—Lipitor, Pravachol, Zocor, Mevacor, Lescol, and Crestor—are the most prescribed medications in the United States. Yet many patients experience side effects, and a whopping 60 to 70 percent eventually stop statin treatment. Here, for the first time, is a simple guide that explains how you can use these drugs properly with minimal risk of side effects.

What You Must Know About Statin Drugs & Their Natural Alternatives begins by explaining elevated cholesterol and C-reactive proteins. It then examines how statins alleviate these common problems, discusses side effects, and offers information on both safe usage and effective alternative treatments. Here is a unique guide to taking statins properly and safely.

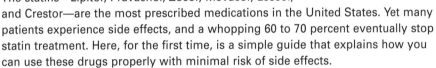

$15.95 US • 224 pages • 6 x 9-inch paperback • ISBN 978-0-7570-0257-1

Natural Alternatives to Lipitor, Zocor & Other Statin Drugs
What to Use and Do to Help Lower Your Bad Cholesterol

Jay S. Cohen, MD

To combat bad cholesterol, modern science has created a group of drugs known as statins. While these medications can be effective, the side effects can be serious. *Natural Alternatives to Lipitor, Zocor & Other Statin Drugs* explains the problems caused by statin drugs, and offers easy-to-follow strategies that will allow you to benefit from safe and effective alternatives.

Written by a highly qualified researcher and physician, this concise book highlights the most important natural treatments, providing information on the science behind their claims, their proven effectiveness, and their suggested dosage. If you have elevated cholesterol and C-reactive proteins, or if you are currently using a statin drug, *Natural Alternatives to Lipitor, Zocor & Other Statin Drugs* can make a profound difference in the quality of your life.

$7.95 US • 144 pages • 4 x 7-inch mass paperback • ISBN 978-0-7570-0286-1

THE MAGNESIUM SOLUTION FOR HIGH BLOOD PRESSURE

How to Use Magnesium to Help Prevent and Relieve Hypertension Naturally

Jay S. Cohen, MD

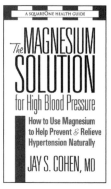

Approximately 50 percent of all Americans have hypertension, a devastating disease that can lead to hardening of the arteries, heart attack, and stroke. While many medications are available to combat this condition, these drugs come with potentially dangerous side effects. When Dr. Jay S. Cohen learned of his own vascular condition, he selected a safer option—magnesium.

In *The Magnesium Solution for High Blood Pressure,* Dr. Cohen describes the most effective types of magnesium for treating hypertension, explores appropriate magnesium dosage, and details the use of magnesium in conjunction with hypertension meds. Here is a proven remedy for anyone looking for a safe, effective approach to the treatment of high blood pressure.

$5.95 US • 96 pages • 4 x 7.5-inch mass paperback • ISBN 978-0-7570-0255-7

A GUIDE TO COMPLEMENTARY TREATMENTS FOR DIABETES

Using Natural Supplements, Nutrition, and Alternative Therapies to Better Manage Your Diabetes

Gene Bruno, MS, MHS

If you are among the 17 million Americans who have diabetes, you are probably working with a doctor to maintain an appropriate treatment program. But what if you could do more to improve your health? *A Guide to Complementary Treatments for Diabetes* reveals natural ways to complement your diabetes management.

The author first explains what complementary therapy means, stressing that the treatments he recommends are meant to enhance your current diabetes program, not replace it. The remainder of the book is devoted to diabetes symptoms and natural methods for dealing with them, as well as important information on potential interactions between prescription drugs and alternative therapies. *A Guide to Complementary Treatments for Diabetes* will help you assume an active role in your diabetes program.

$7.95 US • 176 pages • 4 x 7.5-inch mass paperback • ISBN 978-0-7570-0322-6

**For more information about our books,
visit our website at www.squareonepublishers.com**